cry of the banshee

The Weeping Woman statue overlooks the Jackson Family plot in Riverview Cemetery in Parkersburg.

Cry of the banshee

History and Hauntings of
West Virginia and the Ohio Valley

Susan Sheppard

quarrier press

Charleston, West Virginia

Quarrier Press
Charleston, WV

First Quarrier Press Edition

10 9 8 7 6 5 4 3 2 1

Printed in the United States of America

Library of Congress Control Number: 2008931716
ISBN-13: 978-1891852-59-6
ISBN-10: 1-891852-59-0
Book and cover design: Mark S. Phillips

Originally printed by Whitechapel Productions Press in 2004.

Distributed by:

West Virginia Book Company
1125 Central Avenue
Charleston, WV 25302
www.wvbookco.com

Contents

Introduction

In Appalachia, the word "haint" isn't necessarily a crude misuse of the English language. In old-timey terms, a 'haint' is merely a haunt—a meddlesome ghost or spirit, a mysterious force that is somehow visited upon you, your neighbor or your kin.

Haints are lost souls that haunt crumbling houses, spirits who vex you at the crossroads, wraiths who stalk you in dark hollows or ghosts that chase your sorry self through old, abandoned railroad tunnels. They are the nightmares that ride you and startle you awake at night. Haints can be regrets or feelings of dread that somehow find ways into your consciousness. . . just to devil you, so they say.

In this book, haints become death-shrouded banshees that keen along isolated riverbeds while washing out the bloody clothes of their dead. They are women-in-white who linger along the shorelines of the Ohio River's mystifying islands. Haints are the apparitions of John Brown and his men, abolitionists who lost their fight in the streets of Harpers Ferry. Haints are wisps that wait next to long ago Indian mounds. They are the souls of the unquiet dead who don't have their business settled yet—ones that stalk us in the indigo darkness of West Virginias' foreboding hills.

The Allegheny and Appalachian mountain region of the United States is steeped in the history of ghosts, weird creatures and restless spirits and has been from the beginning. After all, Native American Indians steered clear of what is now West Virginia, because they viewed the hills and valleys as troublesome places, plagued by angry ghosts and even more menacing monsters. Perhaps the terrain itself (once you make it down one hill it is already the time to climb up another one) simply wasn't a convenient place for the Shawnee, Seneca, Delaware and Cherokee peoples to settle. These earliest Americans were superstitious about the lands that fell between the Potomac and Ohio rivers and pretty well stuck to the waterways, claiming their prizes of flint, salt, fish and game along the way.

The earliest European settlers, the Scotch-Irish, the English and the Germans, brought their own views about ghosts.

The Celtic/Pictish peoples brought to the Ohio Valley a belief in banshees, witches, haints, and will o' the wisps. In fact, from the word "Pict" (a diminutive early people of the British Isles) came the word "pixie."

Through the early German/Pennsylvania Dutch came the poltergeists, doppelgangers, hexing and *hexens* (witches). Africans and Guineas added devils, boogers and spooks. Meanwhile the Black Dutch brought the concept of the crossroads as a place of spiritual danger. They combined Rom/Gypsy/Pennsylvania Dutch Powwow magic with beliefs in ghosts and graveyard ghouls who had masqueraded earlier in Eastern Europe as vampires.

While these groups intermixed, they were still remote to such a degree that words that were an archaic form of the Queen's English were still being spoken in the foothills and valleys as late as the 1960s. This isolation created a unique blend of mythologies when it came to ghosts, spirits, boogers and things that go bump in the night.

In the mid 20th century, Appalachian haints assumed a modern persona through a surprising number of UFO and creature sightings in West Virginia and the Ohio Valley. None more famous than the West Virginia Mothman, the Flatwoods monster and the UFO contactee tale of Woodrow Derenberger and the alien Indrid Cold. Many such strange stories parallel ancient European fairy tales, where the unsuspecting are abducted by fairies, spirited away at night into alternate realms of awareness and experience.

That explains the folklore, but what about the science of ghosts? If anything, ghosts and their related folklore don't just belong to the past. They also belong to the here and now where hauntings—such as those at the Blennerhassett Hotel in downtown Parkersburg and sightings of John Brown at Harpers Ferry—are ongoing and ever evolving. Reports of ghosts are now being studied with tools of the 21st century, such as digital cameras and recorders, electronic voice phenomena, electromagnetic detectors, camcorders, infra-red photography, thermal imaging and other kinds of equipment that now belong to the over one-hundred-year-old science of ghosts hunting that evolved from 19th century Spiritualism.

It is getting more difficult for skeptics to disprove that "something isn't out there;" that things of a more spiritual nature exist. In this book, *Cry of the Banshee*, we look at the various related phenomena considered to be our haints, ghosts, apparitions, contactees, mothmen, banshees and other unexplained occurrences that can only fall under the category of the paranormal.

During my study of ghosts, I returned time and time again to the classic movie *The Wizard of Oz*, of a scene in the haunted forest that takes place at the crossroads. It is here that Dorothy, Tin Man, Scarecrow and the Cowardly Lion reconsider their quest for the witch's broom. The first sign points up a winding road that reads: *This Way to the Witch's Castle* while the second sign says: *I'd Turn Back If I Were You!*

Are the perils of chasing ghosts worth the trouble? Yes. Every human being has a right to explore the mysterious—even against risk or ridicule.

My Haunted Parkersburg Ghost Tours takes place from mid-September throughout the first weekend in November (private tours are also available throughout the year) and has achieved national prominence. The tour won the 10th Most Popular Ghost Tour in the Nation in 2008 given by the Haunted America Tours in New Orleans, Louisiana.

The Haunted Parkersburg Ghost Tours have helped to revive interest in downtown and the older historical section of Parkersburg. The tour teaches local history and covers famous paranormal tales from the area. It is not at all unusual for ghostly activity to show itself during the Haunted Parkersburg Ghost Tours. Ghost hunters, psychic mediums and local theater students lead the tour. The tour has given birth to two local ghost hunting groups: the Haunted Parkersburg Ghost Hunters led by Kristall Chambers and the Mid-Ohio Valley Ghost Hunters led by Tom and Jim Moore.

As ghost hunters and ghost tour researchers, our midnights have been spent in 200-year-old graveyards, haunted tunnels, Civil War hospitals and abandoned prisons. On summer afternoons, we have crawled through foul empty buildings possessed by angry ghosts. We have sat in darkened places waiting for spirits to come. We have scrutinized dozens of mysterious photographs sent in by enthusiasts taking the ghost tour. We follow up on ghostly leads, and have attended and led séances.

We embraced the light. And we embraced the gloom.

It is through such connections in spirit that we tunneled our way out of our fears and allowed those fears to see the light of day.

I am once again reminded of the scene in *The Wizard of Oz* when near the end, Scarecrow, Tin Man and the Cowardly Lion all receive their badges and degrees of honor. After the ceremony, the Wizard reminds the Cowardly Lion that he was really courageous all along. His answer is much like ours:

Hain't it da truth! Hain't it da truth!

— **Susan Sheppard**
Parkersburg, West Virginia
October 31, 2003
(Revised February 25, 2008)

ONE
Tales of Appalachian Banshees

Double, double toil and trouble,
Fire burn and cauldron bubble.
Cool it with a baboon's blood,
Then the charm is firm and good.
O, well done, I commend your pains.
And now about the cauldron sing
Like elves and fairies in a ring.
By the pricking of my thumbs,
Something wicked this way comes.

— From **MacBeth** by William Shakespeare

Not all fairy tales have happy endings. Not all fairies bring goodness and light. Among the Irish and Scottish people there is a supernatural creature they call "the Banshee."

The Banshee is an attendant death fairy, one that brings an omen of doom to Irish or Scottish clans. It is the Banshee that announces the death of a family member, usually over bodies of water with her keening or *caoine*, a shrill crying for the dead.

But the Banshee doesn't just stay near bodies of water washing out the grave clothes of her dead as it is told. She also travels to the homes of those about to die, sometimes mounted on a pale steed or riding a black funeral coach with two, pale headless horses leading the way.

There are various descriptions of the Banshee. The Irish Banshee is called *Bean Sidhe* in an older tongue. Depending upon what source you use, "Bean" means woman and "Sidhe" (*shee*) means fairy. But other sources say that Bean Sidhe is translated as "woman of the hills." Some ancient lore says the Banshee can even be the ghost of a young woman who has died in childbirth, especially if she was not given the last rites of confession.

The Irish Banshee is said to materialize as a beautiful young woman with streaming auburn hair. She wears a green woolen dress with gray cloak clasped about her shoulders. The Irish Banshee hangs out at rivers and waterfalls. The only hint that this beautiful Banshee is a messenger of doom comes from the fact that her eyes are blood red from crying for her Irish dead.

The Scottish Banshee, the "Bean Nighe," is more menacing. The Scottish Banshee dresses in moldering grave clothes, her face covered by a tattered veil. Often, she rides a prancing white steed. Her age and features are difficult to make out but she appears to be a decrepit crone. And yet, the Banshee's movements are lithe and she rides her pale horse sometimes with a black hearse following behind her. Rarely, the shroud of the Scottish Banshee is crimson, reddened by the gore of blood.

The Mid-Ohio Valley was settled predominantly by people of Irish and Scottish ancestry. Along with the Welsh and French, they shared ancient Celtic ties and are descended from clans. The Celts believed in unique forms of mysticism, such as sorcerers, witches, leprechauns and fairies, and not the least of them—the Banshee.

Stories of Banshee spirits went underground as Irish and Scottish immigrants moved into the verdant hills of the Ohio Valley. But the legend of the Banshee is not entirely forgotten, as you will see by reading the following pages.

Let us travel back to the shores of Scotland on a blustery winter day in the year 1590. A group of women, known later as the Berwick Witches, summoned their powers at the ocean's edge. Over the icy waters of the North Sea, King James VI and his new bride Anne of Denmark made their way back to Scotland when their boat nearly capsized. Later, rumors circulated that King James was in great danger from a plot or a curse put upon him by the witches of North Berwick.

This quickly caught King James' attention, since he had always been fascinated by witchcraft. It wasn't long until the supposed witches were captured and put on trial. One young woman, called Gilly Duncan, confessed under torture that she and other witches cursed the King, and were intent upon murdering him by chanting spells and evil curses. She also claimed that she and other witches were in cahoots with the Earl of

Boswell, first in line to the throne after King James' death. King James' morbid fascination with witchcraft only fed his paranoid delusions about the mysterious powers of women. When James authorized the *King James Bible*, his translators changed the Hebrew word for "poisoner" into the English word for "witch," two terms that are hardly interchangeable. The word stuck however, and the rest is sad history of the murder of many innocent people, mostly women.

King James had earlier written a treatise against witchcraft. Wild claims about the Devil being intent upon murdering King James were made and rumors flew. It was reported back to King James that a group of Scottish witches had gathered at night near a castle in Edinburgh where they fashioned a waxen image, or witch's poppet (a European version of a voodoo doll) of the King. In front of a raging bonfire, the witches passed the wax doll amongst themselves, chanting in unison:

"This is King James the VI, ordained to be consumed at the instance of a nobleman, Francis Hepburn, Earl of Bothwell." The witches' poppet was tossed into the flames where it melted away instantly.

Were such dubious claims likely? It is highly doubtful. Most of the women charged with witchcraft identified themselves as devout Christians, and would not likely talk ill against such a powerful and paranoid ruler.

But the story fit in perfectly with what the King already believed, making him even more determined to hunt down the "witches" who were "persecuting" him. More "witches" were brought forth and the King himself interrogated them. It was alleged that 200 witches met at a Church in North Berwick on All Hallows' Eve to curse King James again. It was then told that the Devil himself presided over the meeting wearing a black mask, preaching obedience to himself and bringing great evil against the King. Unable to stay quiet a moment longer, King James interjected and called the witches present liars.

For some inexplicable reason, one of the witches gestured for the King to come closer. She whispered words King James had spoken to his wife on their wedding night. No one knew why the woman would do such a thing. It sealed their doom.

The witches were later executed at Edinburgh's Castle Hill. But it did not end there. In later years, Scottish witches were "brought to justice" at MacBeth's Hill near the town of Nairn. Witchcraft had a strong hold in Scotland. Scottish rule executed 4,400 alleged witches. Only a handful of witches were executed in England and Ireland. Next to Germany, Scotland murdered more people during their witch trials than any other country.

In light of our tale, if the names of "Duncan" and "MacBeth" sound familiar, there is a reason for it. It has long been thought that King James held great influence over William Shakespeare and was even responsible for Shakespeare's unflattering portrayal of Scottish witches in his play "Macbeth."

King James was certainly one of the most literate of all British kings and Shakespeare's *Macbeth* was written only seventeen years after the initial royal paranoia about the Berwick witches, a long enough time for the imagination to fodder and to take certain liberties with the actual story.

Most of the scenes for *MacBeth* took place at Glamis Castle, allegedly the most haunted castle in Scotland. This was even acknowledged in the day of Shakespeare. But Scotland's influence on public thought having to do with witches and witchcraft did not end there. Many trials and executions were to follow later.

And yet the powers of witchcraft still lurked in Scotland's remote forests, its lonely crashing shores and mystic mountains of gloom.

North of Aberdeen, there is a haunted place called the "Forest of Marr." It is believed this is the area where some of the Scottish witches escaped. As they went underground, the women's occult powers grew.

It was conjectured that the ghosts of the executed witches eventually became Banshee spirits and continued to roam the countryside, bringing persecution and death to the Scottish Clans who backed King James.

From the Aberdeen area of Scotland to Wood County, came a family named "Marr." Some have said that their lives were marred by the earlier witches' tragedies. And now we begin our first tale moving from the dark reaches of Scotland into the even darker reaches of West Virginia.

The Banshee of Marr

On certain lonely, moonless nights in the Mid-Ohio Valley, under a sky littered with stars, riding over the hills of Marrtown, there appears a shrouded figure on a white horse—one that is known as "the Banshee of Marrtown."

Marrtown was once a small farming community southeast of Parkersburg. The family of Scottish immigrant Thomas Marr settled Marrtown in 1836. Thomas later married a local woman named Mary Disosche whose family owned a local brewery. The Marr family brought to America many of the ancient beliefs and superstitions. The daughter of a widow, Mary Marr was an autumn bride, considered to be an ill omen by the Scottish people. In years to come, Mary would lose six of the eight children that she bore. Only two would carry on the Marr name. Times were hard for Thomas and Mary Marr but they did not lose their dream of a better life, pouring their energies into a simple tract of land that is now Marrtown.

Soon, a picturesque white farmhouse stood against shadowy woods thick with sumac, milkweed and blackberry brambles, framed by a sweeping green valley. To the west of the Marr homestead was a steep hill that ran directly into the Ohio River. To the north was Fort Boreman Hill, where Union troops camped during the Civil War, and where a Pest House housed locals and soldiers who had contracted typhoid fever, small pox and other diseases.

The years of the Civil War, as for most, were not happy ones for the Marr Family. They lost two of their children to typhoid fever. From their front window Thomas and Mary witnessed small clashes that turned into bloody battles between Yankee and Confederate soldiers. There were public hangings on nearby Fort Boreman Hill. As the Civil War drew to a close, marauding soldiers from both sides stole freely from the

Marr family, making off with what food and stock the family had put away for themselves.

Shortly after the Civil War, the Marr family's Scottish brew of bad luck appeared to come to an end. Thomas landed a job as night watchman at the toll bridge that crossed over the Little Kanawha River from lower Parkersburg to the road leading into Marrtown. Mary would stay home to tend the farm and children. Still, there were ominous hints of what was about to unfold.

Thomas told his wife that while traveling to and from his work, he had seen a robed figure riding a white horse. He had come upon this rider nearly every night in the identical spot not far from his farmhouse. Mr. Marr said he was not able to determine the gender of the person on the horse, but it was as if their paths were fated to meet. Some sense told Thomas that the person was a woman but he couldn't be sure. The face remained covered by a ragged hood. Whenever Thomas tried to approach the shrouded figure, the white mare reared. Horse and rider then disappeared into the mists of morning.

On a cold February night in the year 1876, Mary sat by the front window awaiting Thomas to come home from his job. Earlier, Mary had awakened suddenly and was eager to see her husband. The middle-aged woman heard footsteps coming up the road. She stood up to peer out the window. But instead of Thomas, a white horse loped up to the front gate of the house and then stopped. Sitting atop the horse was a rider whose face was covered by a tattered veil. It looked to be a woman. Alarmed, Mary moved from her chair and walked outside into the frigid night air. The rider, dressed in the threadbare clothing of a beggar, remained silent.

As bitter winds gusted, Mary pulled her woolen shawl close. Mary asked the rider what she wanted. There was no answer. Plumes of icy air billowed from the nostrils of the white horse. As Mary repeated her question, rider and horse inched closer. The aged woman sat stiffly in her saddle. Underneath the gauzy veil, Mary saw that the woman's eyes radiated an eerie red glow.

After a few moments, the woman on the horse spoke. "I am here to tell you, Mary Marr, that Thomas Marr has just died. Say your prayers, Lady. I bid you well." Rider and horse turned abruptly and galloped away.

Mary collapsed onto the front stoop. Through tears, she watched the shrouded woman and her horse vanish. Within the hour, a man who worked with Thomas came to deliver the dreaded news.

No one knows for sure what happened to Thomas Marr that fated winter evening. Some say that while working at the toll bridge Thomas was shot by an assailant's bullet, and then fell and drowned in the Little Kanawha River. Others claim that it was the cry of the Banshee that startled Thomas into meeting his end in the river below. Others reported Thomas Marr dead along the B & O Railroad tracks only a few yards away from the turbulent waters. After all, it is known that the keening of the Banshee is most often heard over bodies of water. The truth is, Thomas Marr did die on February 5th, 1878 when the Marrtown Banshee made her visit, and she had to cross water to do so.

In years to come, the Banshee did not abandon her Marr clan. The ghostly rider continued to make other visits to the family. Mary Marr lived to be ninety-years old. Such advanced years were an exception for the time. As Mary lay as a corpse in the parlor of her home many years after her husband's death, family members heard the rattling of chains in the attic. Others claimed to hear the shrieks of a wild cat near the house around the same time.

A few years after Mary died, one of the Marr descendants had his arm cut off in a tragic accident. As family members sat up with the boy, they heard snarling and growling sounds on the porch. When the women went outside to see what it was, the stoop where Mary met her Banshee was covered with blood as if a terrible struggle had taken place.

What has become of the Banshee of Marrtown? It is said she still rides, giving dreaded omens to those of Scottish blood. Not Scottish or Irish, you say? You would still be wise to avoid Marrtown on certain still, dark and moonless nights.

Center Point Banshee

Banshees aside, if you have ever had the opportunity to fly over West Virginia and the Mid-Ohio Valley in a small plane, you may have noticed the foliage below appears as dense and electric-green as that of a rainforest, an excellent place for harboring fugitives but terrible for your sinuses!

In a time where most of the wilderness in the U.S. is vanishing, West Virginia is still "wild and wonderful," as the slogan says. But the "wildness" may mean something other than what the travel ads claim.

Native American tribes were afraid of these lands. The Shawnee Indians were especially spooked by the land east of the Ohio River, and avoided it as much as possible. The Native Americans did not make a habit of settling into what is now West Virginia, believing it cursed by ghosts and strange beasts.

There is a community in a remote part of Doddridge County called Center Point, a place that is now a ghost town. Center Point is typical of small mountain communities reclaimed by the woods. The village used to have a post office and the Ross Country Store, but that is all gone. A craggy, brown creek courses through lush foliage with leaves as big as mud flaps. Modest white houses cling to the sides of hills with sloping yards made muddy by children at play.

In Center Point, there isn't much for children to do other than chase each other with sticks or head for the creek in search of the little brown clots with pinchers known to West Virginians as "crawdads."

Nothing much had ever happened in Center Point until the summer of 1918, when the Black Flu hit. That was the year when the people of Center Point thought the entire world was coming to an end. The rest of the world did, too. Millions had already died.

And…unless you were a seven-year-old girl named Pearl White who loved to play in the woods, one who dreamed of flapping her arms and flying away like a bird, a place like Center Point could be pretty dull. But there was plenty for Pearl to do. She had drive and imagination. She wasn't worried about the Black Flu. Sickness happened to people older than she was and Pearl was invincible. Why, she almost knew how to fly already!

It was near dusk in late summer. Pearl was staying with her Grandmother at Center Point on the farm while relatives traveled to Pennsboro to help those already stricken by Black Flu. Like so many of the flu victims, Pearl's young, unmarried uncle had taken sick but appeared to be doing fine. His flu didn't seem to be much worse than a chest cold. It was odd how the Black Flu preyed upon those in the full bloom of life. Many victims that succumbed to the Black Flu were young, only in their twenties and thirties. But Pearl's uncle was in good spirits, sitting up and talking as the days wore on.

One late August evening drew in a bit more somberly than before. The indigo of twilight was upon Pearl and her grandmother. The night was clear. There was not one cloud among the stars. Flickering lights studded the evening sky. Pearl counted the Big Dipper, the belt of Orion, and the North Star, and dreamed of flying to all of them. Center Point was small, but the world was still hers.

Pearl's grandmother was in the process of taking her granddaughter to the outhouse one more time for the night before retiring to bed. As darkness enclosed, the clip-clop sound of horses' hooves sounded up the road. The trot was slow and measured. Whoever it was didn't seem to be in a hurry. They looked around to see a rider on a horse. Grandmother thought perhaps it was the mailman paying a late visit. After all, the Black Flu had taken its toll on Center Point. Many people had died. Mail could arrive at just about anytime of day or evening.

Pearl and her grandmother paused to watch the rider and horse make their way toward the farmhouse. Crickets sang in the shadows.

It seemed strange how the figure sat erect on the horse and was enshrouded in pale, fluttering rags almost like a mummy. The horse itself was also pale like a ghost. The gender of the rider could not be made out either, although something told them it was a woman.

Pearl felt an urge to draw near the figure. She was curious and ran toward the front porch, where the horse and rider seemed to be intent upon stopping. Her grandmother followed Pearl. Now they could see that the rider looked more like an old woman but still, the little girl was not sure. The rider's face was covered by what was a torn, ragged veil. Garnet red eyes glittered beneath the gauzy fabric. The hands looked old and waxen, too, like those that had been sealed within a coffin.

Pearl's grandmother recoiled but still the little girl ran to meet the figure on the horse anyway. They sauntered up the front walk. The sun was entirely gone, the world left in shadows. The rider tugged on the bridle and the horse stopped. In later years, Pearl would say that she was so close to that Banshee's horse that she could feel its hot breath on her face.

Yes, those of Celtic blood called this creature a Banshee. Pearl and her relatives were of Scottish descent and this is a classic way that the Scottish Banshee appears, usually as a shrouded figure.

And yet, on that fated night in Center Point, the Banshee spirit issued a warning. She pointed a bony finger at Pearl's Grandmother and proclaimed in a rasping voice, "One of yours is to die this very night!"

A keening cry split the evening's stillness. Banshee and horse instantly vanished.

Shaken and left in shadows, Pearl and her grandmother hugged each other. But there was no time to think about the terrible thing that had just happened. Already sounds were coming from the house, sounds of someone struggling for air.

It was Pearl's uncle. The two ran inside just in time to realize that the young man's lungs were filled with fluid. Blood foamed from his nose and mouth. This was the way people died when they had the Black Flu. Grandmother knew it. There was no saving him. Within moments, Pearl's uncle had drowned in his own blood. After the death rattle, all became still, except for the sound of horses' hooves galloping away. It was then something squalled like a wildcat in the distance.

Despite the evening when she witnessed her uncle's terrible death from the Black Flu, Pearl White grew up and she did learn to fly. She became a pioneer in the field of aviation and was the first woman to parachute out of a plane. Pearl was a member of the famous "Barnstormers," a name given to pilots who performed dangerous stunts. Pearl performed her stunts all the way from the Pennsboro Fair in 1935 to the movies in Hollywood, California.

In her life, Pearl White feared very little. In fact, as a young woman she was attracted to danger. When she was just sixteen, men would strap Pearl's body to the belly of a plane, go up and then swoop down so she could pick up small objects off the ground. She broke her back once at Ravenswood, West Virginia in 1935, and yet she recovered.

It was strange how in later years, Pearl was often afraid to sit outside on her front porch at her modest home on upper Juliana Street in Parkersburg. There was something that disturbed her. . . the oncoming of night.

Pearl was not afraid to be strapped to a plane and fly through the air. She was not afraid to jump out of one as a teenager. After meeting up with the Center Point Banshee as a small child the only thing Pearl White was ever afraid of—was the dark.

The Coach-A-Bower-Of-Mineral Wells

The Banshee has a power that she shares with witches, and that is the power of *glamoury*. Glamoury is a Gaelic word that simply means to "shape shift" to alter one's self at will. It is also the Scottish derivative of the Old French "gramaire," from which our word "grammar" came from which meant to "recite a spell!"

To some, glamoury is an illusion. To others glamoury is real. Witches are said to master glamoury by turning into birds, animals or even a more attractive or younger person. But in Ireland, Scotland and West Virginia the Banshee sometimes takes on another form, one that is neither animal nor human.

Along Route 14, between the small communities of Mineral Wells and Elizabeth, the Banshee assumes the disquieting form of a death omen. In Gaelic it is called the *coiste-bodhar*, or the 'Coach-A-Bower,' a black hearse with a coffin strapped to the top and lead by two white headless horses.

In Ireland and Scotland, the Coach-A-Bower often precedes the visit of the Banshee. And since the Banshee appears at households to announce a death, you would best do well not to open the door when you hear the rumbling of a carriage outside. This is when the darker side of the Banshee's fairy powers of the Coach-A-Bower becomes evident. Those who are unwise enough to open the door are met with a basin of blood tossed into their faces.

However, even in the quiet meadows and mossy woods of West Virginia, the Coach-A-Bower is updated. It is a phantom black hearse that winds its way along Route 14 between Mineral Wells and Elizabeth. And yet, the hearse is not entirely modern. It appears to be one from the time of the 1950s, perhaps even earlier.

A spiritualist group meets in Mineral Wells once a month upon every full moon. They have done so for a few years, and many evenings are spent communicating with spirits from other realms. No one had given a thought to the idea of a Banshee appearing!

In the spring of 1998, one séance lasted well past midnight. As one of the participants got into her car to go home, she noticed that the air had grown quite chilly and the full moon, that now looked to be the size of a pearl, had slipped behind veils of black clouds. As the woman proceeded with her drive on Route 14 toward Parkersburg, she soon noticed that she was trailing a black hearse.

As the hearse ambled through the hills, it looked shiny but dangerous, like a loaded gun. In the mist and fog, its' taillights blinked like a pulse. The woman thought that it was odd that a hearse would be out at such a late hour. What was stranger was the fact that the hearse, with pulled velvet curtains, appeared to be from a different era, like a relic put in antique car shows, or those dusted off for community parades as curiosities from the past.

The woman followed closely, it would seem rude or disrespectful to pass a hearse. Within moments the hearse had vanished. Curious, the woman sped up a bit to see if she could catch another glimpse of the black, snaking vehicle. By the time she got to the interchange that would take her back to Parkersburg there was no sign of the hearse.
But seeing the old-fashioned hearse was so unusual the woman did not forget it and later asked the others if they had seen the hearse on the way home. No one else had.

Within the month, one of the members of the spiritual group experienced a wrenching family tragedy so terrible that it would be sacrilege to reveal in a format like this that is meant to entertain. The woman often talked of visiting Scotland and was proud of having Scottish blood. She dreamed of a time when she could see first-hand ancient Scotland where a belief in psychic powers and omens remained strong. Was it the Banshee's Coach-A-Bower or just a strange mix of circumstances that foreshadowed the tragic event?

As with many mysteries, we will never know.

And yet, it is important to remember that every Scottish and Irish clan has its' own Banshee. According to the Irish poet Yeats, important people often have an entire chorus of Banshees that sing upon their demise.

Luckily, I've not met my Banshee yet.

Let us hope you won't meet yours any time too soon.

TWO
Otherworldly Tales: Woodrow Derenberger & the Men in Black

The date is November 2nd, 1966. The time is 7:15 p.m. You are driving down a lonely stretch of highway, somewhere between the valleys and sloping hills of western West Virginia. Your car radio is tuned in to a ballad sung by the late Patsy Cline or maybe a Willie Nelson tune. . .before he grew his hair out and got famous. Over your right shoulder, the sky is tinged a faint pink. The hills are inky black. As a light rain falls, you turn on the windshield wipers but you barely need them, so you switch on your wipers every minute or so. Rainfall is minimal and it's less distracting that way.

A few passing cars catch you in their beams. Your trip home is relaxing as you travel through the slanting landscape. The world inside your truck is so comforting and insulated that you struggle to keep your eyelids open. Perhaps you dream of your wife's famous homemade vegetable soup and putting your soaked feet up by the fire and making small talk with your better half about what happened at work today. Business was slow, but should pick up shortly, as many homemakers would be expecting a new Singer sewing machine on Christmas morning—because that's what you sell at your store in Marietta, Ohio—brand new Singer sewing machines.

Almost dreaming, in a place between wakefulness and sleep something enormous and dark rushes up behind you. The force makes your entire vehicle rattle and shake—just like a Jerry Lee Lewis song. The thing is huge and dark and menacing . . . A tractor-trailer truck veering out of control? Can't be. . . there aren't any lights. Hey, what kind of a crazy nut would drive without his lights on anyway? Now, the thing pushes you off the highway. It's barreling down. Cripes! You struggle with your steering wheel and try to bring your vehicle under control. After a few tense moments, you get your truck to the side of the road. The "craft" (as you will learn to call it later) swerves slightly then rolls over you. Just like a ball of fire. And yet, there is no light to see by. As you clutch your steering wheel, with beaded sweat on your brow, you notice a door opening in the craft. It's some kind of hatch. You see warm light and a man pass through it. A human arm helps him out the door. A tall stranger steps from the craft walking toward you in an unhurried manner. As he gets closer to your car, the dark gray craft shoots seventy feet straight up and hovers suspended in space.

You hear the man's words over and over: "Do not be afraid. I mean you no harm. . ." words that will eventually sear into your brain like a brand and yet his lips do not move.

Your name is Woodrow Derenberger and your life will never be the same. . . .

*   *   *   *

To most readers the name of "Woodrow Derenberger" may not be a famous one. But to a select number of UFO enthusiasts and older residents of West Virginia and the Ohio Valley, the name "Derenberger" still holds meaning. After all, Mr. Derenberger was at the center of one of the most bizarre and fascinating UFO cases in U.S. history—one that would help spawn a Hollywood movie thirty-five years later.

Woodrow Derenberger was a man of modest means. He worked as a salesman, commuting from his farmhouse in Mineral Wells, West Virginia to his job in Marietta, Ohio, a distance of about twenty miles. Up until November 2nd, 1966, Woody Derenberger could only be described as your average Joe, serving as Deacon at his local church, going about his routine as a husband and father of two small children.

However, life for Woodrow Derenberger would change after that date, in ways that he could not imagine. Depending upon whom you ask, opinions of Derenberger vary. Some consider Mr. Derenberger to be the first person to go on record by reporting his "close encounter" to the authorities. Others believe the stresses of every day life may have been too much for Derenberger and he fashioned a story of an alien encounter for the attention or some other complex, emotional reason.

No matter what we believe, something extraordinary occurred to Woodrow Derenberger on that early November night, whether real or imagined, as he drove south on I-77 home to his farm in Mineral Wells. Derenberger's claims were so mind-boggling that service men from West Virginia and the Ohio Valley listened to reports of the Derenberger's close encounter over the radio while serving in the jungles of Vietnam. This fantastic tale of a brush with a UFO proved so compelling that media from Australia and Japan descended upon Parkersburg.

Derenberger's meeting up with the UFO took place sometime after 7:00 p.m. A slight rain misted. The highway was completely dark except for the headlights of the occasional cars that he met along the route home. Derenberger was nearing his turn off at State Route 47 when his panel truck rocked with the force of something large coming up behind him at a high rate of speed. As he glanced into the rearview mirror, he could see a dark object on his tail. But at that point the object did not touch the ground. The UFO then rolled over the top of Derenberger's vehicle forcing him to the side of the road.

Derenberger later described the craft as being similar to "the shape of a glass chimney of an old-fashioned kerosene lamp lying on its side, with a dome-like top." Derenberger also stated the UFO was charcoal gray in color and until its hatch opened, he never saw any lights. He claimed the spacecraft never touched the ground at anytime and instead, floated about twelve inches above the berm of the road.

Within minutes Derenberger glimpsed a harsh yellow light as a hatch opened in the side of the craft and a tall man wearing what looked to be dark trench coat climbed out. Derenberger later described the individual as, "Like any man you would see on the street" and added "there was really nothing exceptional about his appearance."

As the stranger walked toward Derenberger's vehicle, the alien craft shot vertically into the air to a height of approximately 75 feet and that is where it stayed for the entire duration of the conversation.

Mr. Derenberger saw that the craft's occupant appeared between 35 and 40 years old, was close to six feet tall and weighed about 185 pounds. The man had a tan complexion and dark brown hair, which was slicked back. The man's clothing described as gray and shimmering was covered partially by a dark overcoat.

As rain fell lightly on the vehicles the stranger talked to Mr.

Derenberger in a friendly, almost soothing way. Derenberger thought it strange he understood what the man was saying so easily because his car window was rolled up. The stranger again reassured Woodrow: "Do not be afraid," the dark-haired man repeated, "I mean you no harm. I only want to ask you a few questions." (Later Derenberger claimed the man continued to repeat throughout the conversation "Be not afraid. Why are you so frightened? We only wish you happiness.") But the Marietta businessman was alarmed because while the man talked, his lips did not move at all. He apparently communicated with the salesman through mental telepathy.

The tall man introduced himself as "Cold" and pointed toward the city lights of Parkersburg that glowed in the distance. Cold asked, "What do you call that?"

Mr. Derenberger answered, "That's Parkersburg. I call that a city."

Indrid Cold then said, "Where I come from, we call it "a gathering." The alien being would later tell Woodrow Derenberger in other visits that he was from "a place called 'Lanulos,' a country less powerful than yours."

This struck Derenberger as curious since Cold claimed to have traveled to Mineral Wells from another galaxy, a feat believed technologically impossible on earth.

Even so, Cold held a 10-15 minute conversation with Derenberger, discussing topics such as cities and towns, the climate, population, and oddly, the farming of livestock in the area. Throughout the conversation Indrid Cold smiled and had his arms crossed over his chest, with hands hidden under his armpits. During their talk, Derenberger couldn't recall ever seeing Cold's hands. And even stranger, as Indrid Cold spoke to Woodrow Derenberger the alien's lips did not move. At times there seemed to be an echo behind his words. In fact, Cold's voice at times seemed to be nothing more than echoes reverberating in Derenberger's head.

There was another eerie feature to this strange tale. Derenberger claimed that as he talked to the alien visitor, other cars passed under the craft, unbeknownst to what was suspended above. The Mineral Wells resident saw no lights.

Once the conversation ended and Indrid Cold gave his farewell, the alien walked back toward the craft, which by this time had settled down to its former position. As Cold entered the ship, Derenberger reported that a second arm appeared from the doorway to help him inside. After the hatch shut behind the stranger, the space ship shot into the air and flew away at a high rate of speed with a fluttering sound.

Derenberger sat in the darkness of his car wondering what to do next. As soon as the UFO was out of sight, the Mineral Wells resident turned on his ignition and drove to his house in a daze. His wife met him at the door and was startled by his paleness and trembling. "What has happened to you?" she asked as she helped him inside. After explaining his frightening encounter to his wife, she promptly called the West Virginia State Police.

A media storm in the Mid-Ohio Valley followed the initial telling of Derenberger's story. A press conference was called the next day with local media and law enforcement as well as officials from the Wood County Airport. Once again, Woody Derenberger told his strange tale the afternoon of November 3, 1966. Derenberger was to give a live interview on WTAP-TV, the local NBC affiliate, when interviewed by veteran reporter Glenn Wilson and Wood County Sheriff Ed Plumb. It was in that format that Derenberger chose to enlighten the world of his encounter with Indrid Cold, the visitor who came from a "country less powerful than yours" that still holds sway over our imaginations.

The tale of alien visitors told by Woodrow Derenberger is not a simple one. Yet the middle-aged sewing machine salesman never deviated from his original story. No amount of criticism or ridicule caused him to recant his original tale of alien visitors and Indrid Cold— at least not in the beginning. . . .

Television/Government Interviews

While conducting research for the Haunted Parkersburg tour in 1996, we happened upon one of the more fascinating elements of the story: the actual reel-to-reel audio tapes of Woodrow Derenberger's live press conference in November of 1966.

The tapes were in the possession of veteran newsman Glenn Wilson who interviewed Derenberger at least twice for more than an hour. Wilson decided to donate these rare tapes to the Haunted Parkersburg team for historical value and safekeeping. Until they were transferred to cassette, the tapes had not been listened to for over thirty years. At times

Derenberger is flustered and repeats himself, or tries to clarify what he has previously stated. As the tapes progress, so does the sincerity of Mr. Derenberger's words—a man who is clearly still frightened.

Woodrow Derenberger, November 1966 during WTAP-TV, Channel 15 live interview Parkersburg interview

Tape #1

The first taped interview is moderated by Glenn Wilson (WTAP Anchor), and Ronald Maines (WTAP General Manager). The running time of tape #1 is approximately 27 minutes. It simply covers the story of Derenberger's experience on I-77 of the previous evening.

At one point in the interview a reporter asked Mr. Derenberger if he drank alcohol or had stopped at a bar on his way home. As a deacon of a Christian Church on Parkersburg's South Side, Derenberger emphatically stated that he did not drink alcohol, nor was he drinking at the time of his encounter.

Wood County Sheriff Ed Plumb mentions to Derenberger that there had been a story similar to his written up in newspapers and magazines weeks before. Plumb asked Mr. Derenberger if he had previously read that reported tale of a UFO.

Woodrow Derenberger states, that no, he did not, because up until his encounter with Indrid Cold he did not believe in UFOs, therefore, he had no interest in the subject and he would not have read such an article.

Tape #2

On this tape Derenberger relates how the UFO forced him to the side of the road, how long it took him to stop and how close he was to Cold's craft. The reporters questioned him about the distance between his car, the spacecraft and the highway. Other questions had to do with what time it started raining, when the rain stopped and how Derenberger was able to talk with the alien visitor since his window was rolled up?

After describing Indrid Cold and his clothing it was asked how Derenberger was able to see such detail since it was dark and rainy. Mr. Derenberger stuck to his guns and said that throughout his conversation with Indrid Cold other cars passed under the suspended craft, and shone light on both of them enabling him to see what Cold looked like. Derenberger said Cold's face was not one he would likely forget.

At one point in the tape Woodrow Derenberger draws a picture of the spacecraft. What has happened to the drawing, we do not know. During the interview you can also hear Derenberger emphatically beating his knuckles on the desk while he is answering questions as if frustrated over not being believed.

Tape #3

It is mentioned on Tape 3# that officials were en route from Wright-Patterson Air Force Base in Dayton, Ohio to question Woodrow Derenberger and Derenberger said he had no objections. The middle-aged man commented that he had nothing to hide since he was telling the truth and he did not care who questioned him. (What happened during this interview is not known because no other officials seemed to be present for it.)

This is when the conversation turned more personal and Derenberger was questioned about his private life. He declined to give out any information about his family, saying that except for his wife, they knew nothing of his story.

Sometime during the interview, one asked, "Mr. Derenberger, if this Indrid Cold told you to 'be not afraid,' and did not threaten you in any way, why are you frightened? Would you be happy . . . to see him again?"

"I would be happy to, BUT. . ." It is then Woodrow Derenberger contradicts his earlier words, "Cold said 'we will see you again,' and I'm afraid. . . I'm afraid he will and I don't want him to." When saying this Mr. Derenberger's voice fades out. . .

The MIB Visitations

After the initial press conference, Woodrow Derenberger's life careened out of control, turning into a surreal circus. Initially, Derenberger did not want to call law enforcement after being stopped by Cold's spacecraft for fear of public ridicule. However, his wife convinced him that he should do so for the safety of the general public. Derenberger's fears of becoming an object of ridicule indeed came true when many residents in the Mid-Ohio Valley scoffed over Derenberger's "flying saucer" and his "Martians."

Reporters from across the globe began to harangue Derenberger for further interviews and "more details." Local citizens stopped him on the street, occasionally to offer support, but just as often to make him the target of their insensitive jokes. Finally, Derenberger decided to avoid the general public as much as possible. What the sewing machine salesman had thought would be a marginal tale with a simple truth had turned into a fiasco. Woodrow Derenberger's simple life had changed, and he was more alone in this bizarre experience than any person could ever be.

And then there were the visitations—No, not Indrid Cold exactly. (That would come later, if not in a physical way, then telepathically.) Derenberger was visited by the "Men in Black." Just when he thought things couldn't get worse, three visitors dressed entirely in black and driving a black Cadillac came rolling up his driveway. Thinking they were government officials, Derenberger invited the men into his home. The men were odd in their mannerisms, almost robotic and they had a quick, mechanical way of speaking. The Men in Black questioned Woodrow about his encounter with the spacecraft.

At first they acted interested in Mr. Derenberger's story. But intermingled with the questions were vague threats for Derenberger to keep quiet in the future or something very bad might happen to him or members of his family. At the time, Mr. Derenberger believed the Men in Black to be members of the Mafia.

For a while, fearing he was being threatened by the Mafia or the United States government, Mr. Derenberger backed off and tried to return to a normal family life. That's when he began to receive the messages. At first it started with buzzing and clicking sounds in his head and the familiar words: *Do not be afraid. I mean you no harm. . .*

It was Cold again.

Through mental telepathy, or some other form of mind control, the alien said he was coming back. He told Woody that he was supposed to prepare a place for his ship to land, on top of a ridge beyond Mineral Wells, at an area called Bogle Run. At various times, Mr. Derenberger and several others went up on the ridge to await Cold's spacecraft, but the alien ship never materialized for anyone other than Woodrow Derenberger. Family members also speak of several times when Derenberger told them, in an effort to verify his telepathic communications with Indrid Cold, for them to "look up into the sky for certain colored lights in the east, west or south," and they would be able to "see Cold's spacecraft at a specific time in the evening." Sure enough, when family members looked for the colored lights in the sky they always appeared at the EXACT time and in the direction Woodrow Derenberger said they would. Generally, the lights were green, yellow or red and flashing. Not an easy feat for someone on the ground to accomplish. Derenberger explained that Cold always told him where he would be during his visits to earth and when he would be flying over.

What really happened to Derenberger after Cold's visitations is open to speculation. Some say that Woodrow Derenberger went about his life as normally as possible, ignoring the public's sympathies and insults. He became more active in his church for a while. Yet, he claimed to remain in contact with the space aliens, and said that he was visited by Cold in the flesh on several other occasions. There are claims that after a few years of stress and confusion, Mr. Derenberger recanted his original story. But many believe this was after a particularly frightening visit by the Men in Black at his Mineral Wells farm.

What did the Wood County resident really encounter on November 2, 1966 as a mid-autumn rain misted around his modest panel truck on I-77 during that chilly, damp night?

Were Derenberger's words at the TV news conference the day following his encounter the ravings of a lunatic or the boasting of a sad, lonely man craving attention? Was Woody (as his friends called him) simply a pawn in the secrets our government continues to keep? Or was he a prophet for the enlightenment of a new age?

In some published correspondences, writer John Keel said he was not convinced about Derenberger's account of his meeting with Indrid Cold. Keel wrote that Derenberger may have "made it up." But if so, how did Derenberger know that less than two weeks later, another spectacular sighting would occur—an event that frightened residents throughout West Virginia and that had little to do with Indrid Cold.

These spectacular sightings were of a red-eyed, winged creature that came to be known as the Mothman. How had Woodrow Derenberger known what was about to unfold? When the Mineral Wells man reported his encounter to the West Virginia State police, the state had not experienced such a spectacular event since the Flatwoods monster in the mid-1950s. Was Derenberger a prophet, a victim trapped by insane circumstances or a misguided hoaxer?

There is no clear answer. For this reason, the mystery of Woodrow Derenberger's astonishing encounter may never be solved. Maybe he was waiting for a time when others might verify his encounter with alien beings. Perhaps another person would eventually meet up with the strange man dressed in a black overcoat who introduced himself as Indrid Cold. That time never came for Woodrow Derenberger. He died with most of the general public disbelieving him.

However, before coming to an answer as to whether Indrid Cold even existed, there were other witnesses with a similar story to Derenbergers'. At the exact time Woodrow Derenberger was having his conversation with Indrid Cold, residents of the nearby Cedar Grove community reported experiencing interference with their television sets. Authorities received a report from a Cedar Grove man who claimed his TV set went "berserk." He wondered if there was a strange electrical incident or accident in Wood County that was causing it?

On the same night Woodrow Derenberger had his visitation near the turn off at Route 47 near Parkersburg, an elderly gentleman was driving home toward Point Pleasant—fifty-some miles down river from Parkersburg—who claimed to have had a similar encounter but without seeing a UFO. The older man reported that a tall man had stopped him along the edge of the highway. He asked him a number of seemingly pointless questions like whether he knew what the weather was going to be or did he know of anyone who had livestock? Afraid he was about to be robbed he never rolled down his window completely. This senior citizen didn't stick around for the entire interview, but instead spun away quickly, leaving the man standing by the side of the road.

Instead of calling the police, the older man dropped in at a local newspaper the next morning to see if anyone else had witnessed or reported the same experience. (The Derenberger story had not yet hit the newspapers.)

Around this time handfuls of people from around the world claimed to experience similar visitations from benevolent beings from other worlds. Although only Derenberger said the craft came from a planet called Lanulos, the style of encounter reported by the contactees was always the same. The visitors would scout out a solitary person, approach them, and then ask questions that seemed to have little relevance. The beings always appeared human-like, attractive, and friendly.

Often, the messages took on a more serious tone, claiming Earth was on the verge of a major evolutionary leap and that their mission was to choose selected people to help prepare for the day when the first official contact would be made.

Perhaps the next most famous visitation of this type was that of George Adamski. Adamski was reclusive man who claimed to have communications with "the Space Brothers," whose warnings were that the people of Earth needed to start thinking globally and stop fighting one another. Humanity "needed to find forms of renewable resources," as Adamski was told, "Before we destroy the ecosphere."

Adamski's visitation from aliens matched Derenbergers' visitor nearly to the letter, down to Cold's description of gatherings and the peaceful vegetarian lifestyle. The description of Adamski's "Space Brother" was similar to Cold with the exception of his visitor having long flowing sandy hair, whereas Cold's hair was dark and combed straight back.

It's been thirty-five years since the initial visit of Indrid Cold to the Ohio Valley, and several unanswered questions remain. Was Indrid Cold a Space Brother flying down from a place called Lanulos to warn us, or are these just the tales of imaginative or deluded individuals? Could these stories of Indrid Cold visitations be based on reality—a reality the rest of us are blind to?

No matter what the tried and true facts are, the accounts of Indrid Cold reach much farther than a visit with a tired sewing machine salesman on a rainy November night on a lonely stretch of road in rural West Virginia.

Another, Perhaps, Related Sighting

This letter appeared as a posted message on a UFO sighting report on the Internet:

"I want to relate a sighting that another witness and I had in 1997. I was training a new driver for a produce delivery route that I had in West Virginia. We were about 10 miles or so south of Marietta, Ohio. This was about six miles north of Mineral Wells.

"As I was proceeding down the highway (I-77), my partner yelled, "Look at that!" He startled me so bad that I almost lost control of the truck. Anyway, I looked out my window, and to my total amazement, I witnessed a large, black triangle, heading eastward just above the hills.

"I gathered my senses and pulled the truck to the side of the road. We both got out of the truck to look at it. As I stood, I held my arm straight up and made a fist. It was about twice the size of my fist. If I had had a rock, I could have hit it! I could see plainly that it had a non-reflective, kind of flat-black, surface. On the bottom of this craft were four lights. They looked as if they were on dim. That is to say, they did not shine brightly, but were definitely visible.

"The one thing that caught my attention was that the craft appeared to make no sound what so ever! It just seemed to float. It was moving so slowly that I could have out raced it on foot. We watched it for at least 10 minutes; then it moved over the hills and we lost sight of it. We got back into the truck and went south a few miles and I pulled over to see if I could see it again. We didn't see anything again that night."

What is most fascinating about this posting is the driver who wrote this obviously knew nothing about Derenberger's Indrid Cold encounter thirty-one years before, and yet this is almost the exact spot where Derenberger claimed he was stopped by Cold's craft.

Gray Barker: Prankster, Media Genius or Flying Saucer Boogie Man?

One can hardly discuss UFOs in West Virginia—the Mothman, Men in Black or the Flatwoods monster without bringing up the name of a man from Clarksburg named Gray Barker.

As has been written of the West Virginia Mothman, similarly Gray Barker has been called a "strange bird." For a number of years, Barker managed a local bijou in his hometown of Clarksburg promoting Saturday matinee horror films, while writing and publishing on the side. In 1957, Barker published his famous book *They Knew Too Much About Flying Saucers*, introducing to the general public stories about the conspiracies involving UFOs and strange tales concerning "the Men in Black," an idea introduced to Barker by his friend UFO investigator Albert Bender in Connecticut. (Bender had formed the UFO investigation group called The International Flying Saucer Bureau, and had encouraged Barker to form a West Virginia chapter.)

The Men in Black have become a much talked about enigma. Dressed entirely in black, they were said to threaten witnesses of UFO's into silence. It was written about by Albert Bender (and later by Gray Barker) that when some individuals report sightings of UFOs, or claimed encounters with aliens, they are soon visited by bizarre, rather menacing men who arrive in vintage 1950s Cadillac's or old model cars. These men uniformed in black are said to threaten witnesses into not talking anymore about "saucers" or to retract their stories. Usually with tanned or often pasty pale complexions, almond-shaped eyes and a strange mechanical way of speaking, the Men in Black were theorized to be government agents or even the aliens themselves.

Probably the strangest feature about the Men in Black is that they usually come across as intellectually slow or just plain stupid. It is hard to believe such cretins could frighten anyone, yet apparently they do. (So much so, that writer John Keel discourages children or young people from getting involved with UFO sightings, especially the Men in Black. Albert Bender had to retire from investigating UFOs because of chronic migraine headaches. Bender felt this was a type of "extraterrestrial interference.")

It is hard to apply the word "dangerous" to the Men in Black, because they apparently are fairly inept. For instance, in Point Pleasant during the Mothman scare, one of the Men in Black was witnessed swaying back and forth on a street corner chirping with the birds in the trees. Others were reported trying to drink their bowls of Jello in local restaurants. One MIB showed up to question and threaten a witness while wearing bright orange lipstick. (And not applied very well, at that.) Other than making ridiculous demands on UFO contactees to keep quiet about their saucer sightings, the Men in Black come across as pretty dumb.

Stories about the MIBs were quickly noted and written about in UFO circles. It was Gray Barker, Albert Bender and later John Keel who enabled the tales of the Men in Black to become a fixture among American pop culture. It was only after Gray Barker died in the 1980s that his ideas about saucers, government conspiracies and Men in Black came under fire. Some couldn't help but notice that Gray Barker appeared to be "a little too close" to these strange unfoldings of UFOs, the MIB and the Mothman.

Associates of Gray Barker pointed out that the Clarksburg writer always showed up when anything of a paranormal nature surfaced in West Virginia—this included the Flatwoods monster in the 1950s and even Derenberger's Indrid Cold encounter in the 1960s. Some of Barker's "friends" claimed that he was quite the hoaxer and could have fabricated any or all of the above stories, sightings, or events, and would have done so to make a buck. That may have even meant dressing up like the Mothman or posing as one of the Men in Black.

So, was this mischievous merry maker of Harrison County really our Mothman? Did Gray Barker dress up in a Halloween suit and appear in Point Pleasant so he could later sell his paranormal monster books?

Frankly, Gray Barker portraying the hoax of the Mothman or Indrid Cold is unlikely. How could he and why would he? Along with being an oddball UFO guy, Gray would have had to have premonitions of the bizarre events ready to unfold.

Many of Barker's detractors obviously don't know much about the geography and highways of West Virginia, especially during the 1950s and 1960s. For one thing, the road to Point Pleasant, located along the Ohio River, (where most of the Mothman sightings occurred) was a twisting and turning, grueling three-hour drive over a two-lane road from Clarksburg. To claim that Gray Barker dressed up in a Mothman suit so he could drive three hours or more in order to scare people whom he did not know, and never met, is ludicrous.

To our knowledge, Woodrow Derenberger did not know of nor did he ever come face to face with Gray Barker before the incident with Indrid Cold. Most of the UFO and Mothman sightings occurred in lonely, isolated spots during late hours, far away from the humble abode of Gray Barker in Clarksburg.

No doubt Gray Barker did help fan the flames of these now famous, still controversial tales. He may have stirred things up a bit, but Gray Barker did not start the fires that would later put spooky, brooding West Virginia as a key spot on the United States' paranormal map.

In the months following Derenberger's encounter with Indrid Cold, several other unexplained events began to materialize in surrounding areas.

Men in Black on Shannon's Knob

In March of 1967, two small girls played on a hillside overlooking the picturesque town of West Union. The hill was called Shannon's Knob.

At the top of Shannon's Knob was a power station that provided most of the electricity for the town. As the girls chased each other and hid behind trees, they noticed two darkly garbed men walking along a level spot below the power lines. They were dressed in pitch-dark clothing. One looked to be wearing a black uniform, with a black shirt and pants, while the other wore a dark gray trench coat. One man appeared to have lightened his hair to the color and texture of straw. He also had almond-shaped eyes and the yellow complexion of an Asian person.

There seemed to be something false about the blond-haired man. His skin tone didn't match his hair at all. It appeared as if he was dressed for some "effect."

As an adult, one of the girls who witnessed the MIBs wrote this: "Do you know how you go to a school play and you see a young person portray an elderly person? You see the hair is sprayed white, the wrinkles penciled in—but you still know it is a young person. The posture is too good. The bones are too straight. Well, it was the same for the Men in Black. At first they looked normal. But as you watched them—there was something deceptive about the men's appearance. I think that is why we were scared and hid in the weeds."

As the girls watched from the bushes, they noticed the Men in Black said little to one another as they surveyed the area. A feeling told the girls not to get too close, as there was something menacing about the strangers. They reminded the girls of the black-suited spies that were so popular on TV shows in the 1960s. This only gave the girls another reason to be frightened. Finally, the men wearing black disappeared over the knob.

The girls ran home and quickly forgot about the men wearing black. But a few days later, another group of school children came upon the same site and found a circular area where weeds were mashed and the ground was singed. The circle was around 25 feet in diameter.

In the mid 1960s, West Virginia had a plethora of UFO sightings and other bizarre happenings. One such sighting was of a creature almost superseding the appearances and hoopla surrounding Bigfoot in the Pacific Northwest and southern states.

West Virginia's creature had enormous wings that unfolded like the wings of a bat, a terrible countenance that stopped the heart cold, and glowing red eyes that electrified witnesses with a sense of dread. This creature spawned a cult-classic book and a major motion picture. And he was uniquely West Virginia spawned and his name was, and still is, "Mothman."

THREE
West Virginia Mothman: Strange Forces, Strange Beasts

The place is Doddridge County, West Virginia. The date is November 14th, 1966. It is 10:30 at night as Merle Partridge watches television with his young son while the rest of the family sleeps. Suddenly, the TV set begins making sounds. The picture blanks out and interference causes the screen to develop a herringbone pattern.

The TV set blanking out was not unusual when one lived in rural West Virginia in the 1960s. This was well before cable channels and satellite dishes. Picking up favorite shows depended upon how deft you were at turning your roof top television antennae to stations in Clarksburg, Wheeling and Pittsburgh. You considered yourself lucky if you got all three.

Otherwise, it was an ordinary night. But what happened to Merle Partridge next was very much out-of-the-ordinary. The television set whined loudly, like a generator winding up. At this point, Bandit, the Partridges' pet dog howled eerily. As Partridge peered outside, he saw that his German shepherd faced the hay barn—about the length of a football field away from the house. Extremely agitated, the dog barked at the dark doorway of the barn.

Merle Partridge grabbed his flashlight and went outside. Bandit had disappeared although Partridge heard the dog wailing in the area of the barn. As he shined his light in the direction of Bandit, it caught two red circles or eyes that looked like bicycle reflectors. Merle was later to describe the red eyes in an interview with writer John Keel, "I certainly know what animal eyes look like. . . These were much larger . . .still those eyes or lights or *whatever they were* showed up as huge even for that distance." (In a 2005 interview, Mr. Partridge clarified what he saw in 1966 as somewhat different than what John Keel had initially reported in his book *Mothman Prophecies*. Partridge said that to him the red orbs look more like "red, rotating lights.")

In an attempt to describe the dread he felt, Partridge added, "It was an eerie feeling like the sort I've not felt before. . . It was as if you knew something was really wrong but couldn't place just what it was."

The snarling Bandit came into focus. He bolted toward the barn. A cold chill swept over Merle Partridge. He hurried inside the house. He slept little that night, keeping his shotgun beside his bed. The next day, he and his six-year-old searched for their pet. They went to where the dog was last seen. The barn had a dirt floor. Partridge found the dog's tracks, but not Bandit. "Those tracks were going around in a circle" as if the dog had been chasing its tail, "But Bandit never did that," added Partridge. And then there were no more tracks. It was if the dog had been lifted up and carried away by something much larger and much stronger. Bandit, the family pet, was never seen again.

Daughter Mary Partridge Stover, a child at the time, remembered going into the barn the next day, as well as seeing huge, clawed tracks left in the mud. When seeing the famous Mothman statue in the public square in Point Pleasant years later, she remarked that the claws were not as large as the ones she saw, nor were the talons or toes spread apart as much as the ones she remembered from the prints left in their barn.

Winter of 1966-1967 marked a peculiar time for West Virginians. During those days, the state was swept up by numerous sightings of a pale, gray, flying creature that was reported by witnesses as close to seven feet tall. Motorists told stories of driving along country roads late at night and hearing a whooshing sound above their vehicle. As the drivers slowed down to look, they saw a large gray creature with glowing, red eyes and a wingspan of about ten feet. Even more strangely the creature seemed to want to race people's cars by flying parallel to the vehicle. Other witnesses who encountered the Mothman claimed that if you made the awful mistake of locking eyes with the creature, you would become paralyzed for seconds or minutes.

Many claimed to hear footsteps walking on their roofs at night. Others reported intense poltergeist activity such as banging and creaking sounds. The few who saw the Mothman on the ground said his stride was clumsy, and he walked in a shuffling gait as if he was not used to his feet, similar to the waddle of a penguin.

Reports of the Mothman, alone, were bizarre enough to make state and national news. However, during the time of the Mothman sightings, there were also hundreds of eyewitness accounts of UFOs and Men in Black throughout the state and the Ohio Valley region.

Woodrow Derenberger's close encounter with Indrid Cold and his spacecraft at Mineral Wells on November 2nd preceded the Mothman sightings by about 12 days. Such bizarre events ended with the tragic collapse of the Silver Bridge in Point Pleasant that snuffed out the lives of 46 people who plunged in the icy waters of the Ohio River below. And yet, what did these seemingly incredible events have to do with one another? What did the Mothman have to do with UFOs, missing pets in Doddridge County, the TNT plant and the Silver Bridge collapse in Point Pleasant? Many believe it all began with a Shawnee Indian, named Cornstalk who cursed the area before he died.

The Curse of Keigh-tugh-qua or "Cornstalk"

The areas surrounding Point Pleasant, West Virginia are lush if not picture-book scenic and many parts remain undisturbed. Where the Ohio meets the Kanawha River is a rich and fertile ground to grow crops. Fish and game are plentiful. Nomadic tribes often used what is now Point Pleasant as a rest area before continuing to their destination. And yet, Native Americans inhabitants were afraid of the lands now known as West Virginia, considering the Alleghenies, wedged between the Ohio and Potomac Rivers to be plagued by evil ghosts and terrifying night creatures.

When the first white men visited the area in the mid-1700s, they saw great potential for farmlands along the river and its gentle sloping hills. In 1765, Major George Crogham of Pennsylvania was one of the first officials to explore and admire the area. Five years later, on October 31, 1770, George Washington made a trip to the area and decided that he found one of the most sublime stretches of land ever. A settlement was constructed and the first settlers built permanent homes. Soon, the local Native Americans were forced out of the area.

Chief Cornstalk, a Shawnee chieftain, thought making peace with the Europeans would be the best way to preserve at least some of the Native American way of life. He realized that an overt act of hostility against the white men would prove devastating for his tribe because the settlers possessed many firearms while his group did not.

However, subordinate chiefs from his group attacked the settlement of Fort Randolph leading to one of the most violent battles in the area. Cornstalk commanded nearly 12,000 troops, which matched Captain Matthew Arbuckle's army. The battle of Point Pleasant took place in October 1774 and is considered by many historians to be one of the first conflicts leading up to the Revolutionary War.

Three years later, on November 8, 1777 (a particularly bloody year for natives and settlers both), Cornstalk led a party of Shawnee to Fort Randolph to pay the settlers a visit to see how they were faring along the Ohio lands. With him, the chief brought his son Elenipsico and a trusted friend, Red Hawk. They soon found themselves surrounded by a group of Virginia militiamen, already angry because one of their trackers had been ambushed earlier by a group of renegades. The Shawnee came to the fort a few hours later. It was convenient for the whites to seek vengeance on Chief Cornstalk and his son Elenipsico. Arbuckle attempted to stop the settlers from attacking Cornstalk but he was overpowered.

Cornstalk and his son were pushed to the front where the white men opened fire. The son fell mortally wounded. Chief Cornstalk stood and showed no sign of fear or pain as the musket balls ripped his flesh. Red Hawk was strangled in the skirmish.

After the first volley of shots was fired, Cornstalk remained standing, much to the surprise of his attackers. The Indian raised his right hand, indicating that he wanted to speak. The militiamen were stunned at the toughness of the dying chief. The words that came from the Chief's mouth have haunted the people of the Ohio Valley for over 200 years.

"I was the friend of the border men. Many a time I have saved him and his people from harm. I never warred with you save to protect our wigwams and our lands. I refused to join your pale-faced enemy. I came to your house as a friend, and you murdered me. You have murdered by my side, my son, the young Chief Elinipsico."

The militiamen soon realized they had made a terrible, fatal mistake, but it was too late. Witnesses later said that Cornstalk seemed to grow stronger for an instant. His slanted dark eyes burned with vengeance as he uttered these unforgettable words:
"For this, may the curse of the Great Spirit rest upon this spot; favored as it is by nature, may it ever be blighted in its hopes, its growth

dwarfed, its enterprises blasted, and the energies of its people paralyzed by the stain of our blood."

As Cornstalk ceased speaking, he fell to the ground. Within moments, the man who was called Cornstalk by the whites (but whose true Shawnee name was Keigh-tugh-qua, signifying a blade, or stalk of corn) was no more. His lifeless eyes stared and his body slumped next to the battered remains of his son Elinipsico.

By sunset of the same day, the militiamen led by Arbuckle dug a grave for the three slain Shawnee Indians right outside of the wall of Fort Randolph. In silence the men dug into the frozen ground to bury the remains of the men they had mistakenly killed in a fit of anger.

After the fort was demolished and the village of Point Pleasant grew into a beautiful town, Cornstalk's skeleton was exhumed and moved to the Mason County Courthouse Lawn. Years after that, his bones were transported once again and buried at the Tu Endi Wei Park by the Ohio River. By the 1950s, all that was left of Cornstalk were three human teeth and fifteen bones. They were put in a metal box and buried. A granite monument marks the resting place. The stone depicts the battle of Point Pleasant. As you will learn later, removing the remains from the original grave is considerably dangerous in terms of curses.

Following his death, Cornstalk's curse became legend among the people of the Ohio Valley. The story was passed down from generation to generation. Parents often warned unruly children about the curse and most of the time, the children behaved upon hearing it. A few residents still avoid the area where Cornstalk's remains are buried for fear of stirring up the curse. People in Point Pleasant with native blood often offer homage and leave tokens of appreciation at his gravesite out of respect and in hopes of ending the curse.

There is some validity to the Cornstalk curse. One shouldn't kill someone and later move his remains. Spirits don't like that. This is especially true among natives who believe they cannot enter the afterlife unless all of their remains are intact.

What might happen after an Indian curse?

At least two major eerie events took place within a month of the anniversary of Cornstalk's death. The first event was a series of sightings of the Mothman in and around the TNT area in the fall of 1966 and early 1967. The second event was the tragic Silver Bridge collapse in 1967 that took the lives of 46 people. But the curse wasn't limited to November and December 1967. In 1968, nearby Kanawha County experienced a Piedmont Airlines crash which killed 35 people. On November 14, 1970 a Southern Airways DC-10 exploded into a hillside near Huntington, West Virginia, killing all 75 on board.

In March of 1976, an explosion that killed five people, two civilians and three police officers blasted the Mason County jail in Point Pleasant. Held there was Harriet Sisk, who had been arrested for the murder of her infant. On March 2 her husband came to visit with a suitcase filled with explosives. Sisk and her husband were killed instantly along with police officers.

In 1977, in Pleasants County, upriver from Point Pleasant, close to one hundred men died during a scaffolding collapse at the Willow Island Plant.

Many claim there are too many eerie incidents and tragedies—the Silver Bridge, Willow Island, the Mason jail explosion, airplane crashes, the TNT area, the UFO sightings, the Mothman—to ignore the Cornstalk curse. What is definite is that some strange forces have been at work in the Ohio Valley area since the massacre of Chief Cornstalk. The anniversary of Cornstalk's murder is November 10th. The first Mothman sighting was on November 12th. The dates are perhaps too close to deny a connection.

The Point Pleasant TNT Area

A place where the "Mothman" was said to take refuge was the TNT plant near the city limits of Point Pleasant. The monster's red, disc-shaped eyes were glimpsed by locals. Oddly, most Mothman witnesses first believed the eyes looked more like "lights" rather than animal eyes. Some residents of Point Pleasant will still not go near the plant.

The TNT plant had been a military complex that manufactured explosives during World War II. After World War II, the 9,000-acre complex was closed down and abandoned. Empty shells where left and some of the igloos still held explosives. The roads once used by hundreds of military vehicles daily became lonely areas. This abandoned complex grew into the perfect spot for teenagers to pass countless summer nights. By 1950, the TNT area had become the most popular place in the area for youths to congregate on the weekend.

The strangeness began simply enough. Soon after the plant closed down, shortly after World War II, mysterious events began to take place. Lights were seen flying above the TNT area day and night. As strange as the lights were though, spectral lights alone would not become the reason for people from all over the country and around the world to swoop down (very much like the Mothman did) upon Point Pleasant. The TNT area was the location where some of the first documented sighting of the Mothman took place. Many visitors to the abandoned area came out very frightened, and refused to tell others of their experiences.

Soon it began to have the reputation of being haunted—but by what?

Descriptions of the Mothman

Witnesses to the Mothman agree on these essential facts: The creature was six to seven feet tall, with a wingspan of seven to ten feet. Glowing red eyes, almost two inches in diameter and about six or eight inches apart, radiated from the Mothman's head, or what looked to be shoulders. The being was gray and emitted a shrill noise as it passed over cars. Some said he squeaked like a mouse; others insisted he sounded more like a bird. Still others described a mechanical humming noise emitted from the creature as it flew over them.

The flying creature was apparently afraid of the lights of Point Pleasant, for the strange being immediately ended its pursuit of several cars just on the outskirts of town. Some of the descriptions of the Mothman did vary. Most of the witnesses described him as pale gray with skin wings similar to a bat, but others saw feathers. Some claimed the Mothman was flesh-colored, while some saw him as brown.

Over 100 sightings of the Mothman were reported throughout West Virginia and parts of southern Ohio between 1966 and 1967. According to one author "There were probably at least as many others who were afraid to give their names to the list of those having seen it."

First Sighting of Mothman in Point Pleasant

An unusually tall figure stood in the middle of the road ahead of a woman driving her father along Route 2, in the Chief Cornstalk Hunting Grounds of Point Pleasant in 1960 or 1961. As the figure got closer, the driver slowed the car. The two apprehensive witnesses saw a fleshy gray creature with a human body, but much taller than any man.

The woman later reported what happened next:

"A pair of wings unfolded from its back and they practically filled the whole road. It almost looked like a small airplane. Then it took off straight up. . .disappearing out of sight within seconds. We were both terrified. I stepped on the gas and raced out of there. We talked it over and decided not to tell anybody about it. Who would believe us anyway?"

Scarberry Sightings of the Mothman

Newlywed couple Roger and Linda Scarberry, along with their friends Steve and Mary Mallette, sighted the Mothman on the outskirts of Point Pleasant on November 15th, 1966. Out for a late drive, the couples were passing the West Virginia Ordinance Works north of Point Pleasant, a part of the old TNT plant, when they spotted something quite beyond the ordinary. Near the Wildlife Station, they saw what appeared to be two red lights. As they got closer, they realized the lights were, in fact, the crimson glowing eyes of large humanoid creature. Nearing seven feet tall, the being was definitely man-shaped with wings folded against its back.

Horrified, the couples left the area and headed for town. Only minutes later, they saw the creature perched on the side of a billboard. Later, it flew over a ridge appearing to vanish. But as Roger Scarberry sped up the car, the couples were petrified to learn the large, winged creature was not only chasing their car, the thing was now directly above them. Linda Scarberry would later report that its wings were so colossal they crashed down on both sides of the vehicle as they beat together.

The young couple drove directly to the courthouse to report what they saw. Incredibly, the creature even followed Linda and Roger home, at times peering in the windows throughout the night. This was followed by poltergeist activity in the home. The next day the couple would find large scratch marks on the sides of the car. "Even now," Linda Scarberry told one interviewer, "I will not look out my window after dark."
Their account and other sightings that occurred, now famous and exhaustively recounted, eventually lead to a reporter dubbing the beast as "Mothman," a character from the popular Batman television show.

After this initial Mothman sighting, armed deputies who visited the deserted power plant found oval-shaped footprints measuring about

4½ inches across and fresh animal droppings that none of the men in the party could identify.

Other Mothman/UFO Sightings

During the one-year reign of terror that followed the late 1966 sightings, Mothman held the citizens of Point Pleasant under siege. A total of over one hundred sightings of the Mothman were reported. These claims came from diverse individuals: Point Pleasant businessmen, to a gravedigger, to the local military.

Kenneth Duncan and some other men were digging his brother-in-law's grave on a Saturday morning when something like a "brownish-human being" buzzed past. "It was gliding through the trees and was in sight for about a minute." Duncan was shocked, but the other men didn't see it.

Dave Peyton wrote later: "The number of Mothman sightings couldn't hold a candle to the number of other unidentified flying objects sighted over the skies in eastern Cabell, Mason, and parts of Putnam counties during this same time period. Eventually there were so many UFO sightings at the *Herald-Dispatch* that they could no longer be ignored. The calls became so numerous that we had to set up a special UFO desk to take all of them. The story of Mothman was big, but the continuing stories of UFO sightings took up more newspaper space."

Not only did civilians see the Mothman and UFOs in Mason County, local law enforcement had sighted them as well. Firemen, police, and National Guardsmen were among those who reported encounters with the Mothman and flying saucers. These included Captain Paul Yoder and Ben Enochs; Point Pleasant police officer Harold Harmon; Robert Spears and Charles Fry of the National Guard; plus George Carson and J.A. Wilson of Civil Defense were among those who had encounters with West Virginia's bizarre appearances of 1966-1967.

In Wood County, north of Point Pleasant, residents that lived on Quincy Hill in Parkersburg reported what sounded like human footsteps walking on their roofs at night during the Mothman terrors. One of the higher points in Parkersburg's downtown area, Quincy Hill, overlooks the business district, the railroad and Blennerhassett Island. A number of schoolchildren in the area still refer to a small cave near the bottom of Quincy Hill as "the Mothman's lair."

Former Haunted Parkersburg tour guide Doni Enoch once shared a hospital room with a woman from the Point Pleasant area. The woman told Doni that the winter following the initial Mothman sightings she and her husband happened to be around the area of the TNT plant on other business. A light snow powdered the ground. The couple soon noticed large tracks in the snow. The woman claimed, "The prints looked just like turkey tracks…except for the fact that they were enormous and about six feet apart! I would never go to that place (TNT plant) alone… not even to this very day."

Back in Point Pleasant, Thomas Ury, a shoe store manager at the time, saw the creature from about 500 yards away as he passed the Kirkland Memorial Gardens, ten days after the first sighting. It chased his car, which had reached speeds up to 90 mph, before it broke pursuit. This was the first reported sighting during the day. Ury thinks it was a huge bird with a 10 to 12 foot-wing-span and an oversized body too big for its wings.

Billy Burdette, 16, Darrell Love, 18, Johnny Love, 14, and John Morrow, 14, informed the local authorities that they had spotted disc-shaped red eyes and a creature taking off at a fast rate of speed when they got close to it. They saw the winged beast again at 3:00 a.m. on Camp Conley Road close to a mile from the highway.

In March of 1966, a Point Pleasant woman claimed to have observed a silver disc hovering above a school. She also saw a male figure, wearing tight-fitting, silver coveralls, floating in mid-air outside the open door of a spaceship, gazing down intently at the school playground. The man had shoulder-length hair and pointed features, but otherwise looked completely human and of the Caucasian race. The woman said that later a similar object landed in her yard and was witnessed by her teenaged children even though they did not see the man that she described seeing at the school.

On November 15th, 1966, back in Doddridge County between West Union and Salem, Merle Partridge felt the red-eyed flying man had something to do with the disappearance of his purebred German shepherd dog, Bandit, who was worth $350 in 1966. Partridge said he sighted the 'thing' in a barn, a football field away from his house in Doddridge County about 90 minutes before one of the Pt. Pleasant sightings. Partridge claimed that his television set "began acting like a generator" and that Bandit "was carrying on something terrible." When Merle Partridge shone a flashlight into the field, he saw something that looked like red reflectors, but later said they resembled red lights (as was the Scarberry's initial impression.) The dog's hair stood straight up and he snarled, heading for the Partridge's barn. There was no trace of Bandit in the morning.

But the weird tale did not end there for Merle Partridge. The following night Mr. Partridge was unable to sleep and was watching television around midnight when he heard a loud knocking at his door. When he opened it he found a man in obvious distress. The man explained that he had just run his jeep into a ditch after something gigantic had swooped in front of his jeep.

Trembling and upset, the man explained, "But this is not what I am worried about. I cannot find my six-year old boy. He has disappeared from the car." Alarmed, Merle Partridge grabbed his flashlight and rifle and went on a search with the father looking for the boy, to no avail. After about a 30-minute search, the men returned to the house and called the police. The policed arrived a short time later and began their search, which took another 30 minutes. By this time, an hour and a half had elapsed and the father was frantic. After another search, they suddenly saw the young boy walking up the road in an opposite direction from where the wrecked jeep was. The child was completely in a daze.

When asked where he had been all of that time, the boy could not remember any of it. Years later, a middle-aged man would visit Merle Partridge in his New Martinsville home to tell him about the night he came up missing and how he still had no memory of the time spent when he was lost.

Mr. Partridge said other oddities followed him years later. Partridge made his living as a truck driver. On his way home once, he stopped his truck to grab a few hours of sleep in his cab. When Merle Partridge awakened sometime later, he was shocked to find that his body was covered in cobwebs.

Mr. Partridge wondered if there was a link to the Point Pleasant sightings (which happened the next night) when he read a newspaper report that the body of a dead German-Shepherd dog had been found along the highway where the Scarberry's had had their Mothman encounter. Partridge thought it might be his dog Bandit, but this was never determined.

Probably one of the most physical encounters with the Mothman happened on November 16, 1966 at the home of Ralph Thomas outside the city limits of Point Pleasant. Mr. and Mrs. Raymond Wamsley accompanied by friend Marcella Bennett, and her new baby daughter were leaving the house after a visit. As they departed the Thomas residence, the group stumbled over something large and bulky that slept in the yard. Startled, the strange animal roused and stood up. Marcella Bennett would later describe it as "It rose up slowly from the ground…a big, gray thing. It was bigger than a man and had terrible, glowing red eyes."

In a start, Marcella dropped her baby as she ran for cover. Raymond Wamsley grabbed the infant, but not before seeing the creature open its colossal wings and chase them back inside the Thomas home. The Mothman then came up on the porch and looked into the window of the terrified witnesses. Law officials were summoned, but by the time they arrived, the red-eyed creature was gone. Marcella Bennett had to seek medical help and was treated for shock.

Near the end of the Mothman sightings, five pilots in the Gallipolis area, Eddie Atkins (WJEH Radio DJ), Everett Wedge, Henry Upton, Leon Edwards, and Ernie Thompson reported seeing a large bird apparently following the Ohio River and traveling at a speed of approximately 70 mph. The men claimed the creature was 300 feet above the shore and had a neck nearly four feet long and a body the size of a small man. Some feel this sighting was the end of the Mothman.

But was it really?

No species of bird in West Virginia, to our knowledge, seeks out human blood. In 2002, John Keel, author of *The Mothman Prophecies*, said in a television interview that the Mothman seemed to be drawn to women during their menstrual cycles. This attraction to blood might have put this bizarre creature under the category of a ghoul rather than any space alien. Other reports had the Mothman chasing a Red Cross bloodmobile in 1967.

Theories About the Mothman

There were nearly as many theories pertaining to the Mothman as there were witnesses who claimed to see the winged creature. A few theorized the creature was actually an exotic bird that had flown off course. Others speculated that the Mothman was a type of ultra-dimensional being able to fade in and out of our own dimension of reality at will. (That means he was able to slip through a tear in dimensions.) Others link the Mothman to UFOs, since he was sighted near areas that were already in a frenzy of UFO sightings. Because of the red eyes, some thought the Mothman was some kind of a devil, come to curse the people of the Ohio Valley. Others even link the Mothman to Banshees, other red-eyed portents of doom.

West Virginia writer and folklorist Greg Leatherman points out that the Mothman has similarities to mythological creatures throughout antiquity, "The Egyptian Seth is identified in the late Greco-Egyptian pantheon as a headless demon whose red eyes are placed in his shoulders, just like the mid-20th century reports of the Mothman. In that pantheon, he is called Akephelos. It is no surprise that in another source, *Grimoire, The Testament of Solomon*, this headless demon is said to carry out things at Crossroads."

Leatherman also added, "The Ohio Valley region has more species of moths than any other place in the Northern Hemisphere. Ghosts reside in cemeteries. The Virgin Mary appears in Catholic matriarchal societies, and the Abominable Snowman is so in tune with his environment, he's practically camouflaged. It seems fitting that we'd have our own Mothman." Leatherman lent another twist to the Mothman tale as a different take on the Rip Van Winkle story. (See Senator Peter Godwin Van Winkle in Chapter 8). Legend has it that a man fell asleep along the banks of the Ohio River on a chilly night. Moths, attracted to his warmth, landed on him and formed a fuzzy blanket. When he woke, his body was crawling with moths, and as the first sunrays hit him, he turned into a 'moth-man.' "This is far-fetched, of course," added Leatherman, "but it's fun to consider in terms of folklore and myth."

Except for the disappearance of Bandit, the Partridge's German shepherd, the Mothman never harmed anyone. He seemed to be curious about the world he slipped into, and just as fascinated with us as we were about him.

Was the Mothman A Hoax?

Jimmy Joe Wedge believed it was all a big joke that got out of hand. "Someone dressed up and was scaring people in their cars." Wedge says that he knows names, but won't reveal them. Even though the people involved are no longer alive, he doesn't want to embarrass their relatives. "I had friends who were crazy-acting, fun-loving people. I knew some of the people who supposedly dressed up [as] the Mothman. They had some fun chasing people."

Dick Thomas claims that he was in the general area as the Scarberry's on that night and saw nothing out of the ordinary. "I was in the basic area of the old powerhouse that first night. I could see everything and I never saw anything out of the ordinary. I think those people ought to change their brand of liquor."

W. Joseph Wyatt, associate professor of psychology at Marshall University, thinks that people are afraid to talk about it to this day for fear of ridicule. After all, human beings can talk themselves into and out of anything once they realize their thoughts are out of step with more normal people, or their peers.

And, of course, there was Clarksburg writer Gray Barker, who many thought a great hoaxer. He seemed to be there when anything of an unusual nature occurred.

There were much later sightings of a winged creature in rural West Virginia however, by Parkersburg resident and Haunted Parkersburg guide Lea Wilson. She had a scare in the mid-1980s when she was staying with relatives in Calhoun County. Not yet in her teens, Wilson said she was with her uncle when she heard a strange scream coming from outside the house. Wilson said the screech reminded her most of the old "lost time movies" that had animation of dinosaurs and other prehistoric creatures. 'Honest to God, it sounded like a pre-historic bird . . ." Lea reported, "Or what movies made those Pterodactyl animations sound like. When we ran outside, this large winged thing flew right over us, blocking out the sky. What I remember most was that it was huge."

Theories of Birds

Sheriff Johnson said that if the thing was a migratory crane, local monster hunters had better not shoot it. The sheriff explained that federal and state law protected migratory birds. He also said he would arrest anybody caught with a loaded gun in the TNT area after dark. There were earlier reports of armed people in the area. Some believe the Mothman was nothing more than a snow-owl, or a Sandhill crane.

One local by the name of George Johnson believed that the Mothman was simply a "freak Shitepoke," or shag, a large bird from the heron family. Yet those who witnessed the West Virginia Mothman were certain that he was no such bird.

Dr. Robert Smith of WVU informed the Mason County sheriff department that the Mothman was probably a Sandhill crane (this was before it was given the name 'Mothman'). Sandhill cranes are found in Florida, Georgia and the Mississippi Valley, but are not common as far north as Point Pleasant. The sand hill crane doesn't really have big red eyes, but has red feathers around its eyes, has an 80-inch wingspan, and does stand six feet or better. It would not attack humans unless provoked. "It is mainly a vegetarian. It does have a large bill, and could potentially kill a dog, but would not eat it."

The Silver Bridge

The collapse of the Silver Bridge between Point Pleasant, WV and Gallipolis, Ohio was the event that most feel brought an end to the Mothman sightings—or perhaps it merely turned attention elsewhere so that a flying beast no longer seemed as important as it once had. The bridge had been built in 1928 and earned its name when it became the first in the area to be painted aluminum shortly after it was erected.

During rush hour, on December 15, 1967, the Silver Bridge writhed like a giant serpent and buckled before collapsing into the black waters of the Ohio. The bridge was packed to its full capacity with mostly Christmas shoppers. By 5:00 p.m. the bridge had completely broken up into the frigid waters. At the time it fell, 67 people were on the broken-up portion of the bridge in 31 vehicles. In the end, 46 of those people were killed, including two people that were never found. Five were killed on the Ohio shoreline. Later, 23 of the lost vehicles were recovered from the river and to this day, eight of them have never been discovered.

One man later reported that he started to drive up onto the bridge, but then reversed his truck back down because he wanted to call his wife to see if she wanted him to pick anything up at a nearby grocery store. The man became one of the Silver Bridge survivors.

Mothmania

Over the years, many books and articles have been written about the Mothman, including one by John Keel, *The Mothman Prophecies*, about Mothman sightings and other paranormal events in WV. Other books by Keel have included *Strange Mutants: from Mothmen to Demon Dogs and Phantom Cats* and *Disneyland of the Gods*. A number of John Keel's books are a smorgasbord of speculation meant to tantalize with his unique vision and dry wit.

Other books on the Mothman have included: *The Silver Bridge* by Gray Barker; *Mothman: The Facts Behind the Legend* by local residents Donnie Sergent Jr. and Jeff Wamsley; and Wamsley's most recent offering, *Mothman: Behind the Red Eyes*; and *Mothman & Other Curious Encounters*, by strange phenomena expert Loren Coleman.

Television shows and documentaries have been based on the Mothman and the Merle Partridge Mothman sighting was partly covered on an *X-Files* episode. There have also been two films made about the case, including a limited release called Mothman in 2000 and the popular *The Mothman Prophecies*, a movie based on John Keel's classic book, released on January 25th, 2002. Interestingly, its star, actor Richard Gere, appeared in the movie *Runaway Bride* with Parkersburg native Paul Dooley who played Julia Robert's father.

In the previous year, Richard Gere sent representatives of his friend the Dalai Lama to Parkersburg to bless and nourish the Ohio River and its people. They did this by building a multi-colored sand Mandela at the Parkersburg Art Center. Later, they marched to the Ohio River and poured the colored sands and cow's milk into the water. We suspect Richard Gere may have somewhat believed in the Mothman, Indrid Cold and Cornstalk's curse, perhaps not wanting another Silver Bridge to occur.

The contactee character "Gordon" in *The Mothman Prophecies* movie is loosely based on former Mineral Wells resident Woodrow Derenberger. It seems the Mothman is one legend that is not about to go away.

Strangely—Mothman Not Unique

Winged, red-eyed creatures have been reported all over the world. If the Mothman was unique to the Point Pleasant area, it could be dismissed simply as mass hysteria or the misidentification of a bird, just as many non-believers claim. However, there is a universal flavor to all of these birdman' sightings—only the names and places are different.

In Kent, England in 1963 four teenagers described seeing a black figure shuffling toward them at least the size of a human. The teenagers, however, described the creature as not having any head but having large wings on its back that looked like "bat wings."

Also very similar to the Mothman legend is one much older in New Jersey. The Jersey Devil, a creature much like the Mothman, is said to have glowing red eyes, great flapping wings, and emits a high-pitched screeching sound, but leaves footprints that look more like hooves. Stories about the Jersey Devil are more than 200 years old, but there are still sightings in the Piney regions of rural New Jersey.

It is interesting to note that the Jersey Devil and the Mothman have similarities to a frightening creature in old British-Celtic fairy lore, called the "Phouka."

The Phouka was actually the inspiration for Shakespeare's Puck character in his play *A Mid-Summer Night's Dream*. Puck, like Phouka, was really an Irish-Scottish fairy.

The Phouka is said to be a night creature and claimed to be extremely terrifying to anyone who chances to meet him. Some say the Phouka closely resembles an ugly horse, (related to the dreaded "nightmare") a goat-like creature or even a large white dog. The Phouka sneaks into homes where he kidnaps unsuspecting people to give them "the ride of their lives," flying and dragging their victims' exhausted bodies across the countryside all night long. But like the alien visitors of the 20th and 21st centuries, the Phouka always tucks his victims safely into their beds the following morning... maybe not too terrifying, after all. But did one of these Phouka visit Parkersburg?

Phouka Over Parkersburg

In the early days of the 19th century, three farmers were planting gardens down by what is now Parkersburg's Point Park early one morning, in the exact area where the Ohio and Little Kanawha Rivers meet. One farmer looked up to see a massive white beast whipping its way through the clouds, seemingly oblivious to all. The beast resembled a cross between a horse and a goat, but it had wings. The men watched in amazement as the animal passed over them and continued south. This Phouka-like creature was never, to our knowledge, reported again.

Tales of a Black Dog

West Virginia has a number of other supernatural creature sightings. Stories are told of a black dog digging around Riverview Cemetery in Parkersburg even though a dog that size could never squeeze under the surrounding fence. As an animal from English folklore, Black Dog appearances are associated with death and tragedy. Numerous accounts report sightings of a black dog in areas where a person has been killed in an automobile accident. Black dogs protect the graves of those who die in some unfortunate manner.

It is suggested the Black Dog appears shortly before a person dies, much in the way the Banshee does, to howl or cry or bring a message about someone's inevitable demise.

So, do such legends of the Black Dog belong in books of folklore or to some superstitious ancient past? Read on and learn about a modern appearance of a Black Dog in the Parkersburg area. An email I received reads:

Many years ago I was working as a nurse in a local hospital. This day, a friend of my mother's had had a catastrophic stroke, and I was sure she would die that day. However, the day wore on and nothing untoward happened. When it was time for me to go off duty, I checked her one last time and left, certain that she was stabilized.

I walked to the parking lot and just as I came close to my car, a large black dog appeared beside me. I had not noticed a dog in the area before, and the parking lot was a huge expanse of concrete with only a few cars left and I thought I surely would have noticed a big dog coming near.

I glanced around but the dog stayed beside me. I finally spoke to the dog, saying, 'Where did you come from?' The black dog looked up at me. Much to my shock the dog's face had completely transformed into my patient's face! This was quite startling.

Despite my shock the thought struck me that the woman had just died, even as I told myself this experience was impossible.

The dog then walked to the front of my car and disappeared.

I got down on my knees, looking under the few cars that were left in the lot. I saw no trace of any dog whatsoever. Just then, someone called my name and asked me what in the world I was looking for under the cars. . .a friend of mine was crossing the parking lot behind me. She saw me looking around in puzzlement. I asked her if she had seen a dog near me moments earlier and if she had, where had it gone? My friend told me I was crazy. . .that she'd been behind me for several minutes and she hadn't seen a black dog. . .only me crouching down, looking under cars. I glimpsed at my watch and it was 4:10 p.m. The next day when I went back to work, I found that my patient had died at exactly 4:10 p.m.

I never forgot this. Some time later, I heard about the "Black Dog," an animal spirit that is associated with death or the passing onto the next realm. I was certain the Black Dog from folklore is what I truly encountered that day . . . . Not just any old stray dog wandering around parking lots. Nothing will convince me otherwise. . . What do you think? Thanks for reading this . . . As you can imagine, I have told very few people.

For a few years I, the author, wrote monthly horoscopes for a local Internet company. One of my readers wrote to me with this unusual tale about a creature she and her husband spotted near Belleville in south Wood County late one night:

My husband is a Capricorn so you know he doesn't usually believe in this kind of stuff, but he was with me when this incident happened. We were driving home late in the evening when an animal about four-feet tall and completely white ran in front of our car lights. At first I thought it might be an albino fox or raccoon until the animal stood up on two legs and tottered across the road, almost like a monkey that wasn't used to standing upright. It ran on two legs! What wildlife in this area is capable of doing that? I can't imagine what it might have been and neither can my husband. No circuses were in the area and no shop with exotic pets was within miles of the place. If you have any idea of what this creature might have been, please let us know. We are baffled by it.

The Flatwoods Monster

It turns out the Mothman isn't the only elusive monster to terrorize the hills and valleys of West Virginia. There was an equally, if not an even more horrible encounter with a monstrous creature near the rural community of Flatwoods in Braxton County.

It all began on September 12, 1952 when the Braxton County Sheriff Robert Carr and Deputy Burnell Long witnessed something bright and burning fall out of the sky. Thinking it was a downed aircraft, the two went to investigate but found nothing amiss.

That same evening, four boys playing football at the Flatwoods School ball field saw another illuminating object hit the earth on the top of the hill of the Bailey Fisher property. Ever curious and thinking it was an airplane, the boys decided to investigate.

However, the youths became frightened as they made their way up the hill. They stopped at the home of Kathleen May. She and her two sons joined the boys to find out what it was that had dropped to earth.

The early September evening was a misty one. Cicadas whirred in the grass like wind-up toys. Where the object fell, there was a strange smell in the air.

Mrs. May later reported there was a distinct metallic odor but she could not pinpoint exactly what it was. "It burned our eyes and noses." The boys and woman soon came upon a glowing object that hissed. On the object were two lights approximately one foot apart.

One of the boys held a flashlight. As he swept the area with his light, the group was shocked to see what the light revealed: a massive creature nearly ten feet tall, in bright green clothing, with a fiery red face and a head shaped like the ace of spades in a deck of cards. The thing's clothing, from the waist down, hung in long folds. The woman and boys could see no feet beneath the folds, and rather than walking or running, the creature floated toward them just like something in a horror movie. The group ran back to the May home at a break-neck speed and called Sheriff Carr. When he came to interview them, the boys were so frightened they could barely speak.

Later, when a reporter went back to the hilltop site, he saw nothing unusual, but it was now quite dark. An investigation the next morning, however, revealed odd skid marks. Sheriff Carr concluded the whole incident was nothing more than a meteor that had inspired the group's wild imaginings after seeing the meteor's descent to earth. Carr did admit later that when he went on the hill later that night he did see odd reflective eyes in a tree, such as those belonging to an owl, cat or raccoon.

Other residents of Braxton County later confessed they had seen the plummeting lights and the monster but were afraid to come forward because of the ridicule they and their families might suffer. Some even claimed to have seen a spherical object resembling a classic spacecraft.

Such conical UFOs were popular props in Hollywood movies of the 1950s so it is possible those who saw such movies might have interpreted strange lights or objects in this way. Still, no one has ever been able to explain away the green-suited monster, with the fiery crimson face and a head like the ace of spades. As Kathleen May later described, "What I saw looked worse than Frankenstein. It could not have been human."

Thus the mystery of the Flatwoods monster that appeared only one time on a hilltop of West Virginia—precisely September 12, 1952—remains just that—an incredible tale filled with many eccentricities, but like the Mothman, never solved and never really explained.

And The Stories Continue...

West Virginia continues to be visited by uncanny creatures. I don't believe we will unravel these mysteries of strange forces and even stranger beasts anytime soon.

As Einstein wrote, "The most beautiful thing we experience in life is the mysterious." Perhaps tales about the Mothman, Irish Phoukas, Banshees, Black Dogs and the Flatwoods monster are not supposed to be solved. Such enigmas of the material realm and the non-material realm are the most fascinating things we encounter in life. A mystery once explained may end up rather dull. But a mystery left unexplained is a much better story, after all.

FOUR
Haunted Rails: Ghost of Silver Run & The East End Ghoul

Tales of phantom travelers is in every culture. The belief is that ghosts will haunt travel routes, trains, highways and even airports that they have some emotional connection to, especially if they failed to reach their destinations because of death or injury. The spirits will continue to appear where the traumatic event happened in an effort to resolve it.

Traumatic events, such as sudden death and especially murder, can leave a residual energy of the deceased that somehow exists outside of our human conception of time. In this way, the actual apparition or ghost has no consciousness, and is more like a hologram or recording getting played over and over again. This type of ghostly appearance is like a terrible scream that continues to resonate. Because of the shock or trauma, the emotional power behind the event is never lost.

The following tales are similar to many phantom traveler and ghostly hitchhiker stories reported over the last fifty years. Ghostly hitchhikers began to be recorded as automobiles became commonplace in the U.S. However, stories of phantom travelers have been told throughout the world for hundreds, if not thousands of years. Some of these tales trace back to a belief in the Crossroads, a place where ghosts and devils lurk.

The appearance of phantom travelers in trains, planes, cars, buses and even on motorcycles are very recent, of course, but they do hint at a parallel realm that we, as frail humans, cannot fully understand. The explanation may be as simple as the phantoms contacting the living in ways the living can understand. Yet somehow the realm of the phantom traveler exists beyond our mortal ability to comprehend matters of a more spiritual nature. It seems the spirits of the dead are

51

more than happy to remind us time and again of their existence by their unexpected visits and ghostly calling cards.

The Ghost of Silver Run

Not far from Parkersburg, in an isolated patch of Ritchie County is the small community of Silver Run, a lonely place where tales of a ghostly traveler still causes flesh to crawl. Accounts tell of a raven-haired apparition with skin as white as moonlight that haunts the old railroad tracks. Dressed in a long gown, the ghost always appears at the mouth of the Silver Run Tunnel.

Anyone familiar with the history of northern West Virginia knows of the pivotal role the B & O Railroad played in its development. While the southern region of the state had its coal wars and family feuds, the history of north central West Virginia is calmer, more subdued, a bit more civilized perhaps.

That is, unless you believe in ghosts.

Today Silver Run is in actuality a ghost town, where flowers with names like Tiger Lily, Snowball and Black-Eyed-Susan strain under the dusty talc of Ritchie County's backcountry roads. If you drive down Silver Run Road today, you can still see the old tunnel and abandoned houses reclaimed by the weeds, as well as the remains of a once thriving marble factory, a place that made marbles with names like "cat eyes." Even still, one can imagine the inside of the factory lit up by the bright orange, molten lava of liquid glass. Such glass plants, so typical of northern West Virginia, even in their hey-day, looked like tin-sheeted, thrown-together, squatter's shacks.

Over one-hundred-years ago, when the B & O Railroad was a considerable force in West Virginia, trains rolled through Silver Run almost hourly. It was then that an event happened that was so strange it is still fresh in the minds of some older residents of Wood and Ritchie counties.

Nearing midnight one August night, as mid-summer fog hung in thick, wet veils across the rails, an engineer making his way toward the Silver Run Tunnel spotted a young woman standing in the dead center of the tracks.

This, by itself, was out of the ordinary. Mostly drunks wandered out on the rails at night, usually ending up scattered in pieces over the

B & O Six St. Station, Parkersburg, W. Va.

The old 6th Street B & O Railroad station in Parkersburg

tracks, never knowing what hit them. But the young woman's face appeared stricken, as if she had lost her way, perhaps after having an argument. The young woman appeared to be upset or confused, and made no effort to move away from the railroad tracks.

As the engineer turned on his whistle to warn her of the oncoming train, the woman turned and stared at him but seemed frozen in time. Although the lady was visible only for a matter of seconds, the engineer saw that she was thinly dressed in a filmy dress. But what was most striking was her black hair and white skin. At the moment the startled engineer thought that his train was about to slam into the woman, he watched her fly up into the air and disappear into the night.

As he tried to control his train, the engineer's heart nearly lunged out of his chest. Striking down any person was bad enough, but hitting a beautiful young woman took on the shades of a nightmare. He could only imagine the horror of maroon blood spattered against that pearly white skin.

After several frantic moments, the engineer brought the train to a stop. He was sure he would find her dead body (or parts of it) along the tracks. With his engine fireman beside him, the engineer embarked on a search for the woman. Neither man was anxious to see the destruction that a train would do to a human body, but leaving it there until the light of the day would be a disgrace.

After searching the tracks for a while the men concluded there was no body. Convinced he'd had too much coffee and too little sleep the engineer pushed this unsettling occurrence out of his mind and continued with his duties. But the young woman had a message to convey at the Silver Run Tunnel, and made several more appearances at the tunnel over the following weeks. Each week a train came to a stop and each time the figure flew upward and disappeared into the darkness of the night. It so happened that this mesmerizing, dark-haired woman was indeed a ghost.

After sharing his unsettling experience with other engineers at the 6th Street railroad station in Parkersburg, the engineer was surprised to learn that the apparition had appeared to other railroad men nearing Silver Run Tunnel over the years and nearly all were familiar with the scene, as he had encountered it. Some noted the ghostly appearances coincided with the moon phases, the spirit appearing most commonly during a full moon. August appeared to be the most active month for the apparition to reveal herself to the railroad workers. No one knew why.

It happened that one engineer by the name of O'Flannery hadn't yet run into the Ghost of Silver Run. He made no bones of the fact that he didn't believe in ghosts, and anyone that did was a fool or a liar. After a pensive silence, one engineer challenged O'Flannery, saying to the effect that all engineers who had passed through Silver Run Tunnel saw the ghost, and up until then, they had never believed in ghosts either.

O'Flannery wouldn't have any of it. He laughed with bitter sarcasm and vowed that no ghost was going to stop his train—he'd run her down first. Of course, those schooled in the science of spirits and apparitions understand that one does not challenge a ghost. Ridicule tends to cause spirits to step up their ghostly activity.

About two weeks later it was O'Flannery who was nearing the Silver Run Tunnel. The time was near midnight. An incandescent moon glowed inside charcoal-colored clouds. A rich darkness surrounded the traveling train.

As he came upon the Silver Run Tunnel, O'Flannery noticed a flutter of pale movement along the railroad tracks. Much to his surprise, he saw that it was a young woman standing there. She made no effort to move. And, as described by other railroad men earlier, the raven-haired apparition flew into the air and was spirited away into the darkness, to be seen no more.

By this time, O'Flannery was unnerved. Sweat poured from his brow. He felt tremendously relieved to get his train through the Silver Run Tunnel. Even so, O'Flannery was still a boastful type who looked forward to bragging to the other engineers about how he ran the Ghost of Silver Run down. Later, as the Irishman pulled into the 6th Street train station in Parkersburg, he noticed the place was in a panic bordering on bedlam. As he walked through the door, he asked another engineer, "Hey—what's all the commotion about?"

The engineer answered, "Man, don't you know? You hit a woman at the Silver Run Tunnel and she rode all the way into Parkersburg on your cow-catcher!" After all, the spirit had made a mockery of the man as she would many doubters to come.

O'Flannery was left uncharacteristically speechless.

Apparently, earlier in the evening, calls flooded the 6th Street train station in Parkersburg from smaller stations that reported a thinly dressed woman was riding the cowcatcher of O'Flannery's engine as it passed by! As soon as the engine made its appearance at the 6th Street Station, the woman vanished.

Many of the B & O Railroad engineers claimed to see or encounter the Ghost of Silver Run well into the 1940s. The reason for her ghostly appearances, however, remains a mystery. There are a few explanations or theories.

One story goes that a richly dressed young woman was riding into Parkersburg to meet her betrothed and never arrived. After an exhaustive search, the woman's body was never found. No one knew what happened to the young bride.

There is another old tale whispered by grandmothers to grandchildren in Ritchie County on mid-summer nights, especially in homes not far from the Silver Run Tunnel. Legend has it that when an abandoned house was torn down at Silver Run, the skeleton of a woman was found walled up in the chimney. The workers knew it was the skeleton of a woman because the skeleton wore a white bridal gown. Although the few remains were never claimed or identified, the skeleton was given a proper burial in the old Irish cemetery above the Silver Run

Tunnel. After funeral rites had ended, some say the Ghost of Silver Run was not seen again. Or was she?

Does the Ghost of Silver Run still haunt the old tunnel? Many say they still hear the ghostly whistle of a train coming up near the Silver Run Tunnel at night and screeching to a stop. Others claim they see the form of a thinly dressed woman floating eerily along what once was the railroad tracks. But the rest of us who have never seen her are left to contemplate her, the one still called the Ghost of Silver Run.

Ghost hunter Virginia Lyons and grandson Damien, standing amidst orbs and ectomist in the old Irish Cemetery above Silver Run. COURTESY KRISTALL CHAMBERS

Hauntings At Eaton Tunnel, Wood County, West Virginia

Another B & O Railroad tunnel in Wood County with tales of haunts is the Eaton Tunnel, where two workers were buried alive on June 7th, 1963 as they were lowering the bottom of the tunnel so that diesel engines could pass through. As the men worked, the sides of the tunnel caved in, trapping them alive with their bulldozer, truck and backhoe. Herculean efforts tried to save them, but to no avail. The men probably suffocated. Their remains were never rescued. A marker was set on the old tunnel. This was the best they could do as a burial for the men.

To this day, the tunnel holds a hollow, resonating energy (one area rock group even recorded an album in the tunnel) and high-pitched moans are often heard throughout the night, mostly on the anniversary of the workers' deaths. Photographs taken here typically reveal ghostly orbs of light, as well as what appear to be phantasms of hooded figures bending over the curve of the tunnel as if in mourning. A number of interesting photographs have been captured by Tom Moore's Mid-Ohio Valley Ghost Hunters in Eaton Tunnel.

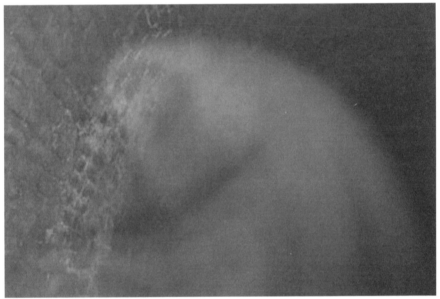

This apparition was caught by Haunted Parkersburg ghost hunter Kristall Chambers at the Eaton Tunnel in rural Wood County. This is where two men where buried alive back in 1962, and one body was never recovered.

Tunnel Green Hauntings, Wheeling, Ohio County, West Virginia

Known locally as "Tunnel Green," the Hempfield Road Tunnel runs underneath a haunted graveyard known as the Old Peninsula Cemetery near Wheeling. It is thought that many of the people buried in the graveyard now haunt the railroad tunnel, including a mysterious woman in a long dark cape and an immigrant worker who was murdered. The worker is said to float above the tunnel on certain nights showing startled witnesses his mangled hand. Others claim the ghost of a man who was hit by a train also plagues the tunnel.

Moonville's Haunted Tunnel, Vinton County, Ohio

It now must seem that many areas along the old B & O Railroad route in West Virginia have haunted tunnels, and this carries over into southeastern Ohio. The Moonville Tunnel is located in Vinton County, not far from the colorful college town of Athens. Over the years there have been tales of a ghostly apparition that swings a lantern in the dark through Moonville Tunnel. Some stories claim that the death of a B & O worker occurred when an inebriated conductor or brakeman fell to his death after a card game when he should have been watching the tracks in early 1859. Through his guilt, the man's ghost still holds vigil over the tunnel.

Another spirit that is said to haunt the tunnel is similar to the Ghost of Silver Run. It is the vision of a young woman at night in a flowing blue nightgown. Many claim that the ghost pulls at her hair and runs through the railroad tunnel screaming bloody-murder.

There are no recorded sources to support the idea of a ghost of a young woman meeting her end on the tracks, however. The only female listed killed on the railroad tracks near the tunnel was an eighty-year-old woman.

There is one recorded source that refers to the haunting of the Moonville Tunnel. It ran in the *Chillicothe Gazette* on February 17, 1895:

The ghost of Moonville, after an absence of one year, has returned and is again at its old pranks, haunting the B & O Southwest Freight trains and their crews. It appeared Monday night in front of a fast freight. Number 99 westbound, just east of the cut which is one half mile on the other side of Moonville, at the point where Engineer Lawhead lost his life and Engineer Walters was injured. The ghost attired in a pure white robe, carried a lantern. It had a long flowing white beard, its eyes glistened like balls of fire and surrounding it was a halo of twinkling stars. When the train stopped the ghost stepped off the track and disappeared into the rocks nearby.

Some ghost! Ghost hunters who have investigated the Moonville Tunnel have witnessed the appearance of a strange light bobbing through the tunnel as if someone carries the lantern or holds it up. Before the light reaches the end of the tunnel, it disappears as if snuffed out. This sounds like the most truthful and accurate telling of spirit activity.

Ghost Hunter Tim Elliot in the Moonville Tunnel, Athens County, Ohio.
COURTESY JUSTIN BERNARD

The East End Ghoul, Parkersburg

If ghosts frighten you, you might not want to consider the thought of being chased by a ghoul. So what is a ghoul, you ask? A ghoul is a hideous, graveyard creature that preys upon the bodies and souls of the dead. The word ghoul comes from *ghul* in Arabic, meaning to "seize quickly" or "grab a hold of." Ghouls are universally malevolent entities. They are like ghosts but are more visceral—you can smell the ghoul's foul breath and touch his rotting skin. Ghouls are physical and not a fleeting apparition.

Ghouls are here to do evil and are more closely related to graveyard demons, revenants or vampires than ghosts or lost souls of the dead. Ancient lore says ghouls will feast upon the flesh of road worn travelers or corpses stolen out of graves at night. This is why ghouls often hang around cemeteries or at the ever-menacing Crossroads.

Most ghouls are content to terrify. Their purpose is to scare the living so bad they wish that they were dead. Ghouls only prey upon the already dead.

The dreaded ghoul has a gruesome face devoid of features. They moan and groan and are unable to make human conversation. These midnight demons are said to inhabit old ruins, abandoned houses and other lonely, isolated places.

In European folklore, ghouls are most strongly attracted to travelers. The reason for this is not really known, except for the fact that travelers seem to be vulnerable. In older Dracula movies, you may remember how they often open with a scene of weary travelers, after being delayed by thunderstorms or losing their way, eventually find themselves at Castle Dracula. Therefore it is no surprise that in Eastern European lore, a vampire and a ghoul are pretty much the same thing. Both are re-animated corpses with evil spirits inside. But only in the cases of extreme evil do human beings ever become ghouls.

Perhaps ghouls are attracted to travelers because travelers are vulnerable, easy to prey upon and confuse. After all, people in route are not immediately missed by family members. That is, if something "unexpected" happens to them.

This is where our tale unfolds, at the Crossroads, a place where the malevolent energies of the supernatural are at their most powerful. The exact place is the East End B & O Railroad yard in Parkersburg, and at the Rowland Boarding House where weary sojourners working the rails chose to rest their heads at night.

The year is 1888. It is the last week of June, more than twenty years after the Civil War has ended. The 6th Street train trestle and bridge have been completed—jobs are plentiful and West Virginia coal is being shipped out west.

The exact place of the haunting is the coal chutes of the B & O Railroad yard in what was then the eastern end of the city. The time closes in on midnight, 'the witching hour,' a tenuous moment when supernatural forces are the strongest and most unpredictable. Tired rail workers were leaving their late evening shifts when they encountered a mysterious being that both startled and terrified them. More than six feet tall and moving at a "funereal pace," the apparition was completely enshrouded in white from head-to-toe.

Although ghostly in appearance, the being was more horrible than any ghost; far more menacing than ethereal phantasms spotted on nearby Blennerhassett Island. What the men encountered was the "East End Ghoul."

The B & O Railroad workers were made aware of the ghoul when they first heard "a clanking of chains." As the men looked in the direction that the sounds came from, they saw something large and white floating along the railroad tracks. Its feet never touched the ground even though the men heard echoing footsteps. The face was mostly covered, and absent of any human features. As this incredible apparition swayed down the tracks, it emitted an unearthly groan that could be heard at both the railroad yard and the nearby oil and gas company.

The workers that didn't scatter immediately took refuge behind some barrels to watch the bizarre event unfold. The ghoul drifted along, moaning all the way, seemingly unaware of the men's presence. The ghoul then came upon the Rowland Boarding House. The hulking phantom hesitated for a few moments as if pondering whether to go in or not. The sounds of the chains were fainter. The thing seemed to have lost its direction. But without missing a beat, the ghoul sped up and coursed down the tracks, past the cemetery, where it came upon an alleyway and vanished into a gray smoke.

This appearance of the ghoul might be easily explained as a hoax except for the fact that it appeared every night for a week in late June and was witnessed by dozens of people. And as such, it was written up in local newspapers.

As with many haunted tales, a skeptic enters the scene to challenge the validity of such frightening and puzzling appearances. In this story, the skeptic is one Mr. Crolley, who did not work for the B & O Railroad but was employed by the Camden Consolidated Oil Company.

Crolley happened to be at the railroad yard one late June night handling a business transaction, and perhaps also to spin a yarn with the B & O workers around quitting time.

As Mr. Crolley left for home, he heard a dreadful groaning near the railroad yard. When he glanced around, he spotted a shrouded phantom exactly as the other men had reported earlier in the week. The apparition drifted up and down the tracks in the area of the coal chutes, approximately one hundred yards from the Rowland Boarding House.

Too shocked even to breathe, Crolley receded quietly into the shadows. The ghoul paused in the area of the Rowland Boarding House as if something inside interested it. Gaslights fluttered at the glass. Songs of drunken men poured out of the second story windows, oblivious to the unearthly thing that was now focused on them.

Of indeterminate sex, the ghoul glided down the tracks. A sweet stench of decay filled the air—it was the kind of smell that reminded Crolley of a back alley behind a funeral parlor. With caution, he inched closer to the ghoul only to realize that he was completely drained, taken over by an overwhelming tiredness. As Crolley fought his fatigue, the ghoul stopped at an alleyway and stared, still not noticing him. The strange being then vanished just as it had before.

Crolley was not a man who was easily frightened or frustrated by unearthly things. He promised himself that he would investigate the ghoulish appearance the very next night. Mr. Crolley was not disappointed.

As Crolley waited, strange echoing footsteps sounded. This was certainly odd, because the ghoul, in fact, had not appeared to have any feet at all as it floated above the railroad tracks.

As with the previous night, the ghoul moved in the direction of the Rowland House and nearby Holliday Cemetery, where it stopped for a few brief moments, then diverted its attention toward the alleyway. Only this time, Crolley started to run after the ghoul. He wasn't about to let this mystery get away from him! What happened next was utterly unexpected.

With a supernatural force, the East End Ghoul wheeled around and approached the man at a high rate of speed. Not knowing what else to do, Crolley leapt behind a tree where he hid for several seconds. As soon as the man regained his courage, he peered out from behind the tree. What he witnessed startled him.

The East End Ghoul was joined at the tracks by another one, an exact replica! But this particular ghoul was dark, its face and clothes completely blackened as if by the sulfurous fires of Hell.

Twin-like, the ghouls moved at a lingering, slow pace, echoing the same movements. Later it was said they resembled photographic negatives of each other. Even so, both ghoulish manifestations seemed to be intent on one Mr. Crolley, who now ran away, feet barely touching the brick-street, glancing over his shoulder all the while. It wasn't long before the ghouls halted. It seemed they had lost interest in the frightened, bedraggled man.

The Ghouls of East End turned and floated back toward Rowland Boarding House where they paused for another few moments as if

Entrance to Holliday Cemetery, Parkersburg. This is the spot were the East End Ghouls allegedly disappeared in 1888

straining to hear the lively sounds of happy men inside. The figures then peered down the alley, hesitated at the gates of the Holliday Cemetery, when in a phantomlike silence they both disappeared. Perhaps, as ghouls are concerned, Crolley wasn't much of a catch anyway. More fun seemed to be had by those spending the night in the Rowland Boarding House.

Nevertheless, the East End haunts were quite the sensation for the rest of the summer. However, the East End Ghoul and his black-enshrouded partner were never seen in Parkersburg again.

What happened to Crolley is pure speculation. It appears his name also faded from the newspapers' pages. One thing that is for certain about Mr. Crolley though—only a fool would chase a ghoul!

Portraits of More Spirits in Black & White

Reports of the black and white apparitions near the coal chutes in the East End of Parkersburg might stand alone on account of their utter strangeness except for similar ghost sightings in August of 1888. These sightings involved the apparition of a little girl who was said to play in the streets near dusk.

An article that appeared in *The State Journal* on August 13, 1888 stated:

The citizens of some parts of the East End are scared out of their wits over an alleged ghost. The children especially are all torn up over the mysterious visitor.

The ghost presents the appearance of a young girl in a perfectly white dress, and has been seen on Latrobe Street and other East End streets. A girl in a white dress on the streets is not a strange or unusual sight, but the actions of this particular individual seem peculiar to the citizens of that neighborhood.

Last week this ghost wore a black dress and was seen on Seventh Street—. The police will probably have him or her in the coop before long if he or she does not quit his or her monkey business.

A more recent sighting of another ghostly figure in the East End was disclosed as recently as the summer of 2000. Shortly after dusk, a resident of the area glimpsed the figure of what looked to be a woman in a white shroud gliding up one of the side streets.

Since the features on this apparition were quite unspecific, this reported spirit appeared to be similar to ones sighted in the 19th century near the railroad yards. It is possible that such creatures of the night still haunt the shadowy rails and alleys of the East End of Parkersburg.

FIVE

Ghosts That Grieve: Eva Zona Shue, Delsie Harris, Margaret Blennerhassett & Mamie Thurman

Margaret, Margaret,
Why are you grieving?
Over Goldengrove unleaving?
Leaves, like the things of man, you
With your fresh thoughts care for, can you?
Ah! As the heart grows even older
It will come to such sights colder…
Nor mouth had, no, nor mind expressed
What heart had heard of, or ghost had guessed:
It is the blight man was born for.
It is Margaret you mourn for…

— From ***Spring and Fall***, by Gerard Manley Hopkins

Grieving ghosts, or "women in white" apparitions, are a universal phenomenon. They are thought to be the ghosts of women with unsettled issues and are linked to tragedies such as suicide, murder, betrayal or even the death of a child. Why some spirits hold on, while others do not, is not clearly known, but in such cases they carry a sense of regret or sadness over some unfair treatment in life.

We have all experienced sad or disappointing circumstances that tend to haunt us over a period of time. But eventually we come to terms with the grief or disappointment, and move on. However, "women in white," or grieving ghosts, are not able to do this—they are unable to let go of the sad circumstances that haunted them in life. They hold on, and linger close to the places where the unfortunate acts took place, perhaps in the hopes of resolving the tragedy. There is urgency to their haunting—appearing again and again until they find resolution—or they appear just long enough for their pleading messages to be conveyed and understood by the living—that they have wrongly suffered.

West Virginia has four famous tales of grieving women ghosts. Why these spirits continue to haunt, you will learn in the following pages.

A Tragic Ghost In Greenbrier County

When twenty-four year old Zona Shue died suddenly in her home on January 23, 1897, few people were suspicious. After all, wherever Zona went, trouble and mishap followed. She had already embarrassed her religious family by giving birth to an illegitimate child in 1895. Everyone thought the girl was easily led astray and lacked "good horse sense." Zona's accidental death only seemed to prove that she hadn't brains enough to look out for herself. However, Zona's mother knew better.

1896 had begun on a happier note for Eva Zona Heaster—at least so she hoped. She met a charming bachelor by the name of Edward (Erasmus) Stribbling Trout Shue who had traveled to Greenbrier County, West Virginia to work as a blacksmith.

Erasmus was a wiry but strong man with oily black hair, and was much more handsome than the men usually interested in Zona Heaster. She needed someone to take care of her and Edward Shue appeared to be the one. At first, she didn't mind the fact that Shue drank, and was mean and crude at times. In fact, his roughness attracted her. She figured he was mean enough to fully protect her.

Mary Jane Heaster, Zona's mother, however, was not convinced that Erasmus Shue was a suitable husband for her naïve daughter. She saw that Shue was sneaky and he never looked her directly in the eye. When Mary Jane visited her daughter in her new home, Shue got up from the table and left the room. Erasmus was edgy whenever Zona's mother came around.

On January 27, 1897, a neighborhood boy discovered Zona Shue's body. The boy was on his way to the store and stopped to see if Zona wanted anything or if he could do any chores for her. Zona's body lay on the floor with her head turned to the side and one hand placed on her stomach. Although the body was mostly stiff from rigor mortis, Zona's head remained loose. The boy ran and screamed for the neighbors.

Local coroner Dr. George Knapp was called in, but it took him over an hour to get to the Shue farmhouse. The Doctor found that Zona Shue had already been carried upstairs by her husband, and placed on the bed in an odd, arranged way. She was not dressed in her usual housedress but in a high-necked dress, the type reserved for special occasions for a young woman in West Virginia. The Doctor had difficulty examining the body because each time he got up to the neck and head of the corpse, Erasmus Shue fell over the body, wept inconsolably, and cradled his wife's head.

Although Doc Knapp noticed some bruising around the corpse's neck and was skeptical, he was buffaloed by Shue and ruled the cause of Zona's death as "everlasting faint." After more pleading words from the greasy-haired man, the Doctor reconsidered and wrote down "childbirth" indicating a sudden, fatal miscarriage. Knapp was relieved to get out of the house—Shue had sweated like a sausage in his clothes. Shue's eyes had grown strange and wild.

The viewing for Zona's wake only added to the suspicion of her friends, family and the residents of Greenbrier County. Even before the viewing at the wake, Shue had placed a pillow against Zona's head "so she can rest easier." A colorful scarf was tied around her throat. Shue mentioned it was Zona's "favorite" even though no one remembered ever seeing Zona wear scarves. As family members tried to step closer to Zona's body lying in the casket, Shue hovered, not allowing anyone near. Whenever her mother stared down at her child, Shue pushed Mrs. Heaster away, and then fell over sobbing and caressed Zona's soft brown hair.

Hushed whispers filled the wake. Those who attended the funeral agreed that "all was not right" when it came to Zona's untimely death—but none as much as Zona's mother, who suspected Shue from the very instant she learned her daughter had died.

For four weeks after the funeral, Zona Shue's ghost appeared to her mother at the foot of the old woman's bed to reveal the true facts of her demise. Not surprisingly, Zona's ghost affirmed that she had been murdered and Shue was the one who did it. For four more days, Zona's ghost returned to add more specifics and details to the case.

Throughout her short marriage to Erasmus Shue, Zona told her mother she had been violated, beaten and abused. One night, when supper was not waiting for Shue on the table at the time he thought it should be, he flew into a fit of rage and killed her. With his rough hands, he choked her into unconsciousness. In doing so, he crushed her windpipe and broke the vertebrae in her neck. After seeing what he had done, Erasmus fled the house and only returned later when authorities notified him that his young wife had died.

After learning of the details of her daughter's death from her anguished ghost, Mary Jane Heaster contacted the Greenbrier prosecutor John Alfred Preston and described in minute detail the circumstances surrounding what she called a murder. Mrs. Heaster informed the prosecutor of the appearance and gave testimony of her daughter's ghost—whom she said had appeared numerous times at the foot of her bed. Whether Preston believed Mrs. Heaster's account or not, one thing was for certain—he was already very suspicious over the odd behavior of Erasmus Shue during his wife's funeral. Preston ordered Zona Shue's body exhumed on February 22nd. The autopsy revealed Zona, indeed, was strangled, her windpipe crushed and her neck broken exactly in the way her ghost had said it happened.

Although the information about Zona's spirit visiting her mother was deemed inadmissible, Erasmus Shue was tried for murdering his wife on very thin evidence. At one point, the defense lawyer brought in information about the ghost, implying that Mary Jane Heaster was a nutcase on a vendetta against her former son-in-law. Even though the testimony of Zona's ghost at the foot of her mother's bed never entered the courtroom, Shue was found guilty anyway. Word does travel… and so do ghosts.

Still, such tales of dastardly deeds do get around—especially in small, mountain communities like those in Greenbrier County. Erasmus Shue was sent to Moundsville prison to live out the rest of his days. He died there in March of 1900. His restless spirit seems to have remained in that spot, perhaps as one that now haunts the famous penitentiary, plagued by a number of unhappy ghosts.

Soul on Fire at Burnt House

Burnt House, a tiny village in Ritchie County, with a few roughly hewn log cabins, was a heavily traveled crossroads between Staunton, Virginia to Parkersburg before and after the Civil War.

One of its earliest settlers was Jack Harris, a large, burly man who came up from Randolph County in the south to set down roots around 1843. Because of the turnpike, any number of travelers passed through the area each day. Jack decided to build a two-story log house and turn it into a tavern.

The Harris tavern was an instant success. It became a major stopping point for the stagecoach with its weary travelers. In 1855, a medicine show arrived. Medicine shows were a popular diversion for locals since they offered various elixirs that promised to heal the sick, and also female dancers to entertain those who were, perhaps, not so sick.

When the medicine show brought a sienna-skinned dancer named Deloris, the crowds were awed. Although this bewitching young woman was rumored to be a slave, she had no trouble commanding attention and was called by the nickname "Delsie."

Delsie was an exotic, mixed-race woman. Some stories claimed that she was, in fact, a captured Cherokee woman, while others told she was a striking mulatto dressed in swirling, colorful skirts and the bangles of a gypsy. Since mixed-race people of black, red and white bloodlines were not unusual in the backwoods of West Virginia at the time, Delsie may well have been all three. Her reddish skin, gold-flecked eyes and raven-hair contrasted mysteriously with the many bright baubles and colorful silks that the young woman adorned her beautiful body with.

No matter what her true heritage was, Jack Harris's son William fell head over heels in love with Delsie. William begged his father to buy her. Knowing Delsie would be quite an attraction for his tavern, Harris did purchase the young slave woman and immediately put her to work as bar maid and singer.

Business was brisk. The mainstay for Harris's tavern was now the many salesmen and peddlers traveling to Parkersburg to sell their wares. Delsie worked well into the late hours. One night, two jewelry peddlers staying at the tavern vanished without a trace.

Soon Delsie turned up wearing jewelry valued beyond anything she or William could buy. Locals and tavern customers talked. How could a mixed-raced girl end up wearing the expensive baubles that only fine white women could afford? An investigator from Richmond was called in by a man related to a judge in Parkersburg who had stayed at the tavern the night of the disappearance.

During his investigation, the detective found out that a stable boy had witnessed William Harris behead one of the salesman while the boy peeked through the window of the tavern. The boy also said he saw Delsie carrying what looked to be a burlap sack that oozed a maroon substance and contained something the size of a human head.

Jack Harris and his son (whether guilty or not) were privy to the rumors and, knowing what a lynch mob could do, fled Burnt House. Like the true cowards they turned out to be—they left the petite woman behind to face the music—and the rope.

But locals went soft on Delsie. After all, she was gorgeous, and some local men hoped she'd be "kind" to them now that she realized that they had saved her neck. Thus, they left Delsie to wile away the months, pining over the loss of the lover who jilted her. Many locals anticipated that the slave girl in her loneliness might share their beds.

But it wasn't long until another owner came in and hired Delsie to continue working there. She already knew the "ropes" of tavern life and most of the customers.

Yet Delsie's depression over her lost love failed to subside. One Sunday evening, the singer and dancer brought her Bohemian clothes out of storage and put them on. . . yards of a scarlet skirt, her apple green vest, the coin necklace and the tinkling ankle bracelets. Gold hoops shone red by firelight through Delsie's ringlets of black hair. She stole into the loft of the tavern and lit a fire. The slave girl, now carrying a torch, danced with that flame. She whirled like a dervish throughout the second story as raging fires spread.

A group from a nearby church gathered. They watched Delsie spin while fire licked her arms and face. The second floor of the tavern collapsed into a hellish inferno. The slave girl's screams rang through the stillness of the valley.

Once the morning came, all that was left of the tavern was ruins. Delsie's physical remains were forever lost in smoking debris.

After Delsie's death, the sheriff made a search of the hollow not far from the Harris tavern and discovered two human skeletons left on an overhang—one of the skeletons was lacking a head. Everyone assumed they were the missing salesmen, but no one ever knew for sure. After that the hollow was given the name "Dead Man's Hollow" as it is still called today.

But it did not take long for Delsie's ghost to return to the lonely, foreboding stop at Burnt House. By dark of night, many describe the apparition of Delsie rising up from the grounds where the tavern once stood. Her ghost appears as dancing fire that assumes the shape of a curvaceous woman. The ghostly form then takes on the energy of a funnel cloud, picks up speed, and disappears into the dark woods. With each disappearance, the ghost screams in self-banishment, writhing in pain over separation from the very place she is doomed to haunt.

In 1883, crashing thunder and lightning storms wrenched trees from their roots at Burnt House. After that terrible storm, the slave girl's ghost appeared to find rest. Many claim that this was the last time Delsie's ghost was seen—careening just like a hellish fire—for one brief moment, setting the woods or perhaps setting the world, on fire. But the mounting flames were dampened, soon vanquished by pouring rains. Perhaps the spirit of the bewitching slave girl of Burnt House found peace in that torrential night of rain in 1883. Yet perhaps she did not. After all, Delsie never recovered the love of William Harris, the man who brought her so much pain.

Why Margaret Blennerhassett May Still Mourn

In the following pages we will explore the history of hauntings on Blennerhassett Island, a lush, scenic, island located slightly south of Parkersburg on the Ohio River.

We would be remiss not to include sightings concerning the lingering apparition of Margaret Blennerhassett on the island. Margaret's ghost fits the classic "woman in white" apparition, which are spirits unable to let go of the emotional complications that held them here in life.

After moving onto Blennerhassett Island in 1801, Irish aristocrats Margaret and her husband Harman Blennerhassett took time, money and effort to turn their remote island into a heaven on earth. After their Mount Vernon style mansion was finally completed on the island, the couple experienced a series of unfortunate events, as you will learn in the following chapter.

Usually in mid-October, especially on the night of October 16th, although the reason is not known, the ghost of a woman in white appears on the island. This apparition has also been viewed during the day. Visitors on the island who have had face-to-face encounters with

Margaret's ghost say she appears with the high sweet scent of perfume. Margaret is dressed in a pale gown, gazing as if eager for human contact once more. Most of the time her spirit walks alone, with hand shielding her brow, looking onward as if searching for someone.

Who the lady in white still searches for, we do not know. Whatever her reason might be, the spirit of Margaret Blennerhassett still watches. . . and she waits.

The Ghost of Mamie Thurman

Murders, even in the present day, are rare events in West Virginia. So it is no surprise that one ghost out of a small community near Logan is still talked about after over 75 years. On June 22, 1932 a doe-eyed, dark-haired beauty by the name of Mamie Thurman was found murdered outside of Holden, on what was then called Trace Mountain. Mamie Thurman was a local socialite, known by just about the entire community. Her trial was in the news nationally and was the biggest event of the year in Logan. Her murder was eventually pinned on a black man by the name of Clarence Stephenson—although most people in Logan, including prominent citizens, never believed he was guilty. Mamie died of two gunshot wounds to the brain and her throat was also slit from ear to ear. Nothing of any value (other than her life) was missing from Mamie's body. She had eight dollars in her wallet, a gold watch was clasped about her wrist and she wore two diamond rings. These were certainly a small fortune during the Depression days and any robber would have taken those immediately.

The reason behind the murder was never solved. We know from the case of the Greenbrier Ghost, that when a person is unjustly murdered and the killer goes free, the spirit cannot rest until he is brought to justice or at least recognized as the murderer.

Some residents of Logan claim Mamie Thurman's ghost still wanders the hills and hollows of Logan, wearing a navy polka dot dress and the finger-wave hairstyle of the 1930s. Mamie's ghost is said to flag down cars on the winding road of # 22 Mountain, where her body was left lifeless and bloodied many years before. When the car slows she just disappears.

Interestingly, even where Mamie Thurman's body rests today is still in dispute. Records show she may have been buried in Kentucky, the state of her birth, while others insist her body was in fact, interred in Logan at the Logan Memorial Park. But Mrs. Thurman's grave is not noted, and it is claimed her ghost continues to haunt the cemetery, seeking justice and pleading for a headstone to mark her life, if not her final resting place.

74

SIX

Haunted Island: The Blennerhassetts & Why They Haunt

How many times have I looked
Out this window?
How many times have
I waited here?
Glorious was the sunlight
Upon the stream…
Among the green way
There is a path—
Where I escaped into wonderment—
I still remember the way—
But cold was the moonlight
When all was lost—
Yet in praise I return
To the dream this day.

— by the author while in Margaret Blennerhassetts' bedroom

It is hard to imagine rustic West Virginia, an area mostly known for steep hills and majestic mountains, has its very own enchanted island; with a love story attached. It is a place so lush and pristine that it was once christened "Eden on the River." It may seem just as unlikely that a handsome couple of noble, European breeding would move to an area that was little more than a howling wilderness, at their own peril, in order to create a paradise on earth. And yet, this is precisely so.

But what if tragedy and bitter disappointment befell this promising couple? What if the husband was tried for treason, then felt the shame of being imprisoned? Imagine if during this unhappiness, the couple's two-year-old daughter succumbs to a terrible, sudden illness. What if the

Blennerhasset Island trees

remains or resting place of the baby were lost and never again located?

Harman and Margaret Blennerhassett reached the mid-Ohio Valley in the last years of the 18th century. The couple decided to move to the United States where few knew they were, in fact, of the same blood. Any marriage between them violated church laws in their native Ireland. And there was another reason for the couple to leave Ireland. Harman had joined the Society of United Irishmen, which made him a target for the British who occupied Ireland at the time. It appears life in the United States promised a fresh start for the cultured and ambitious couple.

In the spring of 1796, the Blennerhassettts departed the British Isles on a ship bound for America. It took seventy-three days to travel from England to New York City. During that time, one strange event took place that foreshadowed things to come for Margaret and Harman. During the voyage, the ship's captain suddenly died. The cause of death was never solved but was thought to be poisoning. Later, other eerie and unfortunate events seemed to nip at the heels of the wealthy Irish couple—hints of future mishaps. Even so, the Blennerhassetts arrived safely on American soil on August 1st, 1796.

After traveling from Philadelphia to Pittsburgh, Harman and Margaret moved south toward the small towns of Marietta and Belle Prairie, Ohio, and what would eventually become Parkersburg, West Virginia. Soon, the Blennerhassetts purchased a small island on the Ohio River, which lay south of what are now Belpre and Parkersburg.

After reaching the lush, green island, the Irish couple and their help cleared a section of land to build a Palladian mansion so splendid in its grandeur that it is now a legend. The horseshoe-shaped structure measured 8,200 square feet. Oriental carpets, marble clocks, expensive oil paintings, Venetian mirrors and silver doorknobs were added to the twelve-room mansion that rivaled any in the British Isles.

This was a perfect retreat for European aristocrats, eventually dubbed "Little Eden" by others, forming a destiny that held the Blennerhassetts on the island for less than five years. The mansion took two and a half years to complete, built with natural hardwoods and other supplies imported from Pennsylvania and Europe. Soon Blennerhassett Island and its fantastic mansion, with all of its European niceties, became an awe-inspiring sight to buckskin-clad frontier people as they passed by. But the shock of finding such an estate on the West Virginia frontier was quickly eclipsed by the tragedy befalling the home and its occupants.

The Blennerhassetts became the parents of three children: Harman Junior, who had been born prior to their arrival, Dominic (a French boy they adopted), and a baby girl, Margaret. Margaret, the youngest child, died on the island when she was only two years old. A small, unmarked grave behind the mansion is where the remains of the baby are believed to be.

But Margaret's spirit was so attached to the island that she wrote poetry in her unmistakable, fluent handwriting about her "paradise." Some of her verse praised the natural beauty of the island with yearnings about how she never wanted to leave it, often leaving out the sad story associated with it. Margaret did not know she would be forced to abandon her island home, never to return, at least not while alive.

Before the downfall of the Blennerhassetts, the couple had met a brilliant, troubled man by the name of Aaron Burr, former Vice President of the United States. He had come up with the idea to purchase a vast amount of lands that are now Louisiana, Florida,

and Mexico in order to form a separate country. This made sense to
Harman since he had worked for Irish independence from England
earlier in an underground movement of wealthy Irish aristocrats.

Burr needed a supporter with a large amount of money to invest
in the plan. By this time, the Blennerhassetts were feeling the monetary
effects of their lavish building and furnishing of the mansion. Harman's
finances were becoming depleted, so he eagerly accepted Burr's
proposal in the hopes of replenishing his fortune.

President Thomas Jefferson issued a Presidential proclamation
calling for "all residents of the United States to bring to punishment all
persons engaged in such treasonable enterprises as Burr's expedition."
Harman Blennerhassett and Aaron Burr fled the island and went into
hiding, leaving Margaret and the children behind.

The United States government sent the Virginia militia to seize
Blennerhassett and his island. Margaret escaped to Marietta; Harman
went to Kentucky. When Margaret finally returned home, she found
the house had been ransacked and greatly damaged by the militia.
Later, Burr and Blennerhassett were apprehended and imprisoned in
the Virginia State Penitentiary.

After completing his sentence for treason, Harman and Margaret
were finally reunited but did not return to Blennerhassett. The couple
later attempted to start plantations in Canada and Mississippi, but
those were losses as well. Margaret regretted each day that she could
not return to the island, but the fiasco with Burr slandered their noble
name. She realized it would never be the same on the island.

After its abandonment, the mansion fell into disrepair. Debtors that
Harman owed money to took some of the belongings from the mansion.
Weeds reclaimed the grounds and gardens. The mansion dwindled to
a shell. After the Blennerhassetts left for good, the mansion was used to
store hay and hemp from nearby farms.

One night thieves stormed the mansion. They aimed to steal
whatever remaining liquor there was from the wine cellar. A lantern
brushed against a bale of hay and caught fire. Within minutes,
the mansion was engulfed in flames. In 1811, in only an hour, the
Blennerhassett mansion burned to the ground. All was lost. Or was it?

This compelling story did not end when the Blennerhassetts
deserted their island. It did not even end when the Blennerhassetts died.

Those who understand the workings of the spirit world know that when issues are not settled ghosts will return to haunt.

Numerous accounts claim that Margaret's ghost still appears on the island along with other mystifying apparitions. Over the years, visitors have reported many odd and spectacular sightings that suggest the island is still haunted. Here are just a few of the ghostly tales.

Native American Apparitions

Long before Harman and Margaret Blennerhassett settled on the land, Native Americans consistently populated the island. Archaeologists have unearthed human artifacts from dozens of Native American graves that may date back nearly 12,000 years. The remains of what appears to be important chiefs or leaders (judged by the type of relics found beside the skeletons) were buried beside rudimentary weapons, tools and rich grave goods. Some of the remains of the Indians were enormous, close to seven feet tall. This gives us reason to believe the island may have been a sacred site as well as a burial site for the nomadic groups who traveled through the mid-Ohio Valley.

In the tradition of many native cultures, if a holy place or a burial site is desecrated, whoever defiles the remains can become cursed until the area is returned to its original state. Is this what caused Harman and Margaret's hardships after they built the mansion on the island? We may never know.

However, we do know the Blennerhassetts are not the only former inhabitants to return to the island—if only in spirit. Long before the island was turned into a historical state park, people traveled by boat to camp out. A few that ventured into the woods claimed to see a man with long raven hair, wearing buckskin clothing and a red breechcloth. The man is seen walking between the older trees on the island. It was the specter of an unusually tall Indian.

But no one saw the stranger's face. He was viewed only from behind. Those that saw the apparition agreed that he was a Native American from long ago. The aboriginal stranger acted preoccupied as if hunting for game. . . or maybe tracking something else.

Whenever approached, the native was said to quicken his pace and disappear deep into the thicket. He became known as "the wild Indian of the island."

This is not the moon. It is a ghost orb on Blennerhassett Island.
COURTESY KRISTALL CHAMBERS

An Incandescent Woman

By far the most famous haunt on Blennerhassett Island is that of Margaret Blennerhassett herself. Her ghost typically appears as a young woman in a white empire-style dress whose vision is often accompanied by the sweet scent of floral perfume and sometimes even the smell of horses. (Margaret was an equestrian.) Witnesses describe her apparition as a young woman, under thirty years of age. When approached, Margaret typically fades away into nothingness before the eyes of surprised onlookers.

Live horses (there are weekend carriage rides on the island) tend to get spooked for no apparent reason while on Blennerhassett Island. Horses are just not at ease while visiting there. It is recorded that Micah "Cajoe" Phillips, a slave to the Blennerhassetts, was responsible for bringing the horses over the river to the island. Riding in the boat made Mrs. Blennerhassett's horses extremely nervous. Horses who visit the island to this very day seem to suffer from mysterious anxieties and unexplained nervousness.

Visitors to the island also report seeing a willowy woman along the shoreline dressed entirely in white. With hand shading her brow, she gazes as if waiting for someone to return. Like many haunts, she at first materializes as if in the flesh, then fades.

A woman riding on the *Mississippi Queen* downriver spied two women dressed in white walking on the shoreline of the island. Later, she asked one of the docents on the island "If there was a convent or nunnery in Parkersburg?"

Thinking the visitor meant the DeSales Heights Convent and Academy in Parkersburg, the docent answered that there used to be a convent school in Parkersburg but it had shut down. The woman then told the docent of seeing two women cloaked entirely in white walking up and down as the boat approached. She thought, perhaps, they were Catholic sisters visiting the island. But no one else mentioned ever having seen the two women on that day.

Margaret often waited for Harman on the northern edge of the island. She often wore a white gown on her walks. Was this the apparition of Margaret? If so, who was the second woman? Perhaps she was a servant or friend who dressed similarly to Margaret. After all, the Blennerhassetts were very kind to their servants. Most of them were of African descent or mixed-race slaves. Some were very light-skinned. Such a woman may have walked with Margaret.

After the Blennerhassetts fled the island over the Aaron Burr debacle, the baby Margaret's gravesite was neglected. One legend claims two farmers plowed a field on the island near where the mansion once was and unearthed a tiny skeleton. They immediately reburied it in a small, unmarked grave. To this day the gravesite has yet to be found.

Locals visiting the island claim to see Margaret's ghost search the area where the small bones may be buried. Startled by the sudden presence of an incandescent woman, two farmers claimed the same apparition walked through their crops. One man recognized Margaret Blennerhassett because of her silky, chestnut hair and old-fashioned clothing. The other recognized her by her richly tucked and pleated dress.

Now Margaret's remains and her son's have returned to the island. But like their daughter, Harman has not been located. His body was interred on Guernsey Island off England's coast. Strangely, Mr. Blennerhassett requested to be buried at night. He did not want visitors at his gravesite. Harman did a good job of hiding himself because no one knows exactly where his final resting spot is.

The author in the library of the Blennerhassett Hotel on Halloween Night, 2002. Notice the ghost orb at the bottom of her cape. COURTESY KRISTALL CHAMBERS

An Untimely Visit From Aaron Burr

When lyricist Joyce Ancrile penned the lyrics for the musical drama "Eden on the River," based upon the romance of the Blennerhassetts, she decided to lie down and get some shut-eye after a long period of writing. Only moments passed when Ancrile sensed a presence in the room and opened her eyes to see a hawkish-featured man in early 19th century clothing gazing across the room at her. The gentleman was dressed in a rich, blue jacket and was resting on a settee.

Startled, Ms. Ancrile immediately sat up. The man faded. But Ancrile recognized the apparition from the research she had been doing for the play. There was no doubt. She knew him by his striking profile. The man was Aaron Burr. Later, Joyce would explain, the man's expression conveyed the words to her, "What has taken you so long," as if he had been pressing her to tell his story.

More Sightings of a Political Rogue

Sightings of the ghost of Aaron Burr are not the norm for Parkersburg, but it is interesting to note that there is a long history behind Aaron Burr ghost sightings in New York City.

Apparently, Burr's specter shows up at various addresses in Greenwich Village. One such place is a restaurant that was Burr's former carriage house. Workers in the "One If by Land, Two If by Sea" restaurant, claim that Burr's ghost returns to smash dishes, swing lamps and scoot chairs noisily.

Also in Greenwich Village, Burr's spirit also visits the area of his former stables, now a café called Quantum Leap Natural Food. Many believe he is searching for his daughter Theodosia who was lost at sea. When Burr appears, he reveals intense dark eyes, is always dressed in a ruffled shirt but cloaked in a gloom of guilt and sorrow. Apparently Burr's life did not live up to his expectations. But it was his enemy Thomas Jefferson, who ended up having Burr imprisoned, who wrote these hard words about him: "I never thought him an honest, frank-dealing man, but considered him as a crooked gun, or other perverted machine, whose aim or shot you could never be sure of." Jefferson had earlier penned: "Burr is a great man in little things but he is really small in great ones." It does seem for certain that the spirit of Aaron Burr, even centuries later, had some unsettled business to contend with. His is the case of a sad yet true haunting.

The Tale of The Wandering Reporter

In 1988, a Pittsburgh magazine writer came to the area by boat in order to write an article about all of the sights and sounds along the Ohio River. Blennerhassett Island would be a perfect addition to his article.

It was in October when he stopped at the island and set up camp. Nearing dawn, the writer was awakened by rustling sounds outside. It was odd how strange shadows surged against the side of his tent.

The writer stepped outside and discovered the source of the sounds. Much to his surprise, he saw a pale woman in a white, flowing dress. The lady stood staring, never moving. Stunned, he waited for her to speak but the woman said not a word to him.

Since there was a chill in the air, the reporter motioned for her to sit by the fire and offered to make her coffee. She simply gazed upon him, then receded into the early morning fog.

Not able to figure this visit out, he decided to get a few hours of shut-eye before his trip in the morning. The reporter was traveling with a collection of his own writings and other reading materials. He had them inside his knapsack outside the tent. Shortly after drifting off, the writer was awakened by sounds once more.

Someone was going through his knapsack! Papers rattled as they were being shuffled. When the sounds finally halted, the man opened his tent and was amazed at what he saw. Every book was taken from his bag, and neatly stacked beside the smoldering remains of the campfire. Whoever had discovered them had read every one, and then carefully placed them back into a pile.

The reporter told workers on the island about his uncanny experience the next day. When he described the woman to the small group of people, they were not surprised. The writer had described Margaret Blennerhassett perfectly even down to the fine brown hair.

Margaret Blennerhassett was a bibliophile. The passion she felt for books apparently survived the grave. The writer promised he would return to the island to find out more about Margaret and the hauntings on the island. But unlike Margaret's ghost, the writer has yet to return to the island. It seems he was spooked away by the entire encounter.

Harman and Margaret Blennerhassett had slaves as well as paid servants while on the island. However, the slaves were treated humanely and often as a part of the family. Although Ohio was a free state and freedom lay less than a mile across the Ohio River, not one of the Blennerhassett's slaves, or servants, were known to have even attempted an escape, at least, while Margaret and Harman were still there.

Many slaves remained loyal to Harman and Margaret in later times when the Blennerhassetts ran a plantation called "La Cashe" in the Deep South.

On the island, one slave in particular was close to Harman and Margaret. This slave, Ransom Reed, often rode horses alongside Margaret while they admired the beauty of the island and surrounding valley. Like the Blennerhassetts many of the slaves often referred to the island as their true home. A few of the former slaves moved to the neighboring towns of Parkersburg, Belpre and Marietta, where their descendants live to this very day.

The Smell of Horses

Historian and horseman Henry Robert Burke of Marietta had a strange, daylight encounter with the apparition of Margaret Blennerhassett. Henry was working on the State Road at the time, clearing off some of the brush at the side of the highway when he was overtaken by a sudden fatigue. He decided he would lie down and rest a few moments, but within minutes he had accidentally fallen asleep. The spell was broken when Henry was awakened by the powerful smell of horses, a scent he would recognize since he often competed in horse shows.

As Henry opened his eyes, he suddenly saw the apparitions of Margaret Blennerhassett and what appeared to be a mulatto man riding by on their horses. Margaret was dressed in her usual riding attire, a triangular hat, leather gloves, small whip and what appeared to be a split skirt. The strangest thing, Henry explained, was that Margaret and her riding companion seemed to have been just as startled by his presence as he was by theirs. Later Burke found out the spot was very near where Margaret used to tie up her horses in what is now Belpre, Ohio. It is interesting that Margaret Blennerhassett's ghost most commonly appears in the daytime when least expected.

After the Blennerhassett estate was rebuilt as a state park in the 1980s, some who visited the island described seeing a black man circling the perimeter of the mansion, wearing clothes common during the 18th and early 19th centuries.

Most people thought little of a dusky-skinned man who wore old-fashioned attire, taking a solitary tour of the island. There are various artisans from the island's craft village and volunteers dressed in period clothing. It would not be out-of-the-ordinary to see such a person. When workers were asked about the gentleman, they didn't have a clue as to his identity. No one knew of an African American male who worked at the craft village or as a volunteer on the island.

But if one looks back two hundred years, you'll find an individual who fits the description. It is Ransom Reed, a favored servant of the Blennerhassetts, thought to be buried in Holliday Cemetery in Parkersburg.

So, is Margaret's ghost an earthbound spirit, doomed to haunt her enchanted island?

No, the spirit of Margaret Blennerhassett is able to move as freely about as any other spirit. Ghosts are not so different than the living. They sometimes like to revisit places, people and memories from times past and most of al, spirits still care about the living and how we carry on with our lives.

Sometimes, when conditions are just right, as it so often is on Blennerhassett Island, we can connect with these wandering spirits and are able to see and experience the memories of the souls of the dead exactly as they once lived.

SEVEN
The Crossroads: Parkersburg's other Harrowing Haunts:
Upper Juliana, Market & Thirteenth Streets

Crossroads

Night is a riddle
Hidden within the magician's dark sleeve.

Consider the vagaries of stars
How they tinkle as tiny bells do
On a jester's velvet cap.

Consider your future
Crowded with saints and lunatics.

Consider lying awake all night
To face the funhouse mirror

Where you have only yourself
And yourself and yourself…

Where a blue window slides away,
Becomes a floating tomb,

Where suicides hang like smoke.
What you cannot see

Is a sky wrought with messages
Like an intaglio on the palms.

At the end of the street
Graves have been emptied.

The moon lets go of her stem,
Becomes a ship of bones.

— by Susan Sheppard

Does the possibility of vengeful ghosts make you a bit squeamish? What about elemental spirits and graveyard ghouls? Do tales of spells of voodoo make you shudder? Or are you simply just one who dreads the dead?

Then you would do best to avoid the Crossroads, a place in every town where roads intersect and form a cross. In ancient lore, the Crossroads is a place where spiritual danger and ghostly powers are said to lurk. This is more so if there is a cemetery near by.

Why the Crossroads? Throughout the world, the Crossroads hold a special significance. After all, it is a place where psychic powers, ghostly powers if you will, are the most focused and strong.

The meeting and parting of ways is associated with the Crossroads. This may explain why ancient peoples were suspicious over paths that intersect—especially lonely, isolated roads where the more sinister elements of the supernatural—such as vampires and devils—have long been associated.

All type of unnatural beings hang around the Crossroads like a foul mist, willing and waiting to gobble up your immortal soul. The Devil himself is linked to the Crossroads. This is true not only in African American folk tales but also in European lore. Not only is the Devil associated with the Crossroads, fairies are said to frequent there—but not the benevolent kind in children's tales. These are fairies of evil, so one should never fall asleep at the Crossroads. All manner of misfortune will find you. You may wake up "bewitched" or "fairy led." You may even wake up in the land of the dead.

Long ago, gallows for the condemned were built at the Crossroads. Suicides and victims of murder were buried at the Crossroads as well. This was done so their restless souls wouldn't wander, seeking revenge upon those who harmed them in life. Some believed it was the power of the Christian cross that the Crossroads symbolized, to protect the living from vengeful acts of the unhappy dead.

Contrary to popular opinion, menacing ghosts are not always the earthbound souls of the departed. They can sometimes be an evil component of the personality that survives death. This ghost is usually one that is said to lack authority and direction. It is believed that a malevolent ghost will stand at the Crossroads all night long trying to make up its mind which way to go. Upon morning, the pure rays of sunlight will send the spirit screaming into banishment. Vampires are said to carry their shrouds to the Crossroads in search of fresh victims. In voodoo rites, tail feathers from a black rooster will help protect you at the Crossroads from devils, ghosts and boogers that usually haunt mountain hollows. A rooster claw works as well.

However, the magic and mayhem of the Crossroads traces further into history than the advent of Christianity. This legend appeared in Asia, Africa and North America well before European influences were felt. This is one of the mysteries that surround it.

Ancient peoples all over the world believed that magic was at its most powerful at the Crossroads, and a path associated with witchcraft. Hecate—the Greek goddess of the underworld, howling dogs and witchery—lurks at the Crossroads, looking for someone to haunt.

In ancient times, offerings of food and cakes were set out at the Crossroads to appease Hecate and her mysterious forces of good and evil. Such cakes were then called "Hecate cakes," in which a lighted candle was placed in the center so Hecate could find her way to the Crossroads. This is where the custom of candles on birthday cakes originates.

Voodoo gives great spiritual influence to the Crossroads. Voodoo spells are often performed at the Crossroads, lending magical powers to the spell caster. Crossroads dirt, as well as graveyard dirt, is still used as protection from the Evil.

In voodoo spells, the Priest or Priestess who casts the spell waits at the Crossroads until an apparition (sometimes the Devil) appears. If the apparition does not make himself known immediately, the spell becomes more difficult to work. But if the devil or ghost arrives just on time, you can be assured the spell will work, but in the most dangerous and diabolical way possible. In Hoodoo culture of the Mississippi Delta, the Crossroads holds great distinction—especially for musicians. It was believed that if a musician truly desires to become great at his craft, he should go to the Crossroads at Midnight (sometimes at dusk) and wait for the Devil to appear or for a rooster to crow.

Once this happened, a big black man would materialize. It is important to point out this was not meant to be an African-American man, but a coal black man usually asking to borrow the musical instrument, which in most cases was a guitar. The black man then tunes the guitar and hands it back to the musician. Sometimes the black man asks to trim the musician's fingernails. Upon finishing these tasks the black man vanishes, either walking down a path into the woods, or just disappearing in mid-air. Now the bargain with the Devil had been made. Typically, the musician will, indeed, become great, but lives a short and violent life as his debt to Beelzebub.

How did a belief in the Crossroads make its way to West Virginia? Mysteriously, a group of small diminutive people called "The Black Dutch" eventually settled in the mountain state. They brought with them a belief in the Crossroads—from their places of earliest origin—India, then Romania and later Germany. Some Black Dutch were German Gypsies who settled with the Pennsylvania Dutch not far from the West Virginia border. Other Black Dutch were Shawnee and Cherokee Indians. Gypsy tradition says one should not toy with this mysterious witchery of the Crossroads. Uninvited forces of a malevolent nature might enter your life. . . So whatever you send out comes back to you threefold, and then some. And don't forget: The Crossroads exist everywhere, even in your town. . .

13th & Juliana Streets

Whenever you get an impressive row of old houses together, there are bound to be a few ghost stories. The Crossroads at 13th & Juliana Streets in Parkersburg is no exception. Possibly it is because Riverview Cemetery, the second oldest cemetery in Wood County, is right off the beaten path with its towering hemlocks and pine-littered graves.

Many of the houses surrounding Riverview Cemetery are allegedly haunted. At one time, the graveyard extended to the corner of 13th Street. Some of the houses on 13th and Juliana Streets may exist overtop archaic graves, some dating back to 1801.

Normally, there's no problem if a person happens to sleep on a grave. Most spirits don't mind. People do it in Africa, Mexico and Haiti during their holidays every year. That is, spirits don't mind unless those graves are located at the Crossroads. And unless your street is numbered Thirteen. . .

Needless to say there are a number of haunts reported in this area of Parkersburg. One modest two-story house has the shadowy form of a man who appears at night in a hall and upper room that faces the cemetery. Lights tend to go haywire in the home. No matter what wattage of light bulbs, the light inside the house always seems filmy and dim. Residents of other homes in the area complain of sinkholes, foul odors and a pounding in the walls during the middle of the night. Neighbors noticed phantom smoke, vague apparitions and objects turn up missing, only to appear later in unlikely places. It is believed the bodies of drowned runaway slaves who died in the Ohio River were buried outside the grounds of Riverview and some of the homes sit on those spots.

One home on upper Juliana Street seems to house a lighter, friendlier spirit, and one who presses her warmth against women visitors. The ghost wears an old-fashioned, sweet-smelling perfume and carries with her a feeling of warmth and openness.

The ghost seldom approaches men. Perhaps she is too shy or perhaps she doesn't care. Still, this lady is still there and continues to haunt.

Haunted Buddha

Given the omens and superstitions surrounding the number thirteen, it is no surprise to learn that several houses on 13th Street in Parkersburg are haunted.

Not far from Juliana and Market Streets, there is a modest brick home that has long been plagued by forces of a spiritual nature. But it wasn't until 1979 when local woman Betty Stewart moved in that unexplained occurrences began.

At first, Betty said that the brick ranch had a "warm, welcoming feeling." She loved the house and she had no qualms about moving in immediately. Everything seemed light and airy, plus the house had the extra bonus of being within walking distance to Betty's job at Public Debt, a federal position with great benefits.

It all seemed too perfect. Betty enjoyed looking into store windows and passing by the second hand shops on Market Street as she made her way home in the evenings. One late afternoon, a statue in the window of one of the shops caught her eye.

It was a green statue of a Buddha. Beside it was a coiled cobra with glittering red eyes. The statues looked to be pretty old and were most unusual. Betty appreciates art with an Oriental theme so she walked inside to inquire about a price.

The statues were a little more expensive than she had in mind, but on a whim, and with the few dollars she had, she decided to lay them away. Betty wasn't overly enthused with the cobra. With its red eyes, the statue looked malevolent. It was the green, pot-bellied Buddha that Betty really wanted. But the shopkeeper informed her that the pieces were to be sold together.

The owner suggested the pair should not be separated.

Every time Betty collected another paycheck she paid a few dollars more on the statues. Eventually the two ceramic pieces were hers and she took them home.

For the first week, all was well in the house. Life was routine. Betty placed the Asian statues side by side on an antique table and they looked splendid together. But then Betty had the sensation that someone was always watching her.

Feelings of being watched eventually were so powerful that Betty feared glancing into a mirror, afraid of who might be staring back at her. She had never been frightened in quite the same way before. She did not consider herself particularly impressionable and she didn't believe in ghosts.

She still liked the house; it was near some of Betty's relatives on Quincy Street. A niece gave Betty a cat for company, but the cat always ran away.

One day, a nephew came to spend the afternoon. He reached for a piece a candy in a nearby dish but accidentally hit the Buddha statue, shattering the candy dish into hundreds of pieces. Somehow, this acted as a catalyst for the strange, psychic energies that had already been unleashed in the house.

A stuffed dog that Betty kept on her sofa disappeared and turned up in unexpected places. Betty wondered if a prankster was at work. Muffled and rapping sounds awakened the Stewarts at night. Betty experienced night paralysis, one of the most frightening encounters of spirit infestations. Unable to scream or move, Betty woke up to the feeling of an evil presence in the room.

Doors in the house creaked open, only to shut with a bang. One night Betty awakened to what seemed to be an odd, pensive feeling in the room. She looked up to see a young boy, about twelve years old, standing in the doorway to her bedroom, dressed in a plaid shirt and jeans. "He looked absolutely real, not like a ghost in a movie or anything," Betty later reported. "I thought someone's child was lost and had wandered into our house." Several nights later, Betty's husband saw the same little boy.

Convinced that certain forces had been unleashed in the house, the couple called upon their son for help.

"It's those statues," the son replied. "I especially don't like that ugly snake. No matter where I am, its eyes seem to follow me around the room." That was enough to convince other family members that something was amiss. Betty's brother took the two statues and placed them in a box in the basement. The house quieted down for a time.

Circumstances in Betty's life caused her to change jobs and move. Later, Betty was told that about fifteen years before she had moved into the house on 13th Street, a young boy had gotten lost in the neighborhood and died looking for his mother. Years later, in the 1980s, a young couple moved into the home and decided to throw a party. One of the women who attended the party turned up missing. It wasn't long before odors seeped up from the basement. The party guest had fallen down the stairs and broken her neck. She died instantly. The woman's body lay there for several days before it was discovered at the bottom of the stairs.

Is the house still occupied? It is.

Who knows what now lurks in the basements of the homes on 13th Street? What happened to the statues of the green Buddha and wicked-eyed cobra? Betty put them in a garage sale and they sold right away. Are the spirit-possessed statues still in Parkersburg? No one knows.

Ghost of Runaway Slave off 13th Street

It seems as if every small town along the B & O Railroad has a story of the ghost of a slave that haunts a tunnel. Usually, the slave has lost his head and carries it under his arm. Usually the fugitive slave is said to moan, groan and shake his shackles.

Before the Civil War, central West Virginia and southern Ohio became major routes along the Underground Railroad. Several ghost stories from the region involve the misfortunes of runaway slaves who ventured through this area.

The problem with such stories is the B & O Railroad was not really in use (in what was to later become West Virginia) before the Civil War times, so it's unlikely a slave would be jumping a train in order to escape into freedom before then. Yet, areas of travel, such as railroads and crossroads, remain important in African American folklore. They became places where the two worlds met—the world of the living and also of the unquiet dead.

Not far from Thirteenth Street, a neglected house welcomed a young woman to move in after her diligent search for a generous old home with "lots of character." Part of the house had been broken up into apartments, but her area of the house had a family feeling since it had an upstairs bedroom and a downstairs living room with a kitchen. The apartment had not been updated for a while but was nicely carpeted with new plush carpet. Definitely a plus for the times—the late 1980s.

Shortly after moving in, the woman heard noises downstairs while trying to sleep. She thought it was, perhaps, the settling of boards in the old home and was surprised when in the morning she found bare footprints in the freshly vacuumed carpet. At other times, the woman's radio switched on or changed channels during the night. Later as she listened to footsteps downstairs, she heard identical sounds in the attic.

Feeling vulnerable and unsure over who or what was making the mysterious sounds, the woman moved out, but not before telling a friend. The friend liked the woman's apartment, so decided to move in and take over the rent. After all, she considered herself a brave person and was not particularly worried.

It didn't take long for her to hear the footsteps in the attic as well as the bare footprints to appear downstairs in the carpet. One night, the second woman listened to noises leading from her bedroom into the living room. The woman got up and grabbed a flashlight. As she ventured forward and flashed a beam of light down the stairs, she caught a glimpse of the apparition of a young black man in rags. His hands were chained. The man held up his shackled wrists and pleaded with sad, dark eyes.

Days later the young woman vacated the house off Thirteenth Street. The woman later learned that the old house had been built on a site that was a well-traveled route of the Underground Railroad. She also learned that many drowned slaves were said to have been placed in unmarked graves on the perimeters of Riverview Cemetery not far away.

DeSales Heights Academy: The Once Haunted Abbey

If old buildings could scream, the DeSales Heights Convent and Academy in Parkersburg would be a good candidate. By most accounts, the spirits inside the famous West Virginia landmark were restless if not unhappy. When exploring the cavernous, abandoned building, visitors felt anything but welcome. In fact, the spirits were known to slap, raise welts and even leave bloody scratches on visitors.

So why were the spirits inside DeSales Heights so upset?

Time was not kind to the old convent. Local youth often vandalized the spacious building. Rumors of the place being haunted attracted the curious and those who dared to risk encountering an angry spirit.

Following the Civil War, a convent was built that eventually became the DeSales Heights Academy. A rambling structure with a courtyard and meandering hallways, the one-hundred-year-old Catholic girls school was closed down in 1994 due to low enrollment and aging residents.

Several elderly nuns were placed in nursing homes while younger sisters went on to serve their church elsewhere. Shortly before the closing of the De Sales, the bodies of seventy-nine nuns were exhumed from their crypts and reburied in Catholic cemeteries. Religious relics and some personal objects were sold at auction.

Many of the cloistered nuns who lived and died at DeSales ended up in those crypts. That means they made an oath to never leave. Some of the nuns, over a span of sixty, seventy and even eighty years, never set foot outside the property until their bodies were moved. By most accounts, spirits do not like this. This would be especially true if the spirits had given their solemn oath to never leave the nunnery—and this is precisely what happened when DeSales Heights finally closed down.

There have been several reports and perhaps reasons behind the haunting. One story is that years ago one of the nuns fell down the elevator shaft, but because of her vow of silence after dinner, she did not call out for help during the night. By the time the woman was discovered it was too late. Her injuries proved fatal. Many believed had she cried out earlier, she could have been saved.

There is another alleged account of a young man who stole a gold cross from the convent and then died suddenly before he had a chance to return it. They say the man's ghost is one that haunts the place.

When filming a documentary about the convent and school several years back, two cameramen happened upon a cellar beneath the basement. As they filmed, a cold wind whipped around their legs chilling them to their very bones. Since the room was sealed off at the time, this was impossible. Suddenly the tiny, isolated room became as icy cold as the deepest bottom of the ocean. A mumbling of voices started—barely beyond detection—but definitely creepy. The camera crew ended up fleeing.

Two women visiting DeSales Heights discovered the same area beneath the floors. As they took pictures, they caught a few dingy ghost orbs. The last picture showed a heart-shaped face, almost like a nun's face under her habit. But the face with vacant eyes and leering grin looked more like that of a skull.

While working on a school project, a mother, daughter and a few of their friends snuck inside DeSales Heights in 2002 at night in order to videotape the inside of the building. Within the enclosing shadows, one of the girls grew afraid. To break the tension, the mother cracked a joke to ease the girl's fears. Once they returned safely home and viewed the videotape, they detected a woman's voice over that of the mother's. The rasping female voice hissed the command, "Get out!"

The convent once created an ominous presence, with a wind-weathered cross on the highest peak. Lonely hallways were carpeted with broken glass. Stained glass windows were removed and the windows nailed over with inexpensive boards. The altar remained after the school was closed, but odd things happened whenever a picture was taken there.

Unwanted visitors caught hundreds of ghost orbs in and outside DeSales Heights. One picture showed a dark red funnel shape coming out of the top of the building.

On July 15, 2002, DeSales Heights was torn down after vandals set a fire in the rectory of the building. A candlelight vigil was held a few days later. Not surprisingly, photographs snapped revealed a number of orbs in motion.

Dark rumors still abound. But we will leave them where they belong, left in a dark place unable to be examined. Just like the souls once inside that waited and prayed for peace.

DeSales Heights' creepy reputation made it to Hollywood when the 2001-2002 TV show *Scariest Places on Earth* asked to tape a segment before it was torn down. The request was denied and the old convent was leveled a few months later. The DeSales connection did lead to some of the Haunted Parkersburg Guides appearing on the ABC TV Family Channel show on Halloween Night 2005 at the Shawnee Amusement Park in Bluefield, West Virginia.

Houdini Plays Parkersburg

Many find it surprising that master magician Harry Houdini played Parkersburg in January of 1920 at the Old Camden Theater. Those who know about Houdini's life are aware of the fact that, after his mother's death, this sleight-of-hand escape artist became increasingly interested in proving (or mostly disproving) the existence of an afterlife. Most of Houdini's investigations into psychic mediums proved to be disappointing though, as he (often in a disguise) exposed frauds.

As he was to his mother, Houdini was extremely devoted to his wife Beatrice. He made a pact with his wife that should he precede her in death, he would come back to her in a séance with a special coded message that would prove the existence of life beyond the grave. But if an afterlife did not exist, no medium would be able to break the code.*

Harry Houdini, in fact, did die before his wife on Halloween night, October 31, 1926 of peritonitis, two years before the Camden Theater in Parkersburg burned to the ground.

Although many faithful believed famed medium Arthur Ford broke Houdini's code (which was "Rosabelle" inscribed on Bess's wedding band and the title of the couple's favorite song) others claimed Ford had previous knowledge. Even unto the current day, séances (the official one is in Scranton, Pennsylvania) are held each Halloween night hoping to entice the ghost of Harry Houdini. So far, he has not reappeared, unless of course, he has something to do with the ghost, sometimes referred to as "the Warlock," that haunts many of the businesses of the block that once held the old Camden Theater.

During the fall 2002 Haunted Parkersburg Ghost Tour, the guides paused at the location of the Camden Theater to briefly tell of Houdini's visit to Parkersburg. That night I mentioned that although Houdini was

---

* The coded message was, *'Rosabelle-answer-tell-pray, answer-look-tell-answer, answer-tell.'* Bess's wedding band bore the inscription 'Rosabelle,' the name of the song she sang in her act. The other words correspond to a secret code used to pass information between a magician and his assistant during a mentalism act. Each word or word pair equals a letter. The word 'answer' stood for the letter 'B,' for example. 'Answer, answer' stood for the letter 'V.' Thus, the Houdinis' secret phrase spelled out the word 'believe'."

intrigued by the possibility of an afterlife, he was never able to prove it and as far as we know, has not returned to his earthly realm.

The minute I said that, an empty car on the street began to blare as its burglar alarm suddenly went off. No one came out to check the car and no one stood near it.

Despite the noisy distraction, I continued with my story, concluding, perhaps, that medium Arthur Ford did break Houdini's code, translating this sentimental message "Rosabelle, Believe" from the grave. I then acknowledged to the crowd, "Maybe there was an afterlife for Houdini, after all." At that exact moment the car alarm abruptly stopped and we confused ghost walkers continued our journey down Market Street, wondering about Houdini.

The Warlock of Market Street

Here is a related story contributed by Parkersburg native Kevin Morehead:

My name is Kevin Morehead and I worked at Power Country 99 and WADC AM 1050 from 1995-98. I was told by a friend of mine you were inquiring about the 'ghost of Power Country 99' in the old theatre at 703 Market Street here in Parkersburg. I was Music Director and Assistant Engineer and Program Manager with a radio show on WHCM, 'The Top Ten at Ten,' a request call-in show for the listeners.

It started back when I was hired in 1995. I was learning the ropes so to speak with the late Mark Eveland, who at the time was our Music Director and Program Director/Manager.

Less than a week of working at the radio station I was on the air running Pittsburgh Pirate Baseball on WADC, when the manager came over to my studio and told me about smelling hot, buttered popcorn. I thought I was working with a real cuckoo until about fifteen minutes later, I too smelled popcorn! The manager mentioned the station being haunted and said a person had hung himself in the projector room on the top floor. I never confirmed whether that was true, but working there at nights I sure saw and heard my share of 'What was THAT?'

There would be many nights I worked as the 'Six p.m. to Midnight Jock' where I witnessed and heard many strange occurrences that I am still chilled by and unable to explain. For instance, our production room was right across from our break room, and loading the computer up at night I would always see something that would catch the corner of my eye but nothing would be there when I looked straight on! My youngest brother worked with me until our boss sold out to Results Radio in '98.

I would say the most terrifying time for me was when myself, one of our sales guys, and our afternoon girl and my brother were present. The afternoon girl thought it would be fun to hold a little ritual with candles and other things she brought in because she always believed the place was haunted. She put lit candles in our old WADC studio where it was always cold and could never get it heated up enough to work, even in a six hour shift. The girl said this is the room where the spirits were concentrated.

Not believing a word of this I went along with what she was doing, of course, thinking the whole time she was trying to scare us, since everyone considered the place possessed. All of our studios had sliding glass doors on them so we could be on the air in private and not pick up background noise from the programming room. She put the candles on the counter by the door and closed the studio door. Immediately the candles flickered and leapt around as she said something about how I could find out more about this in the movie called The Warlock. I laughed, not really believing what I was seeing or hearing as I darted back and forth from my studio, for I was on the air that night on Power Country.

After about 20 minutes of this I, being the man thinking there is an explanation for everything, made the comment that it was the air conditioner in the studio blowing on the candles that made them dance like that. I investigated further to find the air conditioner was not running and even checked myself to see if the unit was on. It was not.

The girl went on for about two more minutes and I had about enough of this or so I thought. I went over to her and told her: 'I don't believe in this junk, so please stop this or get out!'

Well, after I got that out, and it was right after, let me tell, you the door that held our satellite switcher bounced wide open with a bang! The door was above my head and I had to reach up to open it. Strong magnets held it in place and sometimes you had to really pull on the darn thing. Besides that, there was no one near it. Nevertheless, this made me an instant believer.

But wait, this is not the end of my story! It seemed like the spirit harassed me the rest of the evening with the ceiling tiles falling down in my studio. My cart rack that held all the commercials, or spots as we say in radio, twisted and toppled to the floor. The cart weighed over 200 pounds and no one touched it.

The radio station had two basements, one a little scarier than the other. A couple of us Jocks would go down to the one closest to Market Street— it was dark but very spacious.

The other basement near the back of the building was the weirdest. My brother *and I explored it and it has a large room sealed off from the alley behind the building. Most of the theater is still intact. If you pry a ceiling tile up in the hallway, you can see the entire theater, where the old screen is, (it's still up!) and the projector room holes where the projector lens would be. There are many more things to tell about working there. Let me just end by saying, to this die-hard skeptic, it was just downright eerie."*

EIGHT
Riverview Cemetery: The Lady Walks at Midnight

This is the light of the mind, cold and planetary.
The trees of the mind are black. The light is blue.
The grasses unload their grief on my feet as if I am a god,
Prickling my ankles and murmuring their humility.
Fumy, spiritous mists inhabit this place.

— From ***The Moon and the Yew Tree*** By Sylvia Plath

Some times at dusk as the veil between worlds begin to part, when diminishing sunlight casts shadows long and deep, the faces of those buried in Riverview Cemetery in Parkersburg come alive in the dark and light that mingle on tombstones.

To people uninitiated in the world of spirits, Riverview invites dreams. Mossy grounds become a carpet of green. Pine needles scatter the paved walkway. Hemlock trees embrace each one that passes through its gates.

The array of ancient graves include Irish crosses, headstones with cryptic Masonic symbols, marble angels, one lonely grave of a young Chinese woman, the plot of a well-loved slave marked "occupied" and three impressive statues. The historical figures entombed at Riverview Cemetery include two West Virginia governors, the French wife of artist Joseph H. Diss Debar, two West Virginia senators, a New England sea captain and the famed Jackson family, for which there are numerous graves in Riverview.

Even to those who do not know the history, Riverview Cemetery is a place where dreams float and fly—where statues are said to stand up and walk. It is within the graveyard that the living energies of those thought gone still remain curiously alive.

Go to Riverview Cemetery at dusk on a summer evening. Wait patiently, watch and listen. Don't be surprised to see shadows dance on stone or spectral lights flying by.

Rumors abound about the mysterious forces inside the cemetery gates. For years, there has been talk in the neighborhood of peculiar sounds coming from the graveyard. Dry sticks snap as brittle as old bones. Leaves shuffle along the paved path. Late into the evening hours there is a shifting of weight and stony pauses, the clicking of heels and mysterious footsteps—perhaps the rustling of a long silk skirt echoes over the rocks.

Might it be the Weeping Woman statue rising up? *Bloody Mary*, some children erroneously call her…

School children swear all of the statues in Riverview stand up and walk. If only in the mind's eye, who says they don't?

A look at the history and personalities of early Parkersburg might explain what is behind these mysterious happenings. The rest, as in keeping with most paranormal activity, might never be explained.

History of Riverview Cemetery

The first grave in Riverview Cemetery was that of B. W. Jackson, who died in 1801 at the age of the thirty-four. There are a number of prominent people buried in the graveyard as well, including cousins of General Thomas "Stonewall" Jackson, and notable historical figures. Sometimes called 'the Cook' Cemetery, the Cooks, the Dils, the Jacksons and the Van Winkles are just a few of the historical families buried inside.

With the exception of the Revolutionary and Gulf wars, veterans of every American war are represented at Riverview Cemetery, including the Seminole War and the War of 1812. Some of the graves have confederate flags, unusual for a northern West Virginia cemetery.

The Captain's Grave

Witnesses claim to see the vision of a man in a black coat leaning over this 150-year-old headstone that has the carving of a ship on it. The spirit is seen as often by the light of day as he is at night. Perhaps this historical grave has a tragedy surrounding it. . . enough of a tragedy to cause someone to return to the grave site time and time again, even if the black-coated visitor is a ghost. Captain George Deming was a

Grave of Captain George Deming, Riverview Cemetery, Parkersburg

master mariner from New Haven, Connecticut who moved to what was then Virginia in the 1850s. A successful businessman, Captain Deming was proud enough to mention he was a direct descendant of Miles Standish, the founder of the early Plymouth colony, on his tombstone.

George Deming traveled to the Ohio Valley to seek his fame and fortune in the new oil and gas business. After acquiring a small fortune, the Captain set out to build a quaint home on the corner of 11th and Juliana streets. The Captain's House (also called the Markey House) is easy to spot in the district since it is the only house on the street that does not have much of a yard. In the style of a New England street house, the interior of the home, with high wooden beams and narrow halls, resembles the inside of a ship.

Off of 13th and Juliana Streets near the chain length fence in Riverview Cemetery, the grave of Captain Deming is a three-minute walk from his former home. Completed in 1860 one short year before the Captain's death, the house is alleged to have a number of haunts. Orange-colored embers from the Captain's pipe are still seen glowing in the bay window that faces Juliana Street.

When looking at spirit disturbances and other hauntings, there seems to be one event that surpasses all other in tragedy—the death of a beloved child. As workers were updating the Captain's home in the mid 1990s, they noticed a child's bare footprints in the dust that had settled in the attic. After the footprints were brushed away, they came back as soon as the dust settled. Each time the child's footprints were swept up, they always returned. History shows that Parkersburg had typhoid fever epidemics in the 1860s and 1870s. Perhaps the Captain and his child were victims. They are the only two Deming burials in the graveyard.

As I was researching this book, I was told of this story of a child's ghost in the attic but didn't know what to make of it until we discovered that the Captain's young son had died shortly after he did.

Directly beside the Captain's grave is the small weathered tombstone that belongs to his child. This tells us that the black-coated specter is probably not mourning himself—it is the dead child that the Captain still mourns for.

Sink Holes and Unmarked Graves of Slaves

At one point in its history, Riverview Cemetery was said to extend all the way to where Thirteenth Street is now. It is speculated some of the graves in this section of the graveyard were unmarked burials of escaped slaves.

One legend has it that some runaway slaves that didn't make it across the Ohio River were hastily buried on the edge of Riverview. One resident of the area claims to have found a boat hook by which the slaves were fished out of the river. The jury is still out as to whether this was true or not. There is one grave of a former slave that is marked "occupied" since slaves were not allowed to have their names written on a tombstone in a white only cemetery.

Residents of surrounding houses near the graveyard have their share of strange tales to tell. Several describe impressions of sinkholes in their yards while others report erratic poltergeist activity.

One haunted house is alongside the southern edge of the cemetery. The two-story home with window boxes continues to have a number of occurrences. The dining room and kitchen maintains a shadowy or 'overcast' quality that haunted rooms tend to have.

When the couple's children were smaller, they often complained of the lumbering form of a man who stood in the doorway to their bedroom or waking up and seeing a dark shape standing at the foot of their beds. Later, the mother walked into a room and was surprised to see a white-bearded elderly man race across the floor. (The woman later commented that the ghost looked so old she was surprised at how fast he ran!)

Startled, the owner of the house came to realize this was a former resident of the home. A clairvoyant who visited the home did not entirely agree and thought she recognized the ghost of the man with a shock of white hair as a caretaker of the cemetery.

This same woman later ran across a dated picture in the *Parkersburg News* in a story that appeared about Riverview Cemetery in 1950. In an article by reporter Marie Wood, the clairvoyant recognized the man in her vision. No name was given but he was listed as a 'kindly old caretaker of Riverview Cemetery.' The psychic saw the man as the one she glimpsed earlier in the home.

JFK Visits Riverview Cemetery

During the 1960 presidential campaign, John F. Kennedy and his brother Teddy stopped in Parkersburg on their campaign, staying overnight at the Blennerhassett Hotel. (West Virginia was a major factor in deciding the outcome of the presidential election.) The Kennedy's spent part of the day at a house on Ann Street, two blocks south of the graveyard. Legend has it John Fitzgerald Kennedy actually walked through Riverview Cemetery. There are Kennedy graves in Riverview but this was not who JFK came to see during his visit to the cemetery. He came to see the grave of West Virginia Senator Peter Godwin Van Winkle (1808-1872). The reason this grave was significant to Kennedy is that Van Winkle was one of ten men who decided to vote against the impeachment of President Andrew Johnson on May 30, 1868. If it had not been for Senator Van Winkle's and others deciding vote of 'not guilty,' Andrew Johnson would have been the first American President to be brought up on impeachment charges.

However, politics was not the only arena where Peter Van Winkle made his mark. He also had associations with two famous literary figures of the 19th century. Washington Irving's story "Rip Van Winkle" was based upon an actual person and relative of the Senator. But even more strangely, Senator Van Winkle also had connections with the gothic writer Edgar Allan Poe who published the Senator's works when Poe was the editor of the *Southern Literary Messenger* while in Richmond:

[Text: Edgar Allan Poe to Edgar S. Van Winkle-Nov. 12, 1836.]

Richmond, Va. Nov. 12. 1836

Dear Sir,

At the suggestion of your brother, the Editor of the Natchez Courier, I take the liberty of addressing you, and of soliciting a contribution for the "Southern Literary

The "castle," home of Senator Peter Godwin Van Winkle, during a Haunted Parkersburg Ghost Tour. Notice the ghost orbs and apparition in the right window on 2nd floor.

Messenger" published in this city by Mr T. W. White. It would afford me the greatest pleasure if you could aid us in this way. Mr Peter G. Van Winkle of Parkersburg, Va has written for our Magazine, and your brother in Natchez promises his aid. He informs us that you have by you (most probably) a M. S. on the "Study of the Law in the U. S,"—which it would give us pleasure to insert in the Messenger, if you have devoted it to no better purpose.

> *With high Respect*
> *YrObSt.*
> *Edgar A. Poe*
> *Edgar S Van Winkle Esqr*

Senator Van Winkle rests beneath some shady trees in the graveyard. Echoing footsteps continue to be reported at the otherwise peaceful grave. His mansion, known as "the Castle," is just a block away. In the Senator's former grand and palatial home, exceptionally bright ghost orbs have been photographed in the attic and at the bottom of the stairs on the first floor. In the house, there is a long history of ghost sightings.

The Van Winkle home on Ann Street, Parkersburg. Notice the woman with blurred face looking out the window of the vacant house.

Senator Van Winkle was a powerful political figure, having been instrumental in the formation of West Virginia, as well as having an important role in naming the state. He was friends with Joseph H. Diss Debar who designed the state seal, and whose young French wife is buried close to the Van Winkle family. Van Winkle also knew Lincoln, and Diss Debar created a number of drawings placing Van Winkle and Lincoln conversing together. Many believe it was Van Winkle who pressed Lincoln, his friend, to sign West Virginia into statehood.

Shadow People Witnessed in the Graveyard

Between Captain George Deming's gravestone, the Celtic cross, Van Winkle's grave and a row of hemlock trees, many have reported seeing types of apparitions often referred to as "shadow people." Shadow people never have distinct features and only appear as dark silhouettes anywhere from two feet to twelve feet tall. The figure of a shadow man has been witnessed racing between the trees of Riverview Cemetery. No one is certain what these shadow people ghosts represent—they do not really seem to characterize actual persons buried in the graveyard, but are more like inter-dimensional beings from another realm.

One Lonely Chinese Laundress

Other than the burial sites of small children in the graveyard, perhaps the saddest grave is one belonging to a young Chinese woman who died far away from her native country, in a land to which she probably had little connection. This grave, imprinted with symbols from the Chinese alphabet, is located near the chain-link fence that parallels the alley behind the houses. Her tombstone slants in a melancholy way.

Apparently some of the young woman's relatives ran a laundry business on Ann Street and she moved to the United States to work for them. When the woman died suddenly, she was buried hastily in Riverview Cemetery. Over the years, family members moved elsewhere or returned to China.

But the Chinese have a belief that the spirit can not rest being buried far away from one's ancestral home and so, a young Chinese man came to collect the girl's remains, which he placed in a metal suitcase and carried home to their native land.

It is the only gravestone in Riverview Cemetery that does not have a body. It is also the grave that has the least spirit activity.

Odd Angel

There is only one angel in the cemetery, beautifully carved from marble. Imported from Europe, the melancholy angel holds a bouquet of limp flowers that appear to wither in her hands. The angel, with heavy-lidded eyes and pale lunar forehead, represents a time when early death was not a surprise. Instead, early death was a tragic romance, inviting ghosts.

One legend surrounding the angel says that her image cannot be captured without something unusual happening. Something always goes wrong with the film or picture afterwards. Some photographs show a puzzling mist or spectral lights at the base of the statue. Odd, serpentine shapes also show around the angel in pictures. The voices of small children are heard singing and playing in the vicinity of the angel. Perhaps this has something to do with the mild look and the peaceful energies she exudes.

One evening in Riverview in early October, one woman noticed a green light flickering behind the angel. The woman thought the light came from one of those glow-in-the-dark flashlights kids use for trick-

Angel near the Henry Logan grave in Riverview Cemetery

or-treating. Thinking, perhaps, a child was playing a trick, the woman walked down to investigate but found no one. Photographs taken later during the ghost tour that same night revealed mysterious green lights all around the cemetery.

Other Ghostly Photographs

Ghosts tend to turn up in pictures taken in graveyards, but why do ghosts return to sulk in their lonely tombs? What an afterlife! Let's face it. This makes no sense. Perhaps where the human remains are is simply where the ghosts are.

What are the real reasons ghosts are so often sighted and photographed around burials of the dead? One reason may be that graveyards, like hospitals and battlegrounds, are areas of high emotion. Such high emotions transcend space and time and can be tapped into when the conditions are just right for the haunting to occur. Often these images or "imprints" get played back.

Graveyards tend to hold on to tragic feelings, more so from the mourners than from those buried therein. Perhaps the intensity of emotions attracts sympathetic spirits who come to the rescue of the mourners. Cemeteries usually have less noise and human activity, making it an ideal spot for ghosts to haunt.

Another theory might be that spirits go back to where they once lived or are buried to gain their bearings, perhaps in hopes of finding relatives, especially if they have a message or point they want to bring across.

So, how are such ghosts photographed? There are numerous ways spirits materialize in photographs. And with the new sensitivity in cameras, ghosts are caught easier than ever before.

Spiritualism was a major religious movement in the Victorian

Age. Psychic mediums often faked photographs of ghosts to drum up customers. However, this opened the door for ghost photography and also the hopes that the existence of spirits could eventually be proven by science.

Bogus ghost pictures are easy to spot because, in general, spirits don't photograph as looking like people at all. Rarely do pictures show ghosts as they appeared in life, as fully realized apparitions. But more common spirit manifestations in photographs are ghost orbs, vortexes and mists. Ghost orbs are the most common way spirits turn up in photographs and videos. Many speculate the reason spirits come across as orbs (circular shapes) is that circles are the easiest way for energies to assume a physical shape. Let us look at the various ways ghosts can appear in pictures.

Orbs: First of all, orbs are difficult to see by the naked eye, although the author of this book has, on occasion, glimpsed them. Ghost orbs tend to dart and dance about, somewhat like a bug, often changing directions—not like a dust mote floating down. In picture, orbs appear as globes, something like the one Glinda rode in on to meet Dorothy of Oz, but less opaque.

Orbs are seldom large. They appear smaller on video cameras than they do in still pictures. True ghost orbs resemble dense balls of smoke of any color. There are red orbs, white orbs, green orbs, blue orbs and purple orbs. Most orbs are pale grayish or almost tan in color. Some orbs have interesting details, such as what looks to be a human face—at times resembling infants, at other times appearing as grinning skulls.

Of course, much controversy surrounds ghost orbs. Some claim they are weather related such as the appearance of raindrops on the lens, dust motes or snowflakes. (No ghost-hunter worth his or her salt would go out in anything but clear weather to photograph.)

In the case of extremely haunted areas, ghost orbs can be visible to the naked eye. One West Virginia couple visited a cemetery in Scotland that was 900 years old that has more than 300,000 graves. The minute the couple took a picture and the camera's flash went off, they glimpsed thousands of orbs scatter like moths. The pictures they captured show hundreds of orbs. It was humid, but it wasn't raining.

Mists: Mists are mysterious forms that we already associate with the supernatural. We see them in scary movies such as *Dracula*, a castle cloaked in mists, or the *Creature from the Black Lagoon*, lumbering through some swampy, misty fog. Ghost mists, or ecto-mists however, are different. Like orbs, ghost mists are not normally seen by the naked eye. They just turn up in pictures in areas that are allegedly haunted. Ghost mists are sometimes erroneously explained away as cigarette smoke or humidity in the atmosphere.

Ghost Mist (ectoplasm) at Borland Springs in Ritchie County.

Ghost or ecto-mist has a quality of streaking and often resembles whitish fog with appendages. While some mists look simply foggy, others have amorphous shapes that are wispy—like wafting smoke. Most mists are white, but red, green, blue, and violet mists can occur.

Vortexes: Vortexes, or vortices, resemble coils of light, waves or long tubes, or can be crescent-shaped areas. What manifests as vortexes are sometimes orbs traveling at a higher rate of speed than the camera is able to photograph. The reason many of these spirit appearances are not visible to the naked eye but are captured by cameras is that the spectrum of light in the camera is wider and more sensitive than what the human eye is capable of detecting. It is generally accepted that spirits vibrate on a much faster level than anything in the physical realm is able to do. So for ghosts to appear on film, they must slow down a great deal.

If you slow down the film speed on a 35-millimeter camera, you have a better chance of catching ghost mists, vortexes and especially apparitions.

Weeping Woman Statue

If Riverview Cemetery has a point of legend; it is the Weeping

Woman statue. This impressive statue acts as a watcher over the graves of a local family of note—the Jacksons. A number of Jackson graves in the cemetery contain cousins to General Stonewall Jackson, the famed confederate strategist from the Civil War. The statue of the Weeping Woman was made in Evanston, Illinois, but the exact date is unknown.

Susan Sheppard with the weeping woman statue in 2002. Notice the strange lights at the back of the head of the statue. Kodak analyzed this photograph and could not explain it. In a closer view, there are several orbs inside the light pattern.
COURTESY KRISTALL CHAMBERS

Many say that at midnight, when the moon is full or high in the sky, when psychic energies are the most pristine, "the Lady" will stand up from her spot and walk through the cemetery wringing her hands and crying over all of the souls lost in the Civil War.

Do we believe this much-told tale of statues walking?

To understand the history behind the statue of the Weeping Woman, one must understand some local history. The Jackson's were a prominent family with great ambition. Among them were artists, poets, judges, mayors, governors and Civil War generals. The cemetery contains the graves of Lily Irene Jackson (1848-1928) and her father

Judge John Jay Jackson (1824-1907.) Governor Jacob Beeson Jackson rests in an adjoining plot. Also near the Weeping Woman statue is Clara Diss Debar, the French wife of Joseph H. Diss Debar, who designed West Virginia's state seal. Most resting near the Weeping Woman statue were joined in eternity by their high aspirations. All with their own ideas and purposes, none were more unique than Lily Irene, a talented artist with a national reputation.

After the first couple of years of telling the Weeping Woman tale on the local ghost tour, guides were worried that crowds would be disappointed if the lady did not stand up and walk one Halloween night. After all, Halloween was the night schoolchildren said it happened. Nearing the 31st, one of the guides offered to dress up as the Weeping Woman. She planned to wear a veil and hold a candle so tour goers could spot her in front of the statue pacing back and forth, quite forlornly. This night for certain the Lady would stand up and walk.

Earlier in the afternoon, the guide placed a candle, a veil and a box of matches near the base of the statue. She was to later join the tour but would leave the tour early so she could get up to the cemetery to put on her ghost act.

The evening turned out to be unlike the others. Excitement mounted as people congregated at the cemetery. Fearing damage to the graves and tombstones, a guard was posted at the cemetery gate.

When the tour guide left the group to sneak into the cemetery and play the Weeping Woman, she was surprised to find her candle already lit, fluttering eerily and placed atop the statue. She assumed the guard at the gate had gone up and lit the candle earlier so she could find her way through the dark. Mysterious and beautiful against the darkness, the candle pulsated warmly in the late fall night.

The sound of voices at the cemetery gate reminded the tour guide the group was drawing near. She placed the veil on her head, held the candle in front of her and stood in what was now foreboding darkness. Suddenly, the noise of sticks snapping and the pressure of phantom footsteps surrounded the guide. It was the unmistakable sound of someone walking, perhaps a woman's long skirt brushing over fallen leaves. Although the air in the cemetery was cold, the woman felt closed in and hot. The eerie walking continued with its padding footsteps and rustling silk. The guide heard the tour group laugh as they came up the sidewalk. They had spotted her, she thought, and figured out her trick. The ghostly footsteps finally ceased. Peacefulness resumed.

But who was the one who ended up being tricked?

In the end it was the tour guide who was tricked. She never expected to meet anyone, certainly not a spirit near the Weeping Woman statue.

As the ghost tour concluded on the early morning hours of November 1st, the tour guide was relieved to call it quits. She thanked the guard at the gate for lighting the candle so she could see her way through the graveyard in the dark.

With surprise, the guard asked, "What candle? I didn't light a candle."

Other ghostly appearances soon occurred. There was one incident of a woman on the ghost tour who decided to snap a picture of the statue. As soon as she did, the woman said she felt a cool pressure on her stomach. When she glanced down she saw her belt was unbuckled, her pants were undone and her zipper was unzipped. Much to her embarrassment, she stood with her underwear in full view of everyone.

Several people claim they've had cameras freeze up, camcorders, and digital cameras break and batteries drain in the area of the Weeping Woman statue. Women also report having their hair tugged on when near the Lady, especially in cases when they decide to light a cigarette!

There is another very positive legend that surrounds the Weeping Woman statue. It is claimed that if you have a deeply felt wish, a desire that will also help others, you can make a wish near the Weeping Woman statue and she will grant it. If the Lady decides the wish is, in fact, deserved, she will endow that person with good luck within a year's time of making it. Many have claimed to have great success when wishing upon the Lady for her help.

But who is the person that the Weeping Woman represents?

If you follow the most intensely shining ghost orbs in the pictures from Riverview Cemetery ghost investigations, there seems to be one grave where the brightest ghost orbs show up—right over the grave of Lily Irene Jackson, an important personality from Parkersburg's gilded age.

Of the politically famous Jackson family, Lily Irene was a woman who knew her own mind. As daughter of John Jay Jackson, she lived from 1848 until 1928. Against criticism of the ladies in the community, Lily Irene, although quite a beauty, never married. Instead, she developed her

Ghost Orbs in Riverview Cemetery COURTESY HOLLIE RHINEHART

talents as an artist and chose a life with her pets over a husband.

One young couple came on the ghost tour in 2000. As the legend of the Lady granting wishes was being told by one of the tour guides, the young woman suddenly remembered her wish that was made the year before. She gasped, "Oh, now I remember what my wish last year was. I have a condition where I was not able to get pregnant. Last season, with all of my heart, I wished to deliver a healthy child. My daughter was born in August—only ten months after asking the Weeping Woman to grant my wish!"

In previous years, the guides had not talked about the Jackson graves that surrounded the Weeping Woman statue, including the gravesite of Lily Irene Jackson. We had not told Lily's story of throwing a mock wedding for herself even though she was lacking a groom, or any of her other famous Victorian age antics. We didn't know about them then.

Once Lily Irene's name was mentioned, the young woman gasped once more. "We named our daughter Liliana. We call her 'Lily' for short." Since then a number of pregnancies have been associated with the 19th century statue.

But that isn't the only uncanny or mysterious event connected to the Weeping Woman monument. Just recently, a woman was driving up 13th Street in Parkersburg past the old Nash School (now a dance school) below Riverview Cemetery and noticed a woman standing forlornly in the bend of the road. The somber-looking woman had on a floor-length dress and appeared as if she was dressed up for a costume party, even though the dress was gray and drab.

The driver thought, perhaps, there was a special event going on at the dance school across the street. But before she could pass the woman, the lone figure drifted up gracefully into the air, then glided backwards into the cemetery in close proximity to the Weeping Woman statue.

The woman wondered if this was the spirit that haunts the statue and is the one responsible for much of the hair pulling and clothes undoing!

It is also not unusual to stand in the vicinity of the Weeping Woman statue and hear your name being called. Photographs of the statue have shown the hands poised in different positions.

Black Dog in the Graveyard

Tales of black dogs appearing as harbingers of death originated in the British Isles. Such dogs as death omens are reported to be solid black, larger than average (but usually not terribly large) and have glowing, red eyes that brim with a hellish fire. Interestingly, the ancient Irish associated the black dog with their banshees, or "black fairies."

A large black dog often wanders through Riverview. The animal is said to walk among the headstones, stopping to dig and scratch for a few moments, and then disappear into the trees toward the Weeping Woman statue. At times the dog appears to be followed by three black crows that perch on the tombstones watching over as the animal digs about.

The person who reported seeing such a black dog on a number of occasions wondered how a large dog had gotten inside the graveyard. After all, the gates that surround the cemetery were locked, and the dog was too large to have squeezed underneath the chain link fence on the side.

In Greek mythology, black dogs are connected to Hecate, goddess of the Crossroads, the underworld and also witchcraft. It is said that when you hear dogs howling in your neighborhood late at night, you can be assured that the dark goddess Hecate is roaming about. Black dogs and black goats were sacrificed to honor her in ancient times. Whether the black dog in Riverview Cemetery is a real one or one in spirit form, it is most often seen wandering through the graveyard in late winter or early spring.

Evergreen Cemetery-Route 2 North

There is a more recent cemetery sighting at a graveyard located north of Parkersburg along Route 64. It is called Evergreen North. An older couple that had recently married stepped inside the cemetery at dusk so the man could visit his former wife's grave. The woman was not comfortable going into a graveyard so near dark, and expressed the feeling of apprehension to her husband. The man answered, "This is the safest place you could possibly be, since no one is alive in here. The dead can't hurt you. Besides," the husband continued, "Look over there. I see another couple sitting together on a bench."

The wife turned and sure enough, a couple sat on a bench several yards away. With heads bowed the silhouetted couple appeared to be whispering to each other. But, as the husband and wife came closer, the forms took on a shadowy quality. Black and indistinct, they had no human features. As this fact dawned on the couple, the ghostly figures stood and then floated upward into the evergreen trees and vanished entirely.

When interviewed for this book, the man said, "Look at my arms. See the chill bumps rise? I get them every time I remember seeing that ghost couple. I never believed in such things as spirits and haints. But I do now."

NINE
Haunted City: Strange Goings On
at the Blennerhassett Hotel

There is no clear explanation as to why one building is haunted while another one is not. Spirit activity happens in cycles — a house or room is haunted for a while and oftentimes the activity ceases. Ghost sightings sometimes have little to do with the age of the building in which they occur, or even in what shape it is. On the other hand, many old historical buildings are still notoriously haunted – simply because there are more stories and events that are associated with them.

When a place becomes known for its ghostly manifestations, it has generally experienced paranormal activity over a number of years. They tend to be a mixed bag of various anomalies, usually one major haunting with several minor ones, such as poltergeists, which are unleashed psychic energies. The haunting might start out with poltergeists that evolve into spirit recordings, appearances of apparitions, earthbound ghosts, mysterious sounds, smells, and inanimate objects being moved, misplaced or thrown as if by unseen hands.

Although the reason is not known, renovations, or efforts to bring buildings back to their original state, appear to stimulate ghostly activities. Perhaps a sense of "earlier days" attracts spirits who once lived there. Perhaps the renovations simply set up the perfect energy and opportunity for residual hauntings to occur.

Of course, the Blennerhassett Hotel at 4th and Market Streets in Parkersburg is no exception. This historic downtown hotel first opened its doors in 1889 at the height of West Virginia's oil and gas boom. With its fifty-plus rooms and expansive mirrors in the lobby, the sophisticated air of the Blennerhassett set the tone for West Virginia's Victorian Age.

This could not have been achieved without one individual with a singular vision—a man who wanted to make Parkersburg a better place. The man was William N. Chancellor. After the Civil War, Chancellor built not only ornate hotels, but also elegant homes in the Parkersburg area. A native of nearby Ritchie County, William Chancellor made most of his money during the oil boom and served as the mayor of Parkersburg twice. But of all of the places that Mr. Chancellor invested his money, time and energy, only two still stand—the current Blennerhassett Hotel and his former home on Juliana Street. Both places are believed haunted by unquiet spirits. Apparitions sometimes manifest as fiery gold lights in the widow's walk of Chancellor's 1878 Federal style home. We do not know if Mr. Chancellor's apparition appears at his former home, which is also called the Burwell House. There are reports of ghostly footsteps and sightings of an apparition of an older woman at the front door. Ghosts with unsettled business, such as Mr. Chancellor, often haunt the very places where they invested the most energy in life.

It appears that the Blennerhassett Hotel is the more haunted of the two places. One of the spirits who haunts the Blennerhassett Hotel is so persistent, so determined to communicate with the living, he appears to believers and non-believers alike, often in the same gray suit, with a melancholy expression that implies his work is not yet over.

The Smoking Gentleman

A splendid oil painting dating from the late 1890s hangs in the library of the Blennerhassett Hotel. With muted tones and a precision of line, the painting portrays an older gentleman in various shades of blue and gray. If one looks closely at the portrait, it's as if a wreath of smoke surrounds the distinguished looking man. This may seem to be a trick of the lighting and the eyes, if one had not heard about the strange events that have been reported throughout the Blennerhassett Hotel after reopening its doors as a hotel in 1986. One could even say, the portrait seems have taken on a life of its own.

Unusual balls of lights or orbs have been captured in photographs of the portrait, ones that look similar to the burning end of a cigar and perhaps even a pipe.

The spicy aroma of cigar smoke is common throughout the hotel,

Oil painting from the late 1890s of William Chancellor, which hangs in the Blennerhassett Hotel. The smell of cigar smoke is often found in the vicinity of this painting.

even when there has not been anyone passing through the lobby smoking anything. In fact, smoking is prohibited in the lobby. It's not unusual for cigar smoke to turn up just outside the front doors of the hotel as well.

The very first night of the Haunted Parkersburg Tours was rained out, so the ghost tour guides decided to tell ghost tales in the corridor of the hotel near the white Steinway piano. Only a few people showed up that night—but so did the cigar smoke.

That, for us, was the first time we encountered the ghostly smoke. Since then, not a season goes by that we don't encounter the cigar smoke: sometimes outside the doors of the hotel, or in front of Mr. Chancellor's Juliana Street home, and even inside the cemetery.

Late in the 2003 Haunted Parkersburg season, another tour was called off because of rain. We didn't want to dampen the spirits of the fifty people who had shown up so once again, we told our tales of ghosts in the library of the hotel.

When we talked of Mr. Chancellor, and how his ghost turns up with the smell of his cigar smoke, we noticed the audience fidgeting and laughing. Puzzled, we asked the people why they were so excited. A few tittered and pointed toward Mr. Chancellor's oil portrait. Sure enough, a spicy aroma had permeated the room and wreathed the picture frame. This peculiar manifestation was captured on videotape by one of our guests. Most recently at the hotel, guests have complained of cigar smoke in the non-smoking facility to the point where towels have had to pushed up against the transom of the guest room doors!

So, why is there cigar smoke? Or it is pipe smoke? Could it be that

Mr. Chancellor was once fond of expensive cigars? Or might it have been another hotel manager? Read on and learn the evidence so you can decide for yourself.

The Case of the Mysterious Trunk

One local woman who came on the ghost tour told the story of happening upon quite a treasure at a local yard sale. It was a trunk, nearly one-hundred-years old with nicks, buckles, and gritty character. The woman purchased the mysterious trunk for a modest price and took it home. On the trunk there were stickers seemingly collected during travels from various parts of the world. Whoever owned it was probably wealthy and well traveled.

When the woman opened the trunk, she found a label that said the trunk had belonged to a William N. Chancellor. But she quickly resold it. Why? The woman claimed the trunk reeked of cigar smoke.

Is it possible for a ghost to show up as a smell? Yes, in fact, the first stage of most hauntings is phantom smells.

A universal element of many hauntings is the appearance of smells and aromas. These could be referred to as "apparitional smells." Not caused by anything natural in the atmosphere at the time, the scent can be anything, but usually it is some smell that the person or ghost was associated with in life, such as a brand of perfume or cologne, coffee brewing, flowers, pipes or cigars. One explanation may be that of the five or six senses we have as human beings; the one most linked with memory or the past is our sense of smell. Scientists agree that odors stimulate memories in the human brain more than any other sense. Perhaps the smell is evidence, or at least a clue, that the spirit is sending to help us remember that past or, most importantly, his or her past.

The Smoking Gentleman spirit appears as he did in life, looking solid and dressed impeccably in a three-piece gray suit. The phantom of the Smoking Gentleman materializes in the hotel halls, lobby and elevator as well as in private rooms. Those who report the apparition claim that the man appears as absolutely real, but is wearing old-fashioned clothes. Some hotel guests, who have been awakened at night, report witnessing this older man standing at the foot of their beds. Many eyewitnesses claimed the man stares at them in a melancholy way for a few seconds, then disappears.

Generally, the story about the gray-suited man seldom varies, except for one unusual report that happened in broad daylight in a room on the 2nd floor. After showering one morning, a guest stepped from the bathroom back into the bedroom. The witness, who had never heard of a ghost in the Blennerhassett Hotel, said that a man who appeared to be "up in years," stood by his bed staring at him. Taken aback, the hotel guest didn't give the older gentleman a chance to speak. (Old men can be ax murderers, too can't they?) It was at this time the completely nude hotel guest fled into the hallway, leaving his towel behind. Once the frightened man recognized his lack of attire might offend other hotel guests, he sheepishly returned to his hotel room.

Hotel Builder Mr. William N. Chancellor

So, who is the smoking gentleman that haunts the Blennerhassett Hotel?

Those who have had a chance encounter with the gray clad gentleman emphatically say that the ghost is the same man pictured in the portrait that hangs in the library. Hotel workers and others who met the reserved ghost agree.

Always, with the appearance of the smoking gentleman, witnesses smell cigar or pipe smoke. The spicy odor at times wafts out onto the sidewalks surrounding the hotel.

As far as the apparition of Mr. Chancellor is concerned, he seems to hang out in the 2nd floor hallways most frequently, to check his favorite rooms no doubt. The ghost also enjoys appearing in the elevator to fool with the buttons. It often stops on the wrong floor or not at all. Often the elevator will stop on the 2nd floor whether the button is pushed for that floor or not.

In the past, the smoking gentleman has appeared at late hours in the former area of the front desk. It is almost as if Mr. William N. Chancellor is saying, "See me? I am still here. This is my hotel. I'm the one who made this place."

The smoking gentleman whom we believe to be Mr. Chancellor materialized on October 28th, 2001 around 7:15 p.m to one of the Haunted Parkersburg tour guides. As crowds were arriving to take the ghost tour, one of the guides noticed a tall man in gray slacks walking briskly into the library. Since guests usually gather by the door and storytelling begins in the library, the guide followed the man into the

The home of Mr. William N. Chancellor. His ghost haunts the Blennerhassett Hotel.

library to let him know guests were gathering in the lobby. She entered into a room with the unmistakable aroma of pipe or cigar, but found no living soul inside. The guide gestured for another guide to follow her into the library. She asked, "Did you see a tall man walk into the library?" The male guide shook his head "no." At that very moment, the antique typewriter on a nearby desk typed all on its own. The guides remembered specifically the keys that were struck were "J" and "K."

It was only later they noticed a black & white photograph of JFK meeting and shaking hands with local television reporter Glenn Wilson when he visited Parkersburg during his bid for the presidency. Kennedy and Wilson's picture was placed to the left of the old typewriter. John F. Kennedy also stayed overnight at the Blennerhassett Hotel during his 1960 presidential campaign. None of us who worked on the ghost tour knew this at the time.

I Was Here First!

In the summer of 2003, the Blennerhassett Hotel underwent even more extensive renovations. A man from another area stayed in one of the newer, refurbished rooms. Looking forward to a restful sleep that night, he switched off the table lamp. As soon as the guest turned off the light, he felt a weight at the foot of the bed as if someone had just sat down. With a start, the man opened his eyes and as they adjusted to the darkness, he saw an older man, sitting at the foot of the bed in his hotel room. The gentleman then turned to the ghostly guest who bitterly said to him, "I was here first!" Upon that, the apparition disappeared.

But Mr. Chancellor isn't the only spirit that shows up along with the scent of cigar smoke. As it is with most haunted buildings, spirits tend to multiply. Some theorize the hotel has become a portal for more than a few "out of town guests." You know how it is when you throw a really popular party? A few personalities may show up to crash the party that you don't even know. Many times, this is when the fun begins.

The Four O'Clock Knocker

It is important to keep in mind that ghostly appearances tend to occur in cycles. Spectral happenings will kick in for a while and then it will change into something else. That is why you really can't go somewhere and wait for a ghost to appear.

A home, place or person will experience a great deal of ghostly activity and then the haunts will quiet down for weeks, months or even years. In other words, it is hard to predict when a ghost will appear, or even what form or shape that the ghost will assume. The Blennerhassett Hotel has many such ghosts that may not be a ghost so much as kinetic energy.

There is a doorway at the side of the former front desk, now a coffee bar that leads into the office of the hotel. At certain times, especially when a new employee is working the late shift, there will be three sharp knocks at the door. When the doorway is opened, the hallway is empty. That is, except for a powerful cloud of reeking smoke. This particular ghost has come to be known as The Four O'Clock Knocker.

Recently, there has been a somewhat different appearance of the Four O'Clock Knocker. On Christmas Eve of 2000, an employee who worked at the front desk was watching a movie in the side office. Beneath the floor she heard a knocking that startled her. This happened numerous times. It eventually grew into a pounding. A young man who worked with the woman went into the basement to check out what was beneath the floor of the office. Down there he found an old cathedral ceiling that could be described as spooky, but really, nothing else was amiss. The front desk employee could not remember the exact time the rapping occurred, but she guessed it had happened in the early hours of the morning. . . perhaps, just perhaps, at exactly 4:00 a.m.

Man in the Mirror

On the first floor of the hotel behind the bar in the restaurant (now called Spats), there are some regal antique mirrors.

However, they were not originally mirrors. The mirrors were actually framed door casings from a Victorian era apartment building in New York City that had been torn down. Upon reaching West Virginia, large mirrors were added. The effect of the framed mirrors behind the bar was quite dramatic. Within the recessive shadows of the room, the overhead lights sparkled mysteriously.

Late at night, as the bar was closing up, a compelling vision appeared in the mirror to those sitting at the bar. Guests reported that when they looked up, they glimpsed an elegant man in a white tuxedo and clutching a black cane, floating through the glass.

But the man in the white tuxedo was not the only ghost who chose to haunt the mirror. During the day, a sea captain in a hat and dark coat was seen standing in the corner of the mirror, the side facing Market Street. Under the lights of the bar the brass buttons on the Captain's coat were said to shine brilliantly.

Such murky figments and phantasms appear in mirrors throughout the hotel. However, it is not known whether the apparitions belong to the Blennerhassett Hotel or to the apartment building that was torn down in New York. But with the appearance of both spirits, there appeared a spicy smoke that continues to linger.

The Hotel Library

With its old-fashioned woodwork, oil paintings of hunting scenes, sumptuous tables and chairs, and high windows, the library evokes a sense of Parkersburg's gilded past. Just the kind of haunted place ghosts love to hang around in.

An oil painting of a gentleman hangs in the library, donated to the hotel by the builders' great-granddaughter. The walls of the room are filled with antique books. There is also a window on the rounded corner of the room that was once a doorway to the First National Bank. The sound of hotel guests checking in at the front desk fills the library, as piped-in music drifts softly through the room.

The front of the hotel has always been a busy traffic area. With its high windows, the library is filled with natural light, so that despite the noise there is a sense of serenity to the room. Still, there is a feeling of suspense that hints at other forces lurking.

For one thing, the antique books don't want to stay on their shelves. A few of the books have a habit of flinging themselves across the room. When someone goes in to investigate, he usually finds one of the antique books thrown in a corner.

There is one particularly, beat-up book that travels around the most. Workers at the Blennerhassett Hotel have taken to putting a potted plant in front of it, and still, on occasion, the red leather bound antique book flies from its shelf.

What is so fascinating about this almost 100-year-old text is that it includes pages with suggestions for after dinner speeches and lectures. When picking up the book for the first time to examine it, the pages fell open to page 159, to a speech called "The Sorcerer's Response." This speech is on the subject about how men, given the chance and talent, can also be witches. That is a pretty funny spirit, right? Well, many ghosts love to play jokes.

Bo Kitchens, a paranormal researcher who visited the area suggested that Mr. Chancellor might well have been a Mason. A mysterious group with mystical rites, the Masons may have been indicated by the poltergeists in the library by pointing out this peculiar dinner speech. Turns out, Kitchens was right on the money. William Chancellor had been, in fact, a devoted Mason. In 1914, the Masonic Temple was built directly behind his Juliana Street home on Market Street.

There are other unexplained peculiarities in the library. Unexplained gold lights circle Mr. Chancellor's portrait. These lights often appear as gold balls and have been captured on film. What looks to be the burning end of a cigar illuminates as a tiny red light in photographs snapped of the portrait.

Wailing Woman

Earlier in the book, we gave you tales about a type of a spirit, a death fairy actually, called the Banshee by ancient Celtic peoples. This spirit appears in the form of a keening woman who wails upon the moment of a person's death, especially one who is of Irish or Scottish blood. The Blennerhassett Hotel has a similar apparition of a female spirit that wails but unlike the Banshee, this ghost is entirely harmless.

At certain times when the staff at the Blennerhassett Hotel sets up the microphone for an important event in the ballroom, the piercing sound of a female scream sometimes amplifies through the speakers. This same woman's voice has also been heard over the intercom system throughout the hotel. The staff reports that the scream at times sounds like a woman's surprised shrieks; while at other times it is a woman's high-pitched laughter they hear.

Several years ago, a couple from Youngstown, Ohio stayed at the hotel while they searched for a home in the area. In the middle of the night, the wife was startled awake by what sounded like cats fighting inside her room. It took a few moments for the woman to remember she was sleeping on the second floor of a hotel.

With her husband sleeping beside her, the woman listened intently. She realized the noises sounded more like a woman wailing inside her room. After a moment, the voices ceased. Her husband did not wake up through the entire ruckus.

During the local ghost tour, several of the walkers reported that as the group left the building, a woman's cackle was heard at the back of the crowd. Several people were unnerved by this, and rushed to the front of the group. It is not at all unusual for people joining the ghost tour to hear giggling, screams or words spoken by a feminine voice whispered into their ears, inside the hotel as well as outside on the street. So what might be the reason behind the sound of women wailing throughout the hotel? Or maybe it is just one? We were asked this question by two paranormal investigators from the Washington, D.C. area, but were perplexed.

For the first few years of the ghost tour, we simply did not know what was behind these apparitions of wailing women. In fact, we couldn't even imagine. To our knowledge, nothing traumatic had happened to a woman during the entire history of the hotel.

We were wrong. A local woman on the tour pointed to the library window that was once a doorway when the hotel was a bank. The woman said, "Do you see that window? It used to be a doorway when this building was the First National Bank of Parkersburg."

We nodded in agreement, that, yes, we had heard that.

The woman then said, "No, you don't understand. My aunt was killed in that doorway. She was coming inside to make a bank deposit when a tractor-trailer missed a turn and jumped up on the sidewalk. Her body was slammed into the wall and she was crushed."

Might this explain at least one screaming ghost?

Even so, the woman's ghostly voice is not always a tragic one. Years ago, while some of the staff was setting up the ballroom for a social event, they were all startled by a woman's voice coming across the microphone as "Howdy Boys!" The female ghost will even rearrange silverware when the hotel is setting up for their many special events. Obviously, like Mr. Chancellor, she does not want the staff to forget that she is still there.

One Maid A Mopping

Of course, many spirits are less disturbing. These types of ghosts are as harmless as watching an *I Love Lucy* episode. TV viewers can still see Lucy but Lucy can't see us. (At least we don't think she can, but you never know.) This type of spirit, as mentioned earlier, is called a "spirit recording," and is also known as a "residual haunting." There is a pretty good argument that most ghosts are merely "recordings," no more capable of communicating with the living than you having a conversation with your television set. You can try if you want to, but chances are the people on the air won't hear or see you.

In most instances, a spirit recording performs the same task repeatedly, without changing the activity. Recordings go through the motions over and over again.

The Blennerhassett Hotel has several ghosts that are residual hauntings. One such spirit recording that has been frequently sighted is an old-fashioned maid dressed neatly in a black and white uniform. This maid continues to mop in front of the check-in desk. She never changes her clothes or her methods.

It is interesting to point out that one of the places the maid has been spotted most frequently is nearby the Four O'Clock Knocker's door.

Why in front Four O'Clock Knocker door? No special reason, other than it looks like a door that is just dying to be knocked on—especially in the early hours of the morning.

Kissing Bandit

Women staying at the hotel have reported the pleasant experience of being awakened in the morning by soft, affectionate kisses. As soon as the women open their eyes and are fully awake, the kissing bandit has completely disappeared. Most report the kisses are not frightening, but gentle and lovely. No one knows if the bandit is a male or female spirit, but we are willing to bet it is a guy ghost.

The Elevators

Elevators can be creepy even when they're not haunted. Most kids can tell you this. However, when you toss a couple of spirits in the mix, well, a ride on an elevator can sometimes be a bit hair-raising, especially when you're visiting the Blennerhassett Hotel. The elevators at the hotel appear to be under the influence of the same supernatural forces as the rest of the building. The doors open repeatedly when the lobby is the most quiet and peaceful, usually past midnight. It's as if when the spirits step in, the door closes and takes the ghosts for a ride. The elevator doors tend to stop at the 2nd floor of the hotel and pause, where the ghost activity appears to be the most intense.

All of this could be taken as sheer coincidence except for the "stories" that surround the elevators. It's no surprise that apparitions are often glimpsed stepping in and out of the elevators. One of the more interesting ghost sightings took place when a member of the staff was about to carry some laundry a few floors up.

The worker spotted an expensively dressed woman hurrying toward the elevator. With arms full of linens, he yelled for the woman to hold the door for him, which apparently she did, since the door was left open. It was odd that when he got to the elevator he found no one else inside, there was only the lingering scent of a woman's floral perfume.

Little Boy Lost

Once a building falls under the bewildering forces of a haunting, other spirits will invariably show up. It seems once the phenomenon starts, others will be attracted to the place that has become a doorway for various spirit entities to come through. It is my belief the conditions have to be right for this to happen. Individuals with certain receptivity must be in a place for ghosts to appear. This does not mean the witness must believe in ghosts. It just means that in that moment of time they need to be receptive to the spirit.

One of the more recent and interesting ghostly visitations at the Blennerhassett Hotel happened in the kitchen when the chef was preparing the meals for an important event. As the chef turned to grab a pan, he glimpsed a small boy staring at him. The boy was approximately eight or nine and dressed in the clothing of a newspaper boy of the 1920s or 30s. Startled, the chef stumbled back. When the man regained his bearings to look in the corner where the boy previously stood, it was empty.

The chef mentioned that he was surprised how real the boy appeared. The chef had children around the same age. The same little boy has been spotted in the basement close to the employees break area. There used to be a newspaper stand in the back of the hotel around the time of the 1930s.

A Little Night Music

Like many modern hotels, the Blennerhassett Hotel has pleasant, piped-in music throughout the building. Of course, this is not at all unusual for a contemporary hotel. That is, unless you consider the fact that here, the voices of small children have been heard singing above the music. During the Christmas season one female security guard working late at night reported hearing children singing *Jingle Bells* overtop the piped-in muzak. The guard thought this was just an interesting new feature.

When she mentioned hearing children's voices to a maintenance man, he replied, "You heard it, too, huh? They've been doing that for quite a while. It really messes up the lighting in the hotel whenever the kid's voices come on. I usually have to change the electrical fuses whenever those ghost voices start singing."

The security guard asked, "You mean those children's voices are ghosts?"

The maintenance man replied nonchalantly, "Of course, they're ghosts. Remember where you are. This is the Blennerhassett Hotel." Also, Big Band music is heard throughout the hotel at night, especially in the downstairs ballroom.

The Second Floor

One cannot miss feeling the strong energies on the second floor even if you are not normally sensitive to spiritual things. Many experience a high vibration when walking in the halls. Others report sensing a ghostly presence walking with them or the sensation of carpet rolling under one's feet. After all, it is the second floor where Mr. Chancellor's ghost has been spotted more than once with his pervading cigar smoke. There is also the mysterious sound of running water behind the walls of the rooms on the 2nd floor, but leaks have never been found. Psychics claim some of the hotel rooms seem to be the portals between the spiritual and material realms for these unexplained, ghostly energies.

Recently, the 3rd floor has also been a site of unusual happenings. One evening the electricity for the entire 3rd floor was completely turned off several minutes. Since it was linked to other areas in the hotel, there was no rational reason for the lights to go out. The staff still hasn't figured it out. Some have reported the sound of ice being dropped in the sinks or glass shattering. Once it is checked, there is no evidence whatsoever of the breaking noises. When checked, the sinks are dry and empty.

The Red Room

Something is going on in what used to be the Red Room. No one wants to go in there alone. Everyone at the hotel feels a little weird about this room. People give few specifics about the Red Room—no towering ghosts or ornery poltergeists. It's none of that—it is just a feeling—doors opening, closing but mostly getting stuck, the sound of glasses being rattled when nothing is amiss. The Red Room just has an otherworldly feeling. We generally don't add stories that are vague, but this short tale about the Red Room on the 2nd floor is an exception, since it points out the continuing saga of the haunting that goes on at the hotel. The Red Room (now split into two areas) is used for business meetings and other social affairs. It has a large oak table that dominates the room. The floors are carpeted and the walls are covered in red wallpaper.

One evening, a young man who worked at the hotel was cleaning up the room after a dinner. Within a few minutes, witnesses heard the young man yell. He quickly fled the room with most of the color drained from his face.

The young man wouldn't reveal to the other employees why he was afraid, but he vowed never to return to the Red Room. When other workers reminded him that he would have to work in the Red Room, as they all did, the young man turned in his notice.

More recently, a worker at the hotel was asked to unlock the Red Room in order to prepare it for a luncheon. He slipped the key into the lock but it would not budge. As he turned it, the hotel worker said the keyhole felt sluggish as if there were molasses inside. He tried over and over but the door would not unlock. Thinking he had picked up the wrong key, he called for help. Another worker who came to his aid grabbed his keys and the door unlocked instantly.

The second worker gave the first worker what used to be called "the hairy eyeball" and handed the keys back to him. With some embarrassment the employee went to work making preparations for the luncheon. After finishing, he proceeded to leave the Red Room, but realized that he was locked in! He pushed against the door with his shoulder. Nothing budged. The worker banged on the door and yelled for help.

The young man who opened the door earlier again came to his rescue. Much to the first man's horror the door easily glided open as if it had never been locked at all. Another cause for the old "hairy eyeball" again!

Recent photographs taken in the Red Room reveal strange lights that resemble lightning bugs and typical "plasmoid" orbs with comet-like tails. Is the Red Room still active with ghosts? Most who work there still say yes.

The Ballroom

In the main corridor of the hotel is the Charleston Ballroom where receptions and formal dinners take place. For most events, there is a need for a microphone. Invariably, after the microphone is turned on, it will switch itself off. If the person setting up the Ballroom is persistent in keeping the microphone on, odd voices will eke out—usually talking or laughing. Sometimes, muffled words are spoken, punctuated by giggling.

There have been other reports that after the table settings are set up for formal dinners, the worker will come back to the ballroom to discover that every piece of silverware has been put on the exact opposite side of the table.

Although the Blennerhassett Hotel has a number of dimmer

lights, the lights throughout the hotel, especially in the library and the ballroom, will brighten and dim on their own.

Earlier, one young woman who worked at the hotel was setting up the ballroom for an event. She glanced up as several heavy glasses exploded before her eyes.

Late at night, when the ballroom is closed down, music can be heard coming from within the room. Many claim it sounds like lively music from the flapper age. But these aren't the eeriest sounds heard coming out of the ballroom. Sometimes, when all is quiet, there will be the sound of scratching and pecking on glass, like a bony finger.

Fine Food & Spirits

Contrary to popular opinion, people who study ghosts are not as impressionable as you might think. Therefore, when we began to tell our ghost stories at the Blennerhassett Hotel in 1996, we were just as surprised as anyone when Mr. Chancellor's inevitable cigar smoke appeared just as everyone told us it would.

When first told this story, we doubted it, thinking people pass through frequently smoking cigars until we found out that the lobby is non-smoking. Then, we began to smell it ourselves during practice sessions for our ghost tour, late, into the dead of night when no one else was around.

There was no denying the aromatic smoke and the special place that it appeared.

The smoke would catch up with us just about everywhere. On many occasions, the scent was smelled by dozens of people. In 2000, when reporter and photographer Terry Headley of the *West Virginia State Journal* came to Parkersburg to write a feature story on the ghost tour, I showed him around the hotel. Just as the two of us stepped off of the elevator, in the vicinity of the Red Room, cigar smoke pretty much floored us.

It is important to point out, that once you get used to spirit appearances, they cease to be frightening. In fact, it is a privilege to experience such fascinating mysteries. Not everyone gets the chance.

During the ghost tour, we could not help but notice the smoke that seemed the most intense during the times we told the story of Mr. William Chancellor, the original builder of the hotel. Others think it belongs to Mr. Staley, a former hotel manager.

Nonetheless, there is a smoking ghost. We have smelled him too many times.

After leaving the hotel for our ghost walk each year—mysterious occurrences tended to follow us up the street. As we walked past empty cars in parking lots, it wasn't unusual for headlights to suddenly switch on. Sometimes burglar alarms in the cars went off.

At other points doors would open and close in empty vans. Street lamps and other lights behaved strangely while the ghost tour ventured by. Overhead lights of all kinds flickered, flashed and pulsed all the way up to Juliana Street, the residential area of the tour. By the time we get to Riverview Cemetery in the upper historical district, our flashlights were drained and dim. Spirits sometimes draw upon power sources in order to gather enough strength to appear. You can spend a small fortune on batteries while ghost hunting.

There were also stories from people who came on the tour. One man came back to tell us something quite unusual if not downright scary that happened after he left from the ghost tour. He claimed that when he walked into his house, he spied a box of old photographs strewn haphazardly across his dining room table. The pictures had been packed away in his basement. He hadn't seen them in years.

On the tour, we witnessed a bright object in the sky. When I assured the crowd that the light was most likely the planet Jupiter, the bright light proceeded to move from left to right in a way that no contemporary aircraft could. One woman snapped a picture. Then it simply disappeared.

Perhaps the most unnerving events happened after the ghost tour ended for the evening. One of the tour guides was driving home when something large and black flew through the air and hit her car on the right side with a loud thump. It was only two blocks from her house. Still frightened, the woman continued driving, wondering how she was going to explain the huge dent. Later, when she got out of the car, she saw nothing. There was no dent and no hint of the car having been hit.

One employee at the hotel glanced up as he was bringing baggage through the front door of the Blennerhassett Hotel, and saw the apparition of William N. Chancellor standing there, looking very distinguished in his three-piece-suit, holding his cigar and ready to meet each hotel guest. That ghost still turns up to those lucky enough to see him.

TEN

Haunted Hills: Civil War Ghosts, Quincy Hill, Fort Boreman Hill & Droop Mountain

We cannot dedicate—we cannot consecrate—we cannot hallow—this ground. The brave men, living and dead, who struggled here, have consecrated it, far above our poor power to add or detract. The world will little note, nor long remember what we say here, but it can never forget what they did here. It is for us the living, rather, to be dedicated here to the unfinished work which they who fought here have thus far so nobly advanced.

—**Abraham Lincoln**, From the Gettysburg Address November 19, 1863

Parkersburg is approximately 50 miles south of the Mason-Dixon Line. One can only imagine what the atmosphere was like in this small river town during the Civil War, where brother fought brother, and the loyalties of neighbors were divided. Despite the fact that Confederate General Stonewall Jackson had relatives in Parkersburg, the city remained a stronghold for the Union. And because Parkersburg is where the Ohio River and B & O Railroad converged, it became a critical area for the Union to defend and maintain.

After the battle of Manassas, Virginia in July 1861, sick and wounded soldiers were brought to Parkersburg via the B & O Railroad. The soldiers were actually being shipped to a federal hospital in Ohio, but because the train trestle crossing the Ohio River was not complete, Parkersburg was where their journey ended. There was no effective way of getting so many men across the river. Five Civil War hospitals in the city soon sprang up.

The overflow of the battles' wounded were placed in a tent city on Quincy Hill. Although many of the soldiers were wounded, they were not considered critical, so were placed on Quincy Hill to wait for room in other hospitals. Those soldiers who contracted diseases during their enlistment were also sent there. Naturally, because of the crowded conditions—between 500-1000 soldiers were placed in a space smaller than a city block—disease spread like wildfire. The city experienced an epidemic of illnesses, primarily typhoid fever, small pox and dysentery, which spread among locals as well.

Infection ran rampant, and wounds that could have easily been taken care of instead caused many of the soldiers' deaths. The moans of the sick men on Quincy Hill could be heard at all hours of the day and night. Local women doing shopping on Market Street below heard the soldier's cries of agony and pleas for help. Some soldiers, desperate to find relief, left the tent city and crawled down the hill, begging to be treated at one of the hospitals located on 7th and Avery Streets.

Of course, where there was so much death and suffering, hauntings are bound to occur. The psychic pain a person might experience before death, especially where there are unresolved issues, such as a person dying at a young age and away from the loving arms of family members, can create the right atmosphere for these psychic imprints to remain. Tragedy invites ghosts. Haunts often follow.

There has been no greater tragedy in the annals of American history than the Civil War. Nearly 970,000 individuals (including 350,000 from disease) died during the bloodiest time in this nation's history. Sites of Civil War battles have unleashed a host of ghosts. At Gettysburg, Pennsylvania, troops of ghostly soldiers are sighted at dusk fighting valiantly, only to die over and over again. Such haunts fall under the category of "spirit recording" or "residual hauntings"—the Civil War has created thousands of those.

One likely place to find a haunting is where a terrible struggle has taken place, or where individuals die under traumatic, unresolved conditions. What tragedy is greater than a young man in the bloom of life dying violently and alone in an old man's war for money and power?

Is Quincy Hill haunted or is it not? There are a few tales that creep, crawl and lurk about. . . so listen closely.

The Soldier Who Would Not Die

As with most reports of serious haunts the ghostly events that took place on Quincy Hill started innocently enough. It began with doors suddenly slamming, banging and objects being moved. Loud noises, men's voices, raps, and the sound of footsteps running up the basement stairs began one day in the mid-1970s in one old home not far from the site of Quincy Hill's tent city. The young woman who lived there did not think much of the muffled noises at first. After all, older houses always made noises, didn't they? As for the voices, she did have some neighbors, many of who stayed up until the very early morning hours. Other than being somewhat annoying, the noises seemed normal.

After all, she was a resourceful young woman in her late twenties and didn't have time to be frightened of things that went bump in the night. She was attending night school, having a full-time career during the day, and was involved with a man she was seriously considering marrying.

However, the routine at her Quincy Hill home was to quickly become a lot more intense. She started noticing cold spots and would intermittently find lit candles when she knew she had never lit them.

One night after working a long shift and taking a test at night school, a frightening event caught her attention. A favorite chair in her parlor was moved into a different spot, facing a window where one could see sections of Avery Street. The young woman kept the chair facing and beside her fireplace, so she could stay warm on chilly nights.

The moving of the chair unnerved her somewhat, but she explained it away by thinking that her boyfriend had been sitting there and forgot to put it back. The next day when she came in from work, the chair was once again at the window facing Avery Street. Without thinking, she placed it back in its proper location.

Over the next few weeks, the chair was moved so often that she got used to it. Although her boyfriend claimed innocence, she couldn't think of any other explanation. Always, she put the chair back where it belonged hoping against hope she was just being absent-minded. She didn't have time to think about why it was moving; finals were coming up and she needed to concentrate on her classes.

After she became used to her chair being moved, the unusual activity became much more pronounced. Objects turned up in unlikely places. The unexplained sounds grew louder and more disturbing.

One night, the woman was awakened by thumps. She opened her eyes to discover that every candle in her house had been gathered and placed on her bedroom dresser. The candles had been assembled from all over the house; the emergency candles in the basement, the dinner candles from the kitchen, the votive and decorative candles from the living and dining rooms. Each candle had been strategically placed on her dresser. Lit candles fluttered eerily in the darkness. The woman glanced around and sat up. No doubt about it—there was creaking sounds below. It couldn't have been her boyfriend. He didn't spend the night and she hadn't seen him all day. When she had gone to bed two hours before, her dresser had been clear of everything except a comb and a hairbrush.

Unnerved, the woman walked downstairs. The dining and living rooms had been untouched, so it wasn't a burglar. The kitchen was all right, too. As she approached the parlor, she gasped in disbelief. Sitting in the chair, that was once again facing Avery Street, was a red-haired, bearded man attired in a blue Civil War uniform.

The Union soldier stood up, extended his hand as if to greet her, then vanished. Only the smell of lit matches remained. By this time, the woman was clearly frightened. She didn't believe in ghosts, but one had just extended his hand to her and a Civil War soldier at that!

As with most 20th century residents of the valley, the young woman had no prior knowledge of Quincy Hill's tent. All she knew was that a strange man had been in her house, moved her candles to her bedroom, lit them and then disappeared in front of her eyes.

Needless to say, as her boyfriend listened to the amazing story of the night before, he wasn't sure he believed her. He thought that his girlfriend must have been dreaming, but since she had been so terrified, he agreed to stay with her for a few weeks until life went back to normal. Soon, the home was just a home again. There were no longer any sounds, no candles moved to her bedroom, and most importantly, no Union soldiers in her parlor chair.

About a week after the young woman's boyfriend moved in, she was at night class. Into the evening, he was interrupted by a loud thud in the basement. The man put his book down and listened more closely. It was as if somebody was dragging a large object up the steps, toward the door that led into the kitchen. Somewhere a door slammed.

Immediately, the boyfriend got up, walked into the kitchen and opened the basement door. He had expected to see an intruder and was prepared to defend himself accordingly. What he saw was not what he expected. Stunned, the boyfriend looked at the same Union soldier that his girlfriend had described to him earlier. But now the red-bearded soldier seemed more interested in a confrontation than a friendly greeting. The ghost looked wild as he waved a pistol at the man and pointed it directly at his face.

The boyfriend did not linger at this incredible scene. Instead, he escaped from the house and refused to return. When the young woman returned home to see her door wide open and her boyfriend's vehicle not in the driveway, she ran inside, fearing the worst. All appeared well until she started to look throughout the house. The basement door was open, and the chair was facing Avery Street. The glowing light of a candle caught her attention—one the woman recognized from her bedroom.

After hearing the account of her boyfriend's ghost encounter, she knew they had met the same spirit – one of a Civil War solider who died on Quincy Hill. Much to her relief, she never saw the ghost again. Although there have been no more reported sightings of a ghost in the house, the apparition seemed to be tied to Quincy Hill.

In uncovering some of the history of the house, it was discovered that a Union soldier had once lived there. But there was no record to see if his physical description matched that of the ghost that haunted the young couple. It is more likely that the soldier was, in fact, the ghost of one of the soldiers who died in the makeshift hospital, perhaps of small pox or typhoid fever.

Contrary to what many believe, a ghost doesn't have to have lived in a house to haunt it. It may be that the ghost of the soldier was mainly attracted to the young woman and considered her boyfriend to be a threat. It may also be that the ghost was one of the men who died miserably in the tent city and his spirit still wanders looking for an escape for his tormented soul. The haunted house remains on Quincy Hill, still mysterious and ever so gloomy.

Other Tales of Haunts from Quincy & 13th Streets

Here is an account from Kevin Morehead who once lived at Quincy and 13th Streets: "Your story about the Quincy Hill ghost in the Civil War uniform was chilling!

"I have more to tell about a house on 13th Street and Quincy

Hill that is now a historical bed and breakfast. My old girlfriend once lived there, as well as her mother and brother and uncle. Apparitions appeared there every night back in 1996! Nurses in uniforms came toward us as soon as we flipped out the light.

"If we switched the light back on, there was nothing there. When we turned the light off, the ghostly nurse would walk back down the hall. I had to get my cousin to see this. He too saw the same thing.

"I believed the house to be very haunted. As we came down from upstairs, we often detected a cold chill in the air. It felt like something would go past us or sometimes right through us. I know it sounds crazy, but I have people to confirm all this. I don't like to call them 'stories' for they happened to me just as I told you. I know six other people who must also be 'crazy' since they saw and heard the exact same thing that I did."

A number of tales of Quincy Hill's haunts involve mirrors. One young girl witnessed seeing the apparition of a decrepit old man with straggly gray hair glaring out at her from the bathroom mirror. The old man had a menacing appearance, frightening the girl so much she never looked into that bathroom mirror again. Perhaps he was a rugged old soldier who died up there after giving his life for the Union.

Ghosts of Christmas Pasts

From the lookout on Quincy Hill, one can easily view the offices and homes of downtown Parkersburg as well as Blennerhassett Island along the Ohio River. This spot was strategic for Union troops in the Ohio Valley during the Civil War since Quincy Hill gave easy access to both the Ohio River and the B & O Railroad.

Quincy Hill has a number of historic homes but very few, if any, of them date from the time of the Civil War. Most of the houses are from the Victorian Age while others are from the 1930s.

Each year at Christmastime, the Parkersburg Women's Club hosts an annual Holly Trail to raise money for their club. Owners of stately or historical residences are asked to decorate their houses in festive cheer, and the public is invited in to view the holiday transformations of several old or interesting homes. In 1998, one of the homes featured on the Holly Trail just so happened to be a grand old Victorian located on Quincy Hill.

The woman who owned the house had a number of antiques and

old toys. On her mantle among pine and holly boughs, she placed several antique toy trains and cars that had belonged to her father and brother. The display on the mantle turned out even more charming than the woman had expected, so she grabbed her camera and snapped a picture. She took other pictures of decorations around the house as well.

After the photographs were developed, she noticed something unusual. One was a picture of the mirror above the mantle. In it there appeared to be a crowd of ghostly faces in the glass! The facial features of the men in the mirror were clear. Many could even be seen with beards and moustaches. One was a woman. Some wore hats.

The woman's neighbors knew a local man who was an expert on the Civil War, so he was invited over to look at the picture. In the photo, the historian recognized the faces of characters in the area during Civil War times. Some were soldiers whose faces were linked to the tent city. Although the two-story Victorian was not in existence during the time of the Civil War, the house was located near where sick men had lain, and the Union troops kept a lookout of the Ohio River.

Another "Woman in White"

Apparitions of women in white are generally associated with unhappy hauntings. We have a number of stories about ghosts dressed in white on the Haunted Parkersburg ghost tour. Why there are so many defies explanation, but throughout the remembered history of ghosts, women in white have been associated with tragedies. Maybe after dark on a crowded hilltop like Quincy Hill, a white dress is just easier to see.

A woman in white was reported to haunt the servant's quarters of one of the older homes atop the hill. During a family illness, this guardian spirit in a white dress stayed close to the old man's sick room until he died. The family said her appearance was a blessing, because they always felt someone was watching over him with loving attention. A prominent family built the home and thus, they felt the woman in white must have been an attentive servant to the family. Late at night she is seen carrying a bucket or a basket across the grassy slopes facing Avery Street. Residents in nearby houses say they often hear the woman's ghost either whistling or singing.

Although most people might think this is where the story ends, this is not the case. It was in September of 1996 during the last full lunar eclipse of the 20th century. Two teenage girls were at the lookout on Quincy Hill, to watch the transformation of the moon. As the moon turned brassy red and disappeared into black, the girls heard something large crawl through the weeds toward Avery Street just like the wounded Civil War soldiers had done more than a century ago. When they heard the story of the Union soldier, they screamed in fright and left the ghost tour early. Many claim they still hear the soldiers crawling down Quincy Hill pleading for help from anyone who will hear or listen.

Fort Boreman Hill

After small pox and typhoid fever spread to the general population of Parkersburg during the Civil War, a pest house was built on Fort Boreman Hill that also overlooked the city and river. Fort Boreman became another critical lookout point for Union soldiers—the hill faced north and it would be easier to monitor the traffic flow on the Ohio River surging south. Many soldiers and local people died up there. Along with the deaths from small pox and typhoid fever, two area men were executed by hanging after killing another man in an argument over loyalties divided during the Civil War.

Civil War experts and historians have performed archeological digs on Fort Boreman Hill, looking for remains of the Pest House. But no one is altogether certain where the hospital was. The lookout point, on the other hand, is obvious.

Area historians excavating on Fort Boreman have actually heard the voices of men call out for their mothers and wives as if in great pain. At other times, strange metallic pinging noises are heard, almost like a blacksmith hammering away.

My seven-year-old daughter, Scarlet, claimed that when we went up on Fort Boreman to investigate the many tales of hauntings she encountered a woman in a pink dress and rouged cheeks who told her that her name was "Mary McCarty." There were brothels at the bottom of Fort Boreman. Later someone uncovered pieces of silverware with the name "Margaret Matheny" engraved on them.

During one dig, local historians Terry McVey and Brian Kesterson were working together. McVey suddenly looked up and glimpsed the apparition of a Union soldier pointing toward the ground. Later, the men went over the area with a fine-toothed comb and found important

Civil War artifacts in that exact spot. Over the years, there have been tales of a white ghost horse haunting the paths along Fort Boreman Hill.

Fort Boreman was also an important Native American access trail, and was widely used by Indians who followed the Ohio River, Little Kanawha, and the Hughes River in Ritchie County that yielded an important flint site for the natives.

Fort Boreman Hill is now a historical park with a grand view of Parkersburg and Blennerhassett Island. Whether the souls of Civil War soldiers will stop their hauntings, only time will tell.

We have learned spirits have a need to stay in touch with the living. For this reason, we speculate a place like Fort Boreman Hill will yield even more tales of Indian apparitions and Civil War ghosts.

Droop Mountains' Haunted Horses

Located in Pocahontas County, Droop Mountain turns out to be one of the more haunted Civil War battlefields in the state. On November 6, 1863 there were a total of 526 casualties at Droop Mountain. Once this battle was over, Confederate resistance in West Virginia crumbled.

One report from Droop Mountain describes a Civil War soldier sitting on a cannon smoking. He is seen most often at dusk. Pounding sounds of horse's hooves on packed ground are heard as well.

Another fascinating ghost sighting comes from Ron Nelson, a Parkersburg Police officer active in Civil War reenactments with the 17th Virginia Calvary.

One year, Nelson and his fellow re-enactors set up camp near Droop Mountain. Ron decided he needed to use a bathroom before settling in for the night. He glanced over in a clearing and thought he saw a portable toilet, so he grabbed his flashlight and started walking toward it. Before he got there, he realized he was mistaken. It was actually picnic tables turned on their sides.

As he was leaving, the funneled light of his flashlight caught a white horse in its beams. There was something eerie and mysterious about this pure white horse. "A mist floated about the horse and its eye shone just like diamonds," Ron Nelson recalls. "It looked as if it had been ridden pretty hard. It had that sweaty look."

Nelson commented to his friend who was standing nearby, "Did you see it?"

The friend answered, "The horse? Yeah, I see it." Later the friend remembered it looked to him like a white blaze on a brown horse. But when he shone his flashlight into the black of night there was a strange, misting gray substance—denser than fog or mist.

As the two men left the next day, they couldn't help noticing two chestnut horses and one white horse grazing in a field. Nelson's friend said to him, "There's your horse."

"I suppose it is," he answered. But as soon as Ron turned to give the white horse a last look, it was no longer there. Only the chestnut brown horses were grazing. The white horse that glowed like moonlight had vanished! But Ron isn't the only person to have encountered Droop Mountain's pale, ghost horse. Numerous others have seen it, too.

Riding away with his friend, Ron Nelson realized the horse he saw belonged to another time. A time in November 1863 when a terrible battle was fought and many men and horses died in the bloody mud on a dreary, autumn day, in the quiet mountains of West Virginia.

ELEVEN
Haunted Houses: The Upper Historical District of Parkersburg

When we hear the word "haunted," the next word that usually springs to mind is "house." Unlike any other space, private homes can retain the energies of anyone who may have lived in, died or passed through them. And although any spot of ground can end up haunted, houses are especially prone to spirit recordings, ghost imprints and residual energies left long after the owners have moved on.

This is especially true in cases that involve high emotion that occur within the home, such as a sudden death or emotional shock and even times where the feelings are happy ones, such as those at a party or a celebration.

To explain why some houses are haunted we also have to explain why spirits haunt them. We have some theories and scientific explanations of ghosts, but we really have no definite answer as to why ghost haunt us.

The simplest explanation may be the most accurate. Perhaps ghosts are simply an essence left behind after a person or animal has died. Or, perhaps, some part of the personality that survives death likes to check back in with the people they knew, or where they once lived. There is even some evidence that this could be part of the transition or healing process that follows death.

I believe those who died with unresolved issues are allowed to come back and relive those issues, in order to find some resolution or to somehow convey the sadness they feel over not being able to finish something that was important to them. We all think we know what a haunted house looks like . . . Old, crumbling shell of a house glued together by some distinctly Gothic architecture, a full moon, with wind blowing shrouds of clouds, a black cat hissing on the front stoop—right?

Don't be so sure. Haunted houses have no common visible characteristics. The same ancient, decrepit homes that scream the word "Ghost!" often end up not haunted at all. It's the ordinary looking houses and haunted trailer parks that can really catch ghost hunters off guard.

Ghost appearances are usually quite unexpected in a typical family environment, although there is some bearing on the fact that the older the home is, the more likely events that bring about the haunting have already happened there. The history, itself, makes the home a target for ghosts.

The location of graveyards, ancient burial sites, and a history of violence or death in the near vicinity of the home does appear to have a connection to the haunting—but these are of the more dangerous variety of dark entities and menacing ghosts. Such spots should be approached with caution.

So what are you afraid of? Sure ghosts are icy and they tend to sneak up on us when we least expect them. Other than that, experiences with ghosts hardly ever bring on anything bad, as long as you give respect, stand your ground and try not to take them home with you. In many ways, the mysteries of our world are shrinking and ghosts might be one of the last unknown frontiers of human experience.

So—should you call in a priest, a psychic or an Indian shaman?

Not just yet.

Having a ghost is sort of like having a cold—you really don't need to see a doctor. It goes away on it's own.

Likewise, a haunting typically goes away no matter what action you decide to take. But like the common cold, ghosts often do return—to fascinate, bewilder and enthrall. There's really no problem unless you get a nasty poltergeist, which is far from typical despite what Hollywood tells us.

This brings up a question. Are haunted houses plagued by ghosts who once lived in them?

Well, the answer is yes and no.

Spirits often return to homes they once lived in, or their final resting spots. However, some ghosts gravitate to areas where living residents are most receptive to them. If there is a message behind their appearance, they usually do not give up until that message is understood. This is especially true in cases where a young person has died, and the family does not know or understood how or when the child died.

Once a home or an area becomes intensely haunted, the place does become a portal or 'tear' for other spirits to pour through. The most famous places tend to be areas where lots of witnesses pass through such as hotels, taverns, a theater, castles and homes that have been made into offices.

Private homes may be just as intensely haunted. Usually the family is either scared off or the haunting is cyclical in nature and peters out, leaving the family to question their sanity.

When we watch TV shows about ghosts and haunted places we are lead to believe the hauntings are frightening and extremely rare, and not likely to happen to us. Well, this assumption is basically untrue. Hauntings are not uncommon. They occur every single day—all around us. But only on occasion are we able to experience ghosts and their activities. Many remain unaware of hauntings. Their minds are probably firmly fixed on the physical world. Most of us do not pick up on the signs until they cannot be denied.

There is a philosophy, "if it does not fit into my world or reality, it simply cannot exist." When my family home was being plagued by poltergeists when I was twelve, I sat on the couch thinking, "I know I am watching an iron fly from one room to the next and the normal laws of gravity do not permit this – but there it goes anyway!" Frankly, poltergeists are the best way of being introduced to the paranormal because poltergeists are pretty hard to ignore.

But if you view haunts with a level eye it is really not that scary. Spirits entering your home can be no more threatening than a friend walking into your house unannounced. At first there may be surprise or fear, but once we recognize who the person is, there is no threat. The same is true of ghosts.

Bickel Estates

Witnesses have repeatedly reported the apparition of a woman cloaked in solid black standing along the road outside Bickel Estates, a 368-acre estate in the Larkmead section of Marrtown. The figure is seen especially during lightning storms and downpours. As with most spirits, the woman, though pale and distraught, is said to look real but when drivers turn back to see if they can help the stranded woman, she is no longer there. The ghost of a white horse is also said to haunt this section of Wood County. Many believe a woman dressed in black garb rides the hillsides of nearby Marrtown on a white horse. Both stories appear to have connections to the Marrtown Banshee tale—a Scottish death fairy that people claim still haunts the countryside south of Parkersburg.

The following is taken from a 1920s newspaper article from an unknown author:

"OLD SOUTHSIDE HOUSE IS SAID TO BE HAUNTED"

Built at Marrtown over 70 years ago—
Ghosts said to return to look for Hidden Money!

Among the folk tales that still abound in Wood County is the one concerning a house in South Parkersburg built over a half century ago, that is supposed to be haunted.

The house is at Marrtown hill, a gray frame, two-story structure, rambling and falling into disrepair. It was built some 70 or more years ago. Queer tales were told by the owner, who worked on the same side of the river as the house. At nights, he was often followed by a woman all in black who rode a white horse. As he was employed on the river, he frequently didn't get home until late, and often she was there. He never saw her face and neither did she speak to him.

One night, he stumbled, fell, broke his neck and died. The woman on the white horse was somehow blamed for it. Shortly after that, the man's brother lost his job. He was known to have quite a bit of money saved up, which grows important to the story. He had mentioned where it was to a younger relative before he was killed.

'One day the boy went with some garden tools to the Lubeck Mill to have them ground. While there, the boy's arm got caught in a cog. It was pulled off. Most of the blood drained from his body and he died.

Before the boy died, he was said to try and talk to his family about the sum of money that was hidden. But his mother told him not to bother about it until he felt better. He didn't; instead he died."

After that it began in earnest, this ghosting. At night there were strange noises like the clanking of chains going up and down the old steps. The mother knew it was her son's ghost trying to come back to find the hidden money. Lights were also seen late at night and whenever one went to investigate, nothing was found.

Then one night very late, an old woman was dying in the house, with one neighbor there to watch the flickering of her spirit. It was the granddaughter of this neighbor who has since repeated the story many times. How she sat and waited for the promised arrival of a neighbor and a light flickering outside. She heard the gate slam and waited, but nobody ever came. Instead the light went to the back of the house and disappeared. There was nobody there when she went to look. And shortly afterwards, as the old woman was about to die, there was a great banging as though a wind tore at the shutters of the house. Yet it was a still night without wind. Then the old woman died.

After that for a long time nobody lived there. Then a family moved in but didn't stay long. For a time the house was without a resident, and one morning those who passed the haunted house saw a great trail of blood from the porch to the road, and they could find no end to it. Neither could they find what caused it. Perhaps it indicated a terrible fight had ensued, perhaps over the hidden money.

For a long time again, the house was without occupants. Now it is lived in. The current householders say they don't believe in ghosts, but elderly neighbors who saw strange things about this house, know better.

The Captain's House

Captain George Deming's House on Juliana Street, Parkersburg.

Also called the Markey House; this is another example of a perfectly ordinary looking house being haunted in an atypical way. This Juliana Street home was built in 1860 by New Englander and master mariner George Deming, who died in 1861 at the age of fifty-five. Shortly before his death, his small child also died. Legends surround this two-story home, such as people who live in it eventually are driven mad. Although there is no evidence to support this rumor, the house has other interesting occurrences that could only be considered supernatural. The house has undergone a series of renovations that have even caused workmen to question the existence of spirits.

Often in the attic there are a child's footprints left in the settled dust. Thinking a small child had wandered in, the workmen continued to sweep away the dust. If the attic is left untouched for a number of months, as the workmen return they see that the child's footprints have appeared again.

Strange burning fires are said to smolder as orange reflections in the windows. Many claim the fire is simply the reflection of the Captain's pipe. The inside of the house is graced with low ceilings and narrow hallways that resemble the inside of a ship.

The Captain is buried in Riverview cemetery, only two blocks from his home. On the Captain's grave is the carving of a ship. Beside his gravestone is the small headstone of a child with undetermined dates of birth and death brushed away by the ravages of weather and time.

There are only two Deming burial plots in Riverview Cemetery— the Captain and his small child. Several have asked why the Captain's wife isn't buried beside him. When he died, the Captain was in his fifties and had a small child. This indicates his wife was considerably younger, so probably lived on to marry and have another family. Most likely, the Captain and child fell victim to the typhoid epidemic that swept through the area in the 1860s and 1870s.

Ghostly Hands at the Gerwig House

Built by a prominent Parkersburg family, this Victorian home located on upper Juliana Street is now a stately law office with stained glass windows that resemble the rich, pastel tones of a Monet painting. The elegant structure has gone through numerous transformations as homes and various businesses. Since becoming a law office, workers have reported any number of paranormal occurrences in the Gerwig house.

These include a woman's disembodied hands floating in the area where files are kept. A little boy is seen appearing on the stairs that lead from the second floor into the attic. A distinguished gentleman has been spotted on the landing beside one of the stained glass windows that leads from the first floor to the second story. Those brave enough to work into the evening hours report having heard scratching within the walls. Ghostly sounds also come from the attic.

Pictures taken outside the Gerwig house during the ghost tour reveal classic ghost orbs. One of the most chilling sightings happened on the ghost tour before the guide filled the audience in on the story about the disembodied hands.

Shortly after the story, a woman approached the guide looking pale. She said, "Before you told that last story of the floating hands, the window with the curtain behind you? I saw a woman's hand go around the curtain and pull it back a bit as if someone was trying to spy on us. Then the hand suddenly vanished!" Business hours were well over at the time and the building was pitch-black. Sporadic psychic disturbances still take place in the Gerwig house and will continue until the ghosts get tired of its own tricks.

Camden Clark Memorial Hospital

Also called by locals "City Hospital," Camden Clark got its start as a medical facility when wounded and sick soldiers during the Civil War were taken to the Camden home. It was one of five Civil War hospitals in Parkersburg at the time.

Can hospitals be haunted? Yes, because of death, sadness and other unresolved issues, hospitals tend to attract spirits more than any other establishment—even outdoing funeral homes.

In the older wing of Camden Clark, there is an area that is called "the haunted room." A few young nurses are afraid to go in there. Often when the room is made up for a new patient, within a few minutes of making up the bed, an impression forms of a person's rear end near the bottom of the sheet.

Mineral Wells psychic Millie McNemar worked as a nurse at Camden Clark for a number of years. It was her duty to go in the haunted room and remake the beds. Mrs. McNemar said within minutes, the ghostly imprint would form on the bed—but that she was never afraid nor sensed anything bad in the room. "Just spirits," Millie laughs.

The apparition of a former worker, Miss Ella Blumhart, is sighted throughout the hospital.

Miss Blumhart not only worked at Camden Clark as a nurse, she taught in what was once a famous nursing school. When the ghost of Miss Blumhart materializes she wears the nursing uniform of the 1940s and 1950s. Former nursing students who have visited Camden Clark years later report that when they see Ella Blumhart walking the halls she looks much as she did in life, only younger than most remember her. When addressed, the vision of Miss Blumhart ignores the person speaking but continues walking until she eventually vanishes through the hospital walls.

Blennerhassett Museum

The Blennerhassett Museum houses American Indians artifacts that date back as far as 12,000 years. Yet such historical items are not the only things the Blennerhassett Museum houses—a number of friendly apparitions also like to call the museum their home.

Ghostly figures, such as a little man in straw hat, a seersucker jacket, and full theatrical make-up (many report this ghost appears to belong to the Vaudeville Age) and a rouged woman in a bright scarlet-colored dress, have been glimpsed in the mirrors on the first and second floor. Lights flicker oddly. Visitors have detected the flowery fragrance of a woman's perfume wafting throughout the hallways and near the elevator. The sound of faint drumming is heard near where the Native American artifacts are kept.

A row of photographs on the second floor of the museum showcases Parkersburg's most prominent citizens such as 19th century artist Lily Irene Jackson, Governor Jacob Beeson Jackson and Governor William Erskine Stephenson.

The second floor area of the museum hums and vibrates with a heavy brand of energy that proves too intense for some children or individuals with special sensitivities. It seems that most of the ghost activity is connected to the antiques, historical objects and paintings in the museum rather than to the building itself.   Ghost orbs have also appeared when pictures of the portraits have been taken. Ray Swick, local historian and head of the Blennerhassett Museum, says that on one occasion after he had left his work in the evening, he looked up to see the lights in his office had been switched back on. It seems that the spirits inside the Blennerhassett Museum don't mind working overtime.

Haunts at the Elks Club

Feelings of apprehension, muffled phantom noises, boxes securely on shelves falling over, surging shadows and lights where they should not be, loud spirited meetings that go on in rooms that are later discovered empty—these are just a few of the ghostly happenings that take place in Parkersburg's Elks' Club on Juliana Street. Here is a report of Elks' Club paranormal happenings that we received from a former worker in the one-hundred year old building:

"I have been meaning to write to you for some time regarding the Elks Club building on Juliana Street. I worked at the club part-time for about a year and I sincerely believe that building to be the most haunted place I have ever set foot in. You can literally walk into the building and feel something strange going on.

"For several months while I worked at the Elks, little things happened that I at first attributed to the building just being creaky and old. Lights I turned off suddenly switched back on, boxes that were securely placed flew off their shelves, and mysterious sounds that could not be explained.

"Several times I thought there were meetings going on in distant rooms, only to find them empty. One night, however, convinced me without a doubt that the building is haunted. My daughter and granddaughter were waiting for me to finish up when the jukebox seemed to come on all by itself. This particular song sounded strange.

The tune was very loud and was Big Band music. My daughter walked over and tried to turn the machine down. She asked me how to turn it down and I (assuming that she didn't know how to operate the jukebox) walked over and turned the volume button. It didn't work so I tried a control button that we had on the wall. It didn't work either. It seemed at that particular moment that my daughter and I both realized that the music wasn't coming from the jukebox. I don't know how to describe it but it seemed to be just kind of floating in the air and one just KNEW that it wasn't "real" music. There was no specific spot that it seemed to originate from, it just "was." I reached behind the jukebox and unplugged it but still the music continued.

"We were both terrified and grabbed our things and headed for the door!

"As we passed the kitchen, there was an absolute howl that came from the sink. It was a straight-out-of-a-horror-movie howl! I have never been so scared in my life.

"We ran out of the building leaving all of the lights on, a mess on the counters and the doors unlocked.

"When I went in the next day to explain why we had left in such a hurry, no one seemed surprised. There were a few members who were amused that I was frightened and most agreed that strange things do happen there.

"Some of the members explained that many years ago a young black man who was employed there ended up shot in the bar by an Elks member. It seemed that the man was

having an affair with the member's wife. As it was, nothing came of it and the man was never charged. They believe the ghost of the young man still haunts the bar.

"Also, I was told of a member who had drunk too much one night and passed out in the library. Sometime in the night he had to go to the restroom and as he walked past the ballroom he found that there was a dance going on. He told other members that the people were dressed in 20's style clothing and the music was from that era.

"As I said, there is a certain feeling in the building. The bar still felt safe to me although I always sensed that I was being watched while I was in there. The kitchen and the back hallways were extremely ominous. I don't know how to explain it other than sometimes the hair would rise on my arms and I would be afraid for no apparent reason. I apologize for rambling on so. I just thought that you might be interested in investigating the building or at least being aware of this activity."

Unfortunately, the Elks Club building was torn down in 2006.

Trans Allegheny Bookstore

Trans Allegheny Books
COURTESY TIMOTHY ELLIOTT

People swear this place is haunted. It even has its own black cat that disappears behind the rambling shelves of new and antique books. The stained glass windows give visitors the sense of being inside a chapel. Employees claim that most of the time nothing really out of the ordinary happens, just an occasional apparition browsing the shelves, turning on lights and floating about.

The building, once the Carnegie Library in Parkersburg, is pretty quiet so to speak. . . unless you're used to shadows lurking and books flying through the air.

Overhead lights on the second floor flicker quite erratically. Ghostly footsteps are heard when the aisles are otherwise empty. There are five primary spirits in Trans Allegheny Bookstore. One is a homeless man,

09/29/2004

An authentic ghost orb in Trans Allegheny Books. COURTESY KRISTALL CHAMBERS

who spent his time between the building and the Greyhound bus station during the 1960s and 70s. Another spirit is a retired newspaper reporter who was murdered in her home in 1987. She was killed in her home not far from the bookstore.

A former librarian is said to haunt the place and the apparition of a small girl in a white bonnet sits on the third step of the wooden stairway. In the mezzanine, it is not unusual for the overhead lamps to sway and lights to flutter eerily. Perhaps it is just antiquated wiring in an old building. Many bookstore visitors claim to see a dapper man in a brown or green jacket browsing the second floor. The staff assumes it is just one of bookstore's regular ghosts. Perhaps he is the author of one of their books. Most of the spirits that stay in Trans Allegheny Bookstore do so because they seem to be attached to the peaceful, positive energies of the place.

The Lindsey Home on 26th Street

Located on the top of a hill overlooking Murdoch Avenue, this pale gray Colonial is haunted by a quick paced, impatient ghost. Built in 1950, the apparition of a young man briskly passes the back window leading into the doorway to the house, yet he never comes inside. The ghost is normally seen wearing a white shirt, although on one occasion he appeared dressed in an olive green and burgundy-striped sweater. He has also been glimpsed lingering outside the door that leads into what was once the garage, now an art studio. When the woman of the house works in her studio, it is not unusual for the doorknob to turn, followed by the door creaking open. Naturally, there is no one there, not even a wind that might force ajar the door.

Generally, the spirit of the walking man is witnessed a few times per day for a couple of days. His appearances then vanish for a while. Not wanting to frighten her small daughter, the woman of the house did not mention the jaunty ghost (who most often appears during the afternoon and early evening) but the child later said, "Mommy, I see a boy that walks by the back window." Upon leaving the house once, the owner stepped outside the back door and was suddenly hit in the face by something white. "It didn't hurt," the owner said, "It was just surprising."

On occasion the television sets act strangely. During one stretch, the TV switched itself on every night at 12:30 a.m. At other times, the TV set turns off if anything coarse or unsavory is mentioned in front of the woman or little girl living in the house. At other times, the intercom system throughout the two-story house beeps and the sound of children's voices are heard. The voices never complete a full sentence, but the call button beeps over and over again.

Late into the evening, footsteps and doors opening and closing echo downstairs after the family retires for the night. At other times, the muffled voices of a man and a woman are heard having a heated discussion downstairs.

To the current owners, nothing evil or unhappy ever happened in the house—or they have not been made aware of any such thing. Despite the traffic noise coming from Murdoch Avenue (during Christmas season, the busiest road in West Virginia) it is a peaceful home, warm and calm.

The original builders of the hilltop Colonial house on 26th Street were the Lindsey family, part owners in what was once the Burdette-Lindsay funeral home in downtown Parkersburg. Perhaps when the undertakers moved out they left some of the residual energies of their former clients behind.

Black Caped Figure on Dudley Avenue

An anonymous woman emailed the following stories: "My son and I saw something eerie early one morning near the corner of 23rd and Dudley Avenue in Parkersburg as I was helping him with his newspaper route. It was still dark, and there seemed to be a fog in the area but nowhere else. My son and I always did opposite sides of the street in order to get done faster, so I didn't know exactly where he was. Suddenly out of the fog, in the middle of the street, was a tall dark figure of a man in what appeared to be a long black cape. I pressed myself against the house to be less noticeable, hoping the man would not see me, and scanned the street for my son. When I looked back, the ghastly figure was gone, and I came down off the porch in a flash. My son ran up beside me, wide eyed, and asked, "Did you see that?" We never saw the vampire figure again on the paper route, but neither shall we forget it.

"There was also a report of a haunting at 1514 23rd Street. The ghost appears to be a young man, and some say a young man committed suicide in the house. He plays tricks on people—opens windows and doors, things like that. Sometimes smoke curls up out of nowhere and slips across the floor, and there are loud noises. I heard these from the owner of the house, but I have never witnessed it myself. My husband and I looked at this house when it was for sale, before I knew of the sightings, and I had an uneasy feeling about the place.

"Our former home at 1805 23rd Street may have been haunted. Many times I heard footsteps on the porch, walking over to the wooden swing, and when I looked out, no one was there. The doorbell, which didn't work at the time, would sometimes ring and no one was there! I got used to the creaks and bumps, just called it house settling, but a house built in the 1920s should have been done settling."

Apparitions of Nuns at St. Joseph's Hospital

In the older part of St. Joseph's Hospital, now used as offices and the conference area, the apparition of a nun dressed in a traditional black habit has been witnessed carrying a glowing lantern throughout the rooms. A priest in black robes and sandals is also seen in what used to be the psychiatric ward of the hospital carrying and jangling a handful of keys. Lights also go off and on all on there own accord near what used to be the morgue and autopsy room of the facility. In the 4-

South section of St. Joseph's Hospital an unidentified ghost is said to wander the halls overturning trash cans. Occasionally, a bloodcurdling scream will come from one of the empty rooms.

Bessie Bartlett, the Little Ghost Girl

Bessie Bartlett, the little ghost girl, captured in the basement of a house on Ann Street in Parkersburg. The small girl died of Typhoid Fever.
COURTESY STEVE LONGACRE

Perhaps the saddest ghost stories are the ones that involve the death of a child. On Ann Street there is a home that was built in the 1870s by a prominent dentist named Charles H. Bartlett. Along with his wife and other children, Dr. Bartlett had a ten-year-old daughter named Bessie whom he dearly loved. Unfortunately, a typhoid epidemic swept through Parkersburg in the 1870s. Sadly, Bessie Bartlett became one of its victims.

At first, Dr. Bartlett tried to nurse young Bessie back to health. But his dentistry practice was in his home and he could not risk exposing his patients to the fever. Also, because it was the summer, he put Bessie in the basement, hoping the coolness might break her fever.

Yet there was no bringing little Bessie back to health. Her fever was too high and she was too far-gone. Thus, the basement of the home was where Bessie Bartlett died unexpectedly—cold and alone. Over the years, Dr. Bartlett and the rest of his family passed away. Bessie had an infant brother die after she did. An older brother made it into adulthood. He became a minister but died in California at only twenty-seven years old.

Over a one-hundred-year span, the people that lived in the Bartlett home never reported any activity that could be taken as a haunting. But in the 1980s, a family with young daughters was moving to Parkersburg. The upper historic district appealed to the family. As they drove by the Bartlett home they saw that it was for sale. An odd feeling in the car told them to stop.

The family was surprised that the house was built in the 1870s. From the outside it did not appear to be that old. Once inside, the family could see the age of the house. They decided if they bought the house, they would do some renovations. The father grabbed his camera and took pictures throughout the home.

When the pictures from the basement were developed, one photo featured a striking, but disturbing image of what appeared to be a little girl—one cannot deny what appears to be the image of a little girl in this photograph—even to the point of the puffed sleeves of her pink dress, the fall of her long, dark, parted hair, her forearm and right wrist, and both of her open eyes. It looks as if Bessie is sitting on the edge of her bed, as if she is waiting for someone to tell her whether it is okay for her to leave the basement. It was only when the family did research on the house that they discovered that a young child had died in that basement. At the time, the current owners did not know about the girl's death. The fact that a camera captured the image of the child in the basement suggests Bessie Bartlett is a spirit recording or residual energy type of "imprint" ghost.

Still, the owners claim there have been a number of odd, inexplicable activities in the home, including seeing strange balls of light and energy in the basement, and lights turning themselves off and on—the effects, perhaps, of a ghost imprint. In 2005, the Haunted Parkersburg Ghost Hunters were filming some other stories in the Bartlett home. During that evening, they witnessed the opening and closing of doors on their own, doorknobs being rattled and balls of light flying up from the basement.

When the ghost tour passes in front of Bessie Bartlett's house on Ann Street, and the guides begin to tell her story, the lamp on the front porch typically brightens very sharply, flickers and then dims. It is as if Bessie herself is reminding others to remember her name, and to not forget how she died in that basement chilly and alone.

Bessie Bartlett's grave at Oddfellows Cemetery in Parkersburg. She is buried not far from Arthur I. Boreman, first Governor of West Virginia.

Red Brick on Ann Street

Not far from Bessie Bartlett's house is a red brick home that has spirits of all sorts. It all began when a previous resident woke up in the middle of the night with the feeling of someone pulling the blankets off of her. Sometimes she would wake up cold with no blankets covering her. In the beginning, she thought, perhaps, she was doing it to herself until she awakened to find herself levitating about five feet off the bed. As soon as the thought, "My God, I'm levitating!" hit her, she dropped and her body slammed into the mattress.

Considering the event freakish, she continued to go about her daily routine. The woman did notice, however, that as she drew a bath for herself, she heard the mumbling of different voices over the sound of running water. When she turned off the water, the voices always stopped.

The woman soon moved out because she was troubled by too many nightmares and extreme insomnia. She even felt a demonic rape was forced on her. Haunted Parkersburg guide Kristall Chambers lived in this same home as a small girl, and witnessed a number of puzzling events while staying there.

Kristall writes, "I remember footsteps in the attic, a cold chill in the study on the second floor where I played. Someone used to touch my feet at night and stand at the foot of my bed. My stepfather shot at "an intruder" in the attic, but then found no one there. The elevator in the house (one of the previous owners was confined to a wheelchair) would switch on by itself and go up and down at night eerily." It was here Kristall had dramatic encounters with the spirit world, inspiring her life-long interest in ghosts.

The current owners of the red brick home claim no such things have happened to them. This is not surprising. Ghosts like certain individuals more than others. It could be the current owners are just not sensitive to ghostly things or the woman's ghost attacker left with her and is still tracking her.

Boreman Wheel House

The Boreman Wheel House in Parkersburg is surrounded by a number of historical buildings. Next door, the Vision Care Associates, an eye care facility, was once a Civil War hospital. The parking lot for the Boreman Wheel House sits on the site of the former home of the first Governor of West Virginia. In fact, the Wheel House, itself, is the prior home of the daughters of Governor Arthur I. Boreman, Maud and Lorraine.

Located at 4th & Avery Streets the Boreman Wheel House appears to be the epicenter of most of the haunted activity on that city block. Many of the ghostly happenings occur in the bar area of the restaurant, where some of the most expensive wines and glasses are often tampered with. Glasses will literally explode or shatter on their own, and costly wines will turn up completely missing. Sightings of a Civil War soldier (the Boreman Wheel House is very close to Quincy Hill) in a blue Union uniform have been reported. The soldier is usually seen on the landing leading up to the second floor of this popular bar and eatery. Mysteriously, a ghost meeting the description of this same soldier has been visible in the basement of Vision Care Associates. Many of the employees do not want to venture into the basement alone.

So, why would Civil War soldiers be interested in bars, wine glasses and eye glass facilities? During the time of the Civil War, what medical treatment they had for pain was very limited. Doctors often resorted to getting their patients drunk in order to dull their pain, especially in the cases of the many amputations they had to perform. People who die inebriated leave very confused ghosts. Dying while drunk can leave a spirit earthbound. Of course, the ghosts may want to find their way back to the liquor they still may crave, not realizing they are dead. Medical facilities may be attractive to the ghosts, if they had been injured, and since many of them passed away in the former Civil War hospital.

If you are curious about Civil War ghosts, the Boreman Wheel House is a good place to visit and explore. Ghost hunters get extremely high readings for paranormal activity in the restaurant and bar area of the Boreman sister's former home.

Southside K-Mart

In the early 1970s, two Parkersburg teenagers set fire to their home, killing their entire family. Some years later, the land close to where the house stood was purchased to build a new K-Mart store. Things have never been the same since.

Those who work the midnight shift stocking shelves at the Southside K-Mart report a number of ghostly happenings. Sometimes they hear a radio playing a ball game with names from the past. Others report the lights being switched off throughout the entire building, as well as empty carts coasting through aisles and boxes of merchandise being pushed from their shelves. Some workers at the K-Mart have claimed that after stocking shelves, and going on break, they return to discover every single item they have previously stocked is in the middle of the floor. However, the merchandise is not knocked over in a messy pile, as a prankster might do, but neatly stacked in the center of the aisle.

As strange as this may sound, "stacking" is very common in hauntings. It's good to know that ghosts are polite and do not wish to make too much of a mess of things for their mortal counterparts to clean up later.

TWELVE
Other Tales, Other Towns

No matter where you go, tales of apparitions and ghosts are not so unique. Our lives are filled with mysteries. Whether we chose to tap into these mysteries or not, we live in a world that swims with spirits. It would be far stranger if we lived in a world without wonder. The odds are against us being the only life in the universe.

We believe in the existence of the mind even though we can't see it. We speculate that consciousness lies in the brain. We know love exists, but we can't weigh its reality inside the human heart. The reason ghost stories continue is that the evidence, although sometimes slippery, still sticks.

When you have a ghost tale, you can be assured there is something behind it. Yes, the story may get embellished over time. It is human nature to elaborate, and create a better story—this is what separates tales of folklore from ongoing haunts.

Human beings are natural storytellers and have been since we placed bouquets of flowers on our hairy-shouldered dead in Paleolithic caves. Early humans added mystery to stories to give a special spin in the telling and re-telling. Eventually, a belief in ghosts and an afterlife became universal.

No part of America is as rich in tales of the supernatural as the area south of the Mason-Dixon line. Perhaps Appalachia's remoteness is the very thing that enables these stories to live on. The following are just a few more haunts from West Virginia and the Ohio Valley.

One Spirit-Filled Farmhouse in St. Marys

There was a haunted farmhouse in rural Pleasants County that was torn down years ago. A former owner offered up this very real tale:

"First of all," the man explained, "I don't drink. Secondly, I don't think I'm crazy—but after the experience I had at my 135 year-old-farmhouse, I am not so sure. One night, as nature called," he began, "I got up to go to the bathroom down the hall. I was shocked to see a woman standing at the end of the hallway in a long nightgown. She wasn't an old woman at all—and she wasn't bad looking—except for one thing—she didn't have any feet." As the man continued with his story, he nervously rattled the change in his pocket. "Well, maybe she did have feet—her long nightgown probably covered them. She never looked directly at me or spoke. Instead, she glanced past my shoulder—there was a window behind me—as if she were watching down the road. By this time, I had forgotten all about nature calling. I darted back inside my bedroom. I must have been breathing pretty hard or making some noise as I woke my wife up. When she asked me what was wrong, I could hardly say anything. That's when my wife said, 'You saw her, too, didn't you?'

"In all of my days, I have never had an experience like that one. If my wife hadn't witnessed the identical sighting I had of the young lady or ghost or whatever she was, I might have been convinced I was dreaming that night. But seeing that woman standing with no feet will stay with me for the rest of my life."

It is not generally known, but spirits oftentimes materialize with a part of their anatomy missing—very often it is the head or the feet. Sometimes there is just a set of hands, as we learned about in the previous chapter.

The haunted farmhouse in St. Mary's no longer stands but the enigma of who this young woman might have been still remains.

Lonely Hitchhiker at Huntington's Fifth Street Hill

Every region has a story about a stranded, hitchhiking ghost. Traveling spirits are reported all over the globe, but a young woman hitchhiking in a rainstorm is by far the most prevalent way this type of ghost appears.

More than fifty years ago stories began circulating about a young woman standing alone in a downpour sighted at the stone bridge that runs across Fourpole Creek. The woman often flags down motorists and pleads for a ride. But before getting to her destination, she will vanish.

Usually the hitchhiker is dressed in a thin party dress. Others claim it is a wedding gown. When the driver asks her why she isn't dressed more appropriately for the weather, the girl will answer, "I no longer need a coat." Sometimes she will remark: "I haven't worn a coat in ten years." Often the driver will offer his jacket to the young woman. Sometimes she refuses. At others times she accepts the jacket and it disappears with her.

Over the years many unsuspecting Huntington cab drivers have picked up the hitchhiker. As soon as they reach the hill, the young woman asks to be let *off*. The driver will turn around and discover the young woman has vanished.

During one cold, November night, one cab driver noticed a dim yellow light in house near where the girl asked to stop. The one-story white home pushed back against the hill looked like a skull gleaming in the darkness.

The cab driver wondered if somehow the girl had gotten out and ran into the house in order to get out of paying the cab fee. She also had taken his jacket.

In the pounding rain, the cab driver made his way to the house and knocked on the door. At first, no one answered. The man pounded harder and was surprised when an older woman finally came to the door. She looked at him curiously. The driver asked the woman if she had a daughter or a granddaughter? The woman shook her head 'No.'

As the driver turned to leave, he caught a glance of the mantle inside the home and noticed the graduation picture of a young woman. He recognized that it was, indeed, the young woman who flagged down his cab earlier.

Not wanting to be forward, the cab driver inquired, "If you don't have a daughter or granddaughter, who is that in the picture? That looks like the girl I picked up."

The woman gasped. After taking a few moments to gain her composure, she sobbed, "That's my daughter. She died in a wreck at the stone bridge near Fifth Street Hill ten years ago. Tonight was the anniversary of her death."

Stunned, the cab driver was at a loss for words.

Wiping away tears, the woman then asked, "Did she borrow your jacket as well?"

Shocked, the driver mumbled, "Sorry, Ma'am. Just forget about my jacket. Your loss is more important than an old jacket."

"She did, didn't she?" The woman asked. "I need to know."

The cab driver shook his head. "Yes. Yes, she did."

"Follow me." On that, the older woman picked up a flashlight from an inn table and headed outside. Behind the house was a cemetery that had a few small graves. The woman opened the iron-gate and the cab driver followed her in. The hitchhiker's mother stood by a grave with an angel carved on the headstone. She bent over and pulled away some weeds. "This is where my daughter now stays," she said. "I don't want my angel gone from me. I always told her that. Never go away from me, Sweetheart. I need you. That's why she keeps trying to come home." The woman wept softly.

The cab driver stood in a numb silence. It wasn't finding the girl's grave and realizing he had encountered the ghostly hitchhiker of Fifth Street Hill that haunted the driver for many years. On the headstone was his jacket, neatly folded and left for him to find. It was right there on the girl's grave, in plain view.

Hooded Ghost Dressed in Scarlet at Salem

Between Clarksburg and Salem on certain nights, when an incandescent moon drifts high and full over Route 50, the lonely figure of a woman in a hooded red coat is often spotted walking along the side of the road. Whenever motorists stop to inquire if the woman needs help, as she turns to stare they are shocked to see that she has no face beneath the red hood. If the motorists are unlucky, the red-coated woman will follow them home and later pace outside their house peering inside the windows—again, with no humanly features at all— only a solid black void beneath her blood-red hood.

Haunts at the Capitol Plaza Theatre

A showpiece of downtown Charleston, this grand structure was built between 1909 and 1914 on the site of the former mansion of John Welch, which was originally built in 1798. The Welch family home was razed in 1908 in order make land available for the downtown landmark that has hosted cultural and entertainment venues for almost a century.

Like most old theaters, the Capitol Plaza Theatre has its own hosts of ghosts, mostly tied to the original owners of the property. Although no descriptions of the ghost are given most of the ghostly manifestations in the theatre have been connected to John Welch.

It seems that Welch's ghost has become very protective of the theatre. He also likes to hide items and then have them reappear a short time later in obvious places. Patrons and employees also report walking into cold spots, a sure sign of a haunting. John's daughter, Molly Welch, who is said to have died of pneumonia around eight years of age, is glimpsed sitting in the front row of the balcony watching most of the performances. A few claim to hear Molly humming. Other reports claim ghostly footsteps are heard sounding in the bathrooms as well as the ghostly opening and closing of doors.

The Empty Glass in Charleston

The Empty Glass Bar is a main haunting place for a number of spirits in Charleston. One ghost is thought to be that of a former bartender who was killed in an automobile crash. One night some of the employees came to discover loud rock music already blasting in an otherwise empty bar. It happened to be the bartender's favorite songs. Before they could unplug the jukebox, the tall shadow of a man crossed the wall.

Other spirits came with the building, and are most active on the second floor where employees often take their breaks. Restroom doors tend to get stuck downstairs and objects disappear only to show up later in obvious places.

Many believe the ghost of the bartender misses his job and wants to make sure everyone at the Empty Glass remembers him through his harmless pranks. Humor is every bit a part of the spirit world as it is a part of our own human experience. After all, humor, just like our own unique personalities, never really dies.

Ghost Afloat At Walker

A fellow, who often jogged along the old B & O Railroad tracks that are now a walking and bicycling trail in rural Wood County, felt chills rise one day just as he was nearing a bend in the trail. As the man turned, he saw a floating woman behind him with her mouth open as if to scream. The woman floated over the trail at a quick pace. As the spirit neared the startled man, he made out her words as, "Help, oh

Lord, help me." As soon as the ghost's words were uttered, the distressed spirit instantly vanished.

There are other tales of Walker being haunted. Very near the old railroad tracks a Union soldier was sighted leaning on his musket. Others have seen the apparition of a woman in Civil War period dress with a small child close to what they now call "the Bird Farm" at Walker. The Bird Farm once had peacocks and other exotic birds.

Baffling Haunts of Fayette County

Monsters with red eyes, including a flying beast with the wingspan of a small plane and another creature that resembles a half-man, half-horse are said to haunt an area near Mount Hope in Fayette County. Near Witchy Hollow, it is reported the apparition of an old-fashioned car speeds toward other cars with its headlights on high beam. As soon as the ghost car is about to crash into the other vehicle, it disappears.

Also in Fayette County, is the Blumehaven Inn, once owned by a Dr. M. Malcolm but bequeathed to his son. Both men died tragically and painfully, the doctor of esophageal cancer and the son of tuberculosis a few years later. The doctor died in Room 7. To this very day the sound of coughing is heard throughout the Inn and objects are moved or misplaced in Room 7.

Bell Witch Haunting of Adams, Tennessee

As inspiration for the movie the *Blair Witch Project*, the Bell Witch tale had nothing to do with witchcraft but everything to do with ghosts and poltergeists. The haunting began in 1817 to the Bell family in rural Tennessee, when their home was besieged by rapping and knocking noises that also included scratching sounds in the walls. The family ignored the noises until the blankets were pulled off the beds while they slept.

Twelve-year-old daughter Betsy Bell seemed to be the target or epicenter of most of the ghostly abuse. Early on, the Bell Witch haunting had most of the components of what might be termed a poltergeist invasion. Most of it had to do with misplaced or flying objects, knocking and banging sounds, raps, slaps and bumps. Eventually, the sound of a woman's voice was heard that announced itself as the spirit of Kate Batts—a woman who John Bell, the father, had quarreled with sometime before she died. After hearing the voice, John recalled Kate once cursing him.

After hearing the voice of Kate Batt, frightening appearances of the "witch" occurred daily. Her enraged ghost was said to scream, use profanity, throw pots and pans, and rip the curtains off the wall.

The story of the Bell haunting became so famous that President Andrew Jackson visited the Bell family. Although no activity materialized in the house when Jackson was there, as he stepped back outside the wheels on his wagon would not budge. It had to be supported and carried off by his men several yards from the Bell home before the wheels would turn. It was reported a woman was heard laughing in the distance.

Not long after, John Bell became afflicted with a wasting disease and became bed fast. The spirit of the Bell witch was said to titter and curse his dying body. The morning John Bell expired, the family found a vial that held an odd substance. When they rubbed the black substance on a cat's gums, the animal immediately dropped over dead.

Miraculously, the Bell Witch spirit left the family alone for seven years after John Bell died. Her ghost returned only when Betsy Bell become betrothed to someone the Bell Witch did not approve of. She appeared another time at the home of Betsy's older brother creating her usual antics.

Over the span of the last 150 years, the Bell Witch has been mostly silent.

Livingston Wizard, Middleway, West Virginia

Only twenty years following the Bell Witch haunting, a similar case would occur in the eastern panhandle of West Virginia. Instead of a witch, the Jefferson County case involved an alleged wizard. Like the Bell Witch case, it seemed to have fallen under the category of poltergeists— loud, destructive ghosts that really aren't spirits of the dead but spurts of psychic energy unleashed upon certain areas or homes.

It all began on a rainy night in 1794 when a man appeared at the Adam Livingston farm to seek shelter from the storm. The family gladly invited the stranger in, and offered to feed him, but the man said he was tired and only looking for a warm place to rest. In the middle of the night, the man started coughing violently. In no time the stranger was delirious, his body drenched in sweat, and it became obvious he was not going to make it until morning. However the man was coherent enough to ask Adam Livingston to get him a priest to give him his last rites.

Catholic priests were rare in rural West Virginia. Adam Livingston did not know a single priest in Jefferson County. It also went against his faith to allow a Catholic to perform last rites in his Lutheran home. Livingston said no, and said to the stranger that a Catholic priest would not set foot in his house and utter bastard prayers to pagan idols. The man bitterly turned his face to the wall and died.

Not knowing who the man was, Adam Livingston buried the stranger at the edge of his property and erected a small white cross to mark the grave. He was a little afraid of the grave for some reason, and he and the family tended to avoid the grave as much as possible.

It was not long after the burial that ghostly events began. Items fell out of cabinets. Prime livestock disappeared with no evidence of having been stolen. Screams, chants and cries could be heard throughout the Livingston property. Lanterns would suddenly go out and invisible bells rang at unexpected intervals.

Throughout the day and into the night the sound of scissors were heard cutting their way through fabric, but no clippers could be found. These same invisible scissors would cut items in the home into weird spiral shapes. A woman entering the home knew of the mysterious cuttings, so wrapped her expensive silk hat in a handkerchief before crossing over the door. Upon leaving the house, she took the hat out and discovered it had been sliced into ribbons anyway.

A tailor from town came to disprove the unlikely story about the phantom scissors doing so much damage. Under his arm, he carried a suit wrapped in a paper bundle that he had intended to work on later in the evening. As he talked to Adam Livingston, there was a loud shearing sound. The bundle was then knocked from his arm. When the tailor opened it, he found that the suit he had been carrying cut into pieces and no sign of shears or scissors in sight.

At other times, an invisible rope would form a barrier in the road, preventing wagons from driving up to the farmhouse. When men tried to cut through the unseen rope, they were unable to. Sometimes, one wagon would be allowed through but not another.

Adam Livingston saw he made a terrible mistake by refusing

the dying man a priest and turned to religion for help. He first tried a Lutheran minister to perform a banishing ceremony on the property, to no avail. In fact, the hauntings seemed to strengthen after the minister left. Next, Livingston asked an Episcopal priest and three Methodist preachers to rid the area of its wizard ghost. He had no luck with them either. Finally, one night, Livingston clearly dreamed of a priest named "Cahill." His friends recognized the name as belonging to a priest named Father Dennis Cahill who was from Shepherdstown, West Virginia.

Cahill came and performed the rites of exorcism. In doing so, a satchel full of money appeared and burst open onto the doorstep. It was the same satchel of money Father Cahill had been missing from his diocese for over a year! Heartened by this positive development, the Livingstons and Father Cahill looked for the hauntings to stop. Much to their disappointment, they did not. The story was soon written about in the Baltimore newspapers, where it got the attention of a Father Dmitri Gallitzin. He agreed to try and help the Livingston family, as he was very learned in such matters. But a short visit to the farm was not enough to do the trick. Father Gallitzin had to live with the family three months to keep the spirits at bay. A more intense rite of exorcism followed this. Father Gallitzin called on two other priests from Baltimore, and with the entire family, they prayed over the property for several days. Soon the veil of darkness lifted and family and farm found peace.

Adam Livingston was so grateful he converted to Catholicism and deeded 40 acres of his estate to the church. Many who visit the area claim it remains haunted. A man leading a tour group once had his metal-framed glasses snapped completely in two. Many others have had their clothes unbuttoned, ripped by unseen hands.

A Ghost encounter by Teresa O'Cassidy of Charleston:

"When I moved to Morgantown to attend West Virginia University, I got my first apartment in the Sunnyside district of town. I stayed there that first summer to work and go to summer school since "Reaganomics" precluded my being able to find a summer job in Boone County where I am from.

"I had three male friends who also stayed that summer and rented an upstairs apartment in the old house on McLane Avenue. One of them named Joe worked at the Subway sandwich shop with me. Joe had the closing shift that ended around 2:00 a.m. He usually got home by 2:30 in the morning. We all fell into the habit of hanging out at the guys' apartment on McLane once the bars closed and after Joe got off work.

"The way the apartment was laid out, there was a door at ground level that led to an enclosed stairway on the inside of the building, which led straight into the apartment. The landlady lived in the downstairs. There was only the one apartment upstairs that never stayed rented for very long.

"As time passed, we noticed that almost every night we heard the door open and someone walk up the stairs. The footsteps sounded heavy, like a man's footsteps would sound. Someone would always remark, "That must be Joe coming in." Always, the footsteps would stop about halfway up the stairs and no one would ever come. Later, Joe would arrive. We would hear his keys, the door open and close, and his footfalls all the way up the stairs. Joe would normally come in with some outrageous story about his most drunken customer of the evening.

"As time went by, we figured out that the footsteps always came at precisely 2:00 in the morning and so we wondered what the landlady's boyfriend was doing downstairs at that time every night. Maybe he was coming home from work or was a night owl.

"We were all on very good terms with the landlady. She was young to be a landlady, not quite 40. She and her live-in boyfriend had it written right into the lease that the landlord liked to party and if loud music late at night was offensive, it would be advised NOT to rent from her. One evening when a few of us were at her apartment, we asked her what her boyfriend did at 2:00 in the morning because it always sounds like someone coming up the stairs.

"The landlady got the brightest sparkle in her eye and said, "I see you've met the ghost." She said the ghost had been there as long as she had (over ten years) and she had no idea where it had come from. The house had been built in the 1860s and she hadn't researched its history. She said that when the apartment upstairs was empty, she could hear sounds coming from up there like furniture moving and people walking. When she'd get the key and go into the apartment, everything would be still and it was obvious that no one had been there.

"I went to visit the guys upstairs one evening. I knocked on the door and heard my friend's voice calling down the steps, "Come in. Door's open." I opened the door and saw what I believed to be my friend Andy (judging by his build of the backlit shadow) as he walked away from the door toward the first step. I gasped, "Oh, Andy!" (I was surprised to see him so close to the door.) As soon as I said that, Andy's head popped around the doorway at the top of the stairs. As he answered, "Yes?" the shadow immediately disappeared! I slammed the door shut and ran to the Sunnyside Superette to use the pay phone. I called Andy and told him what I'd seen and asked him to come out for a drink because I really didn't feel like going back. He laughed and said he'd wondered why I turned white as a sheet and took off running."

Run Like the Devil in Lincoln County

Lincoln County may be the only spot in West Virginia to claim that the Devil himself appeared there—and fully formed on a footbridge near a place called Dry Branch Hollow. It just happened that Old Scratch was looking for someone in particular—one Lincoln County resident who had challenged him earlier.

The man's name has since been lost. But the story goes that in Lincoln County in the 1950s one particularly violent and ill-tempered man boasted that he was mean enough to whip the Devil. One night in drunkenness, the man waved his fists in the darkness and challenged Old Scratch to a fight.

It didn't take the Devil long to show up at the end of the footbridge nearing Spry cemetery leading to the man's house. The Devil's hands and face where charred and covered with soot. The air smelled like rotten eggs. A long, spiky, whip-like tail wagged out from under the Devil's waistcoat as he stood watching the man with arms folded over his chest.

"Whip me?" Old Scratch asked incredulously. His teeth gleamed yellow like winter corn. "And how, pray tell, have you decided to do that?"

"Just like I always do," the man spat. "Come over here and I will fight you."

"You know who I am," sighed the Devil. "Besides, I can't cross running water. You know that. It doesn't look like there's much fight in you anyhow. You're wasting my time." Old Scratch snickered. Sparks flew and then, with a bang like a firecracker, he disappeared in a cloud of sulfurous smoke.

The next day, the man—now with a much more moderate temper—brought his son to show him the spot where he had challenged the Devil the day before. To their shock, cloven hooves were branded into the wooden planks of the footbridge. The seared footprints lead into Spry Cemetery.

At Spry Cemetery, where the Devil's tracks were said to lead, there is the spirit of a woman who died in childbirth that haunts the graveyard. Her newborn also succumbed during the especially difficult birth. On nights of a full moon, when their names can be read on their gravestones, the woman is seen rocking her baby in the cemetery. Witnesses say the ghosts are dressed in white frocks and the mother appears to be weeping.

An Incubus & A Black Dog in Calhoun County

Haunted tales are just as appropriate near Christmas as they are at Halloween. It is believed ghost tales were told by Druids around the fire during the longest night of the year, December 21st. Perhaps spinning dark tales near the darkest day of the year helps alleviate any anxieties we might feel about ghosts, and perhaps our own demise since food was less available during winter months.

The following article appeared in *The Charleston Daily Mail* on December 27, 1925.

"Nearly 40 years ago the Calhoun County correspondent of the Cincinnati Enquirer *prepared the following account of Calhoun's most prominent ghost. Interested persons saved the clippings, with the result that the story has reappeared recently in various weekly papers. It combines all the elements of a good ghost story and contains about every characteristic spirits are known to possess, and reads as follows:*

Grantsville, Calhoun County, W. Va., 1886—The following history of the haunted house, situated on the bank of the Little Kanawha river, about three miles from this place, is presented to the scientist for explanation. The skeptical reader is frankly and honestly referred to any one of the persons named herein for verification of the history. Although it is one of the strangest and most unaccountable stories written on this subject within a quarter of a century, every detail is well authenticated. A solution of the mysteries connected with this history will be received with gratitude and pleasure by hundreds of the respectable and honest citizens of Calhoun, Ritchie and Wirt Counties. But back to the history. . .

About three miles from the county seat of Calhoun County there resided, and still resides, Mr. Collins Betts, a farmer, who is well known throughout this part of the state. His house is a one-story, rambling affair, close to the banks of the stream and a short distance from the highway. The house was a frequent stopping place for the wayfaring. Few men in a country famed for its nervy and physical giants would dare to stop over night at Bett's house.

The reputation of the house being haunted was acquired some years later. By many it is ascribed to the disappearance of a peddler in the neighborhood. It is surmised by the most cautious that the peddler was known to have had over $1,000 in his possession at the time; and was probably murdered in the vicinity. Others say his horse had been left and no one ever came for it. Be this as it may, from that time forward Collins' house has borne the reputation of being haunted.

Among the first who tested the truth of these rumors was a Methodist minister — Rev. Wayne Kennedy — who was well known throughout the state; a nervy, courageous man, who was never accused of a particle of cowardice. The reverend gentleman stopped at Betts' one night when belated, and willingly took the haunted chamber as his bedroom. About 12 or 1 o'clock the preacher felt something heavy bearing down upon his chest. The sensation of smothering awoke him. When he had collected his senses he declared that he saw something like a big black dog sitting upon his body in the bed. He said that it was with the greatest difficulty that he able to throw off the incubus and release himself from the deadly pressure.

[Author's note: Technically, an Incubus is a spirit that violates sleeping women. Its counterpart, the Succubus, attacks sleeping men.]

In the morning the preacher left, but before doing so he told Betts that he was not particularly superstitious, but that he would not stay in the house another night. The ghost or phantom appeared in different forms and was not confined to the house, but has been seen as far away as the top of the mountain opposite the house.

One night James Wolverton and his son, a boy about 18 years of age, were on their way home, driving an ox-team. When almost at the top of the hill Wolverton declared he heard the tramping of hundreds of horses and the rattling of so many sabers in their scabbards. Upon looking back, he saw what he thought was a troop of cavalry riding at a gallop toward him. His oxen saw them also, and became frightened, and ran off down the mountain. Wolverton said that just as he thought they would ride over him he threw up his hands and exclaimed, "My God, men, don't ride over me!" He declared that the mystic cavalry disappeared instantaneously just as *he cried to stop. Mr. Wolverton and his boy have always adhered to this story, and as they are men of probity, nobody questions that they saw something.*

Now comes another still stranger story. John Betts, brother of Collins, came to Calhoun from Colorado on a visit. He was a large muscular, rough-speaking man, and when he heard these stories he laughed at them and sneered at his brother and everybody who had the temerity to tell him of the rumors. He declared his intention of sleeping in the room where the phantom was often seen. One night he went into his room a hale, hearty man. In the morning he was found lying upon his back perfectly helpless.

He said that sometime during the night he felt some heavy weight upon his breast. He undertook to throw it off, but was unable to do so, and suffered torment until daylight, when the oppression ceased but he had lost the use of his limbs. Mr. Betts has never entirely recovered.

A strange feature of most of the cases is that the victims seem, although perfectly conscious, but deprived of power to resist the incubus, and suffer its torment for hours.

Many people profess to believe that it is the effect of some sort of gas that arises from the earth and is inhaled, but others disbelieve in the gas theory.

Captain Hayhurst, a visitor also from Calhoun County, stopped at Betts'. What appeared to be a headless man rose up before Hayhurst's vision in the middle of the night and frightened the gallant captain so badly that, as he says, he 'wouldn't stay another night in the house for all the gold in the kingdom.'

Henry Elliott met with a fate somewhat similar to John Betts. He slept in this room and was nearly smothered to death by something he took to be a large black animal. Elliott has been an invalid ever since.

I had a conversation about the haunted house with Mr. Henry Newman, a prominent timber man about 60 years of age. Mr. Newman is not the least bit superstitious, but he fails to explain the mystery. He said he had heard the stories often, but didn't pay any attention to them. One night, however, he stopped at Betts' and was asked if he objected to sleeping in the haunted chamber. He said he did not. Mr. Newman's story is that he went to bed, but being very wakeful he lay still and mused until about midnight.

About that time something started to claw the bed clothing off his person. He threw himself up in the bed, expecting to catch a cat or some such animal, but there was nothing there. A second and third time the act was repeated but he could not see anything. He left the next morning.

Young Hosey, a nephew of Betts, who resides on a farm several miles away, says he had occasion one night to pass the haunted house on his way home. Just about half way up the hill, some strange apparition appeared and frightened his horse so badly that it ran off down the hill through the brush. It could not be found until the next morning. This is another instance when the phantom was perceptible to both man and animal.

John Jenkins, a well-known citizen of Ritchie County, was reported stopped one night. What John saw did not clearly appear, but whatever it was frightened him so badly that he got out of the room as quickly as possible, ran to the stable, saddled his horse and left in a gallop. He never could be induced to go back.

It is claimed that the sound of persons whispering can be heard in the room. A sound of water dropping into a tin vessel is often heard, though no such article is about.

The Betts people as annoyed as are other people. The women say they hear all sorts of odd sounds like water dropping, whispering, and the sound of some heavy body falling.

Two nieces of Betts stopped over night at his residence some time ago. One of them was overcome by fear of some peculiar shape and ran out of the room followed by the other. They say they saw horrible phantoms, but could not describe them.

A sister of Betts, in a conversation about the house, said there was something mysterious connected with the house but she couldn't explain it. According to the lady's story the house has never been haunted until after the death of an old woman named Riddle. Since then the place seemed the abode of some restless phantom.

It is no trouble to find people by the dozen in Calhoun who have heard and had some queer experience with the Betts house. Such men as Captain George Downs, whose word cannot be disputed, declare he saw the phantom of a headless man or some other headless sight. To be stripped of bed clothing in the middle of the night, without any tangible means, was not uncommon. In fact, the reputation of the place appears to be widespread, and no one seems to be rash enough, after such experiences as the above cited, to test the matter or find the solution to the mystery.

Your correspondent had often heard of the haunted house of Collins Betts, and determined finally to learn all he could about the mystery. He has interviewed dozens of respectable people, and all of them, though disclaiming any superstition, seem thoroughly mystified. Everyone who ever stayed there over night has heard or seen something strange or horrible. I have no doubt but that someone will be able to explain this mystery, but until then the haunted house of Collins Betts will be the notoriety of Calhoun County, West Virginia."

Many of the above reports seem to parallel the Old Hag paralysis phenomenon (when people feel they are psychically attacked in their beds) that has been experienced worldwide throughout the ages. Generally, this is not dangerous but it is extremely frightening.

Sawyer-Curtis Haunts, Little Hocking, Ohio

Thought to have once been a station on the Underground Railroad, the Sawyer-Curtis home is one of the oldest in the mid-Ohio Valley. Nathaniel Sawyer built it in 1798 above the sloping banks of the Ohio River. This evocative old house has gone through numerous facelifts and transformations, though its ghosts stay pretty much the same.

Owners have experienced an "eerie presence" throughout the home, especially when visiting the cellar where the candles and soap were made. One former resident reported waking up to see a "beautiful lady" sitting at the foot of her bed. She was playing a music box, sweetly, as if she meant it especially to be heard by the house's surprised owner. Others who have lived in the home heard their names called when no one else was around. Windows slam shut and candlesticks are known to fly through the air.

There is a feeling of unrest to the building, and in researching the history of the house, it was discovered that Sawyer was involved in the Blennerhassett conspiracy and was a close friend of Aaron Burr.

For some reason, Nathaniel Sawyer left the area quickly, perhaps having lost his fortune like his friend Harman Blennerhassett. Up until this very day, the owners speak about Santa Claus statues turning up missing. It seems the Sawyer-Curtis House still holds onto the memories of the people who once lived there.

Haunts at Lakin State Hospital, Mason County, West Virginia

The former Lakin State Mental Hospital and West Virginia Industrial Home for Colored Boys was built in 1927 in the town of Lakin, in Mason County. Lakin was at one time called "The Lobotomy Capital of the East" because of the number of lobotomies performed there. It is alleged that as many as four hundred lobotomies could be performed in one day. Most were crude, without any anesthesia while patients where tied down to the table screaming. Families from all over would send family members to Lakin, so they could get the miracle "cure" or "ice pick surgery"—the two halves of the frontal lobes of the brain were severed, leaving patients docile but mindless.

It is alleged that one of the former patients returned to Lakin, overpowered the doctor who did the ice pick surgery on him, and performed a lobotomy on the doctor. Many claim that if you stand in the fields at night you can still hear the ghostly voice of the doctor pleading for his life, or at least for his brain.

The Industrial School started out as a hospital, and is haunted by the ghost of a nurse who was pushed down the stairs by an inmate. The next morning the nurse was found cold and dead. The inmate had escaped by breaking out a window and slipping through the bars. No one knows why the man killed the nurse. Many believe she rebuked his sexual advances. The hospital and school were closed for good in 1956, and the building was demolished in late 2006.

Harper's Ferry Haunts

Despite its long, troubled history, Harpers Ferry is a garden spot. It is undeniably one of the most picturesque small towns in the eastern United States. Located along sloping hillsides and divided by the waters of the Potomac River, Harpers Ferry was a pivotal point in both the Revolutionary and Civil Wars. But one would have trouble pinning the loyalties to any particular cause. Like the houses that cling to the hillsides, it is a hardy, adaptable town.

But if travails and troubles bring on ghosts, then Harpers Ferry is one intensely haunted town. After all, Harpers Ferry is where abolitionist John Brown met the hangman's noose. Found guilty of murder, treason and inciting slave insurrection, John Brown was imprisoned and hanged in Harpers Ferry on December 2, 1859, ending his dream of freeing the slaves.

But many in Harpers Ferry say that was not the end of John Brown. It appears he still walks the streets looking for wrongs to right. Nearing the anniversary of John Brown's execution, an older man with a shock of snow-white hair and wild eyes is said to wander the streets dressed in old-fashioned tattered clothing. Tourists, believing him to be an actor in a local theater presentation, have asked to have their pictures taken with him. Often, without words, he agrees and poses with them, then leaves without saying anything. When the photographs are developed, there is an empty spot where the man should be.

John Brown is not the only ghost that haunts the cobbled streets of Harpers Ferry.

The town's historic Iron Horse Inn once housed the superintendent for the Union army as well as other officers. Shortly before the Battle of Gettysburg, a young confederate spy stayed at the inn, assigned to determine the strength of the Union Army. For a while, the spy came and went completely undetected.

One day, the young spy's clandestine efforts were exposed. When he was confronted, the boy raced toward the door frantically, but was shot dead by a Union soldier. The very same door is said to rattle furiously on certain occasions. Many employees at the Iron Horse Inn report they can even hear the young confederate officer taking his last fall.

Another ghost tale that takes place in Harpers Ferry is one about a young woman who catches on fire. As the girl ran from her house screaming and trying to put out the flames, she was struck and killed by an oncoming train. Some claim you can still see the blazing torch of "Screaming Jenny's flame running down the railroad tracks — but only when the night is especially clear and dark as the spirits gather high.

Pentagrams, UFOs & Restless Spirits—Athens, Ohio

Would you believe it if we told you there is an Ohio Valley town where five graveyards create the exact dimensions of a witch's pentagram—an ancient symbol of mysterious powers and magic? There is such a town—it is the quaint and mystical Athens, Ohio.

Located 45 miles west of Parkersburg, hometown of Ohio University and famous for its campus Halloween celebrations, Athens has a plethora of intriguing tales.

Ancient Adena Indian mounds dot the rolling hills and twisting waterways of Athens County. Various cultures, including the Shawnee Indians, considered southeastern Ohio, to be an especially sacred area, filled with wandering spirits.

In the 1840s, a number of spiritualists were drawn to the Athens area, searching for a spiritually receptive spot to communicate easily with their ghosts and guides. Mount Nebo, the highest spot in Athens County was where the Spiritualists put down roots. They opened their "sittings" to anyone in the area that might be interested in communicating with "guides." It didn't take long for their séances to develop a large following and to make important spiritual connections in Athens.

In 1852, local farmer Jonathan Koons was instructed by a séance medium to build a specific structure at Mount Nebo in which they could hold their sittings. Koons, as well as all eight of his children, were instructed that they had the gift of spirit communication and should use it. Such séances in Athens grew wildly famous, inspiring the British Psychical Society to state that Athens and Mount Nebo were the most haunted spots on earth.

The fascination has continued to today, as Ohio University students often visit graveyards to conduct their own updated version of a séance—albeit in Bell, Book and Candle style. Such impromptu séances may have stirred up a number of ghostly occurrences in local burial grounds, especially those in the Hanning Cemetery where several public executions took place in the 19th century.

Many report gruesome apparitions in Hanning Cemetery, ghosts of dead men with bluish, bloated faces, drifting through the graveyard. Some believe they are spirits of the men who were hanged. Others claim the ghost of John Simms—the guilt-ridden hangman whose remains are also buried in Hanning—is the one that haunts the graveyard.

Wilson Hall on Ohio University has a famous haunt in Room 428. It is believed a young woman who died or committed suicide in the room in the 1970s haunts the room. Students who have stayed in the room claimed they have heard doors opening and closing, resounding footsteps and have watched objects move on their own. Whether a student unexpectedly died there is up for debate, but the room is no longer used.

The most interesting part of the story of Wilson Hall is that it lies in the center of the pentagram created by the five Athens graveyards. Its location and reputation grabbed enough attention for the TV, "Scariest Places on Earth" to air a segment on it in 2001.

Athens has its share of railroad tunnel ghosts along the once-traveled Cincinnati & Marietta Railroad. One story involves a headless conductor who swings his lantern in an attempt to get motorists to stop.

UFOs are not missing from Athens' mixed bag of paranormal events either. On March 29th, 1966, several Ohio State policemen and about a dozen Athens County residents reported a bright, whirling object flying in the sky. A highway patrolman was the first to report the unexplained object at around 5:15 a.m. Others said the object moved for a while in a "slow drifting motion" until it disappeared from sight. Many later believed that the UFO was simply Venus, since it often appears as a bright object in the morning hours. The patrolman disagreed saying, "I know what Venus looks like, and it was not Venus."

North Bend Park, Cairo, West Virginia

Some years ago there was a blind man named Ed Koons who lived at what is now the entrance to the North Bend State Park in Cairo. He had married a shrewish woman, whom along with her mother, cruelly abused and taunted the blind man throughout their marriage. So much so, that Ed ended up hanging himself from a large tree at the entrance to the park. Some drivers that pass by the place at night claim they catch sight of Ed's lifeless body in their headlight beams, swinging from the limbs of the tree. Young couples that parked their cars at a lover's lane in the 1960s reported having their vehicle being soundly whacked and pounded as if by a weighty fist. Often, as the young couple drove away in a fright, they would see a man's handprints smeared in the dust of the windows of the car.

The strangest apparition to appear near the spot where Ed Koons hung himself is an otherworldly thing that resembles a small metal barrel wobbling on spindly legs through the trees. Those who choose to enter the park at night claim that as they walk over the path near the park's lodge, they can still hear the heavy footsteps of Ed Koons, crunching the gravel and echoing directly behind them.

Mary Greene on the *Delta Queen*

Some souls love their life's work so much that they don't want to ever leave it—even after they've died. This could be said of Mary Becker Greene, whose ghost still peacefully haunts the *Delta Queen* riverboat.

Mary Becker was born in Marietta, Ohio in 1869 and married the riverboat Captain Gordon Greene in 1890. The Greene's were a prominent river-boating family in Marietta. It was no surprise when Mary Greene was the first woman to become river pilot captain along the Mississippi and Ohio rivers, receiving her official license in 1896. When Mary died at the age of 80 in 1949, after many thrilling and fulfilling years on the river, it seemed perfectly logical for her ghost to turn up in the place that she loved.

Mary Greene was a teetotaler and had no tolerance for alcohol. One night in the lounge of the *Delta Queen* during the 1990s after an especially tiring day, a few members of the riverboat crew were enjoying some drinks. Suddenly, the room went cold. Then, as they toasted each other, almost every glass above the bar fell and shattered into smithereens on the counter-top.

Although he has never witnessed the ghost of Mary Greene in any visual way, first mate Mike Williams told of an event that caused him to become a believer.

One night in 1982, Williams felt a cold breath and heard whispering in his ear. As Williams startled awake, doors slammed throughout the boat. He followed the sounds into the engine room and found a broken pipe with water rushing in. As she had done so many times in life, Mary Greene saved the *Delta Queen* from certain ruin. Mike Williams was grateful.

An elderly woman has been witnessed throughout the *Delta Queen*. When a portrait of Mary Greene is later pointed out to witnesses, they are in complete agreement that this is the older woman they have seen wandering throughout the riverboat lounge.

Fantastic Phantoms in Marietta, Ohio

It's easy to step back in time when walking the brick streets of Marietta, Ohio. History abounds in the old buildings, quaint cafes and historical landmarks. It is no wonder Marietta was once considered

the most civilized city west of the Alleghenies. All kinds of historical characters have set foot there— including Lafayette, Harman and Margaret Blennerhassett, Johnny Appleseed and the early settler of the area, Rufus Putnam.

We associate rich histories with haunts and Marietta has more than a few. In the older Harmar section of the small city, there is a house built in 1859 by Douglas Putnam for his wife Eliza. The home is an exact replica of a house Eliza admired on the Hudson

The Anchorage COURTESY KRISTALL CHAMBERS

River in New York. The Putnams had always been one of the wealthier families in Marietta. Sadly, Eliza Putnam did not get to fully enjoy her handsome house, as she became sick soon after it was completed, and died there in 1862.

The author with a strange energy vortex behind her as she walks into the Eliza Putnam bedroom.
COURTESY KRISTALL CHAMBERS

Since then, many have sensed a "presence" that appears to wait at the bottom of the staircase. Cold spots are reported throughout the house. A few people have actually claimed to see Eliza Putnam at the bottom of the stairs, as if she is greeting her guests for a grand party or celebration.

In later years, the Putnam house became the Anchorage Nursing home. Over the years, employees of the nursing home noticed a number of uncanny things. They noticed that after they closed up the kitchen at night, having turned off all the overhead lights, that the lights would be back on for the early morning shift. One woman even took the time to write down exactly when she turned off the lights in a notebook. The very next morning the overhead lamps would be on again. The Anchorage is a historical building open to the public. Eliza Putnam's presence remains—while she is not seen, she is certainly felt.

There are other spirits in the old Anchorage. A spirit called "The Colonel" also haunts the place, especially near the widow's walk, where groups of men used to gather to play cards. The spirit of the Colonel is most active around the 4th of July, when the Putnam family enjoyed speeches, celebrations and picnics on the front lawn. The Colonel appears as an elderly man dressed in a white linen suit with black tie. Also, the ghost of a former druggist in a long white coat over striped pants and a carriage driver with a black moustache haunts the house. The sound of a piano can be heard when Sunday school was held for residents. Apparitions of Civil War soldiers in Union uniforms have been sighted on the property as well.

Another important haunted place in downtown Marietta is the historic Lafayette Hotel. It appears that the former manager and hotel owner S. Durward Hoag still likes to make his presence known. Mr. Hoag often appears as flashes of light—similar to a light bulb going off whenever a picture is taken.

The ghost of Durward Hoag is most active on the 3rd floor of the hotel. Whether this is due to Hoag's presence or the suicide that took place there, we don't know. Light bulbs throughout the hotel tend to flicker and even explode whenever the spirit of Hoag is around.

The Ghost of Johnny Appleseed, Dexter City, Ohio

Located on an overgrown hilltop, where Ohio's I-77 intersects with Old Route 821 north of Marietta, is the old Chapman family cemetery—an unimpressive briar patch where less than a dozen modest graves lie in ruins. It is believed the graveyard is haunted by the specter of a gaunt man dressed in rags, with wild, dark hair and hazel eyes ablaze.

The Chapmans were early pioneers in Washington County, having arrived in the area in the mid-to late 1700s. They were a simple, hard-working family who settled along Duck Creek between Whipple and Dexter City. But it is the one Chapman who is not buried at the cemetery that causes motorists to stop and historians to gawk, someone who inspires families to pose for pictures in front of the large monument paid for by the pennies of schoolchildren along Route 821. These are the graves of the siblings and stepmother of John Chapman, otherwise known as Johnny Appleseed.

Depending on your outlook, John Chapman was an unsophisticated 19th century preacher, a neo-pagan hero, a visionary soul, or just a plain old sower of apple seeds.

Some recent writings claim Johnny was the American Dionysus, Greek god of pleasure, spiritual intoxication and wine. Many point out that when an apple is sliced in half the seeds create a pentagram. Even in the "Witches Tarot," the card for "the Fool," (representing faith and trust, making a leap or taking a chance, encountering the wilds, or facing the rough magic of a wilderness) corresponds to the "mythic figure" of Johnny Appleseed. Yet Johnny Appleseed was real!

There is no doubt the Shawnee Indians were in awe of John Chapman because he did in fact, seem to have unusual powers. To harm or dishonor such a great person would certainly bring misfortune on their tribe. They wouldn't dare harm the wild man. That's why the Indians always allowed Johnny to sleep in their encampments whenever winter closed in.

John Chapman cared more for others than he ever did himself. While his outer appearance was craggy and austere, his inner world of God and spirit was rich and varied. John's only wish in life was to spread his vision of heaven and to love and care for others.

Although Johnny Appleseed died in Indiana around the age of 70, it is said his spirit often visits the graves of his relatives on a hilltop quite visible from I-77.

Many say he left the Ohio Valley in bitterness over a broken-love promise. A girl promised to Appleseed married someone else. Although the young lady's name is no longer remembered, it is said she decided not to marry John thinking him "just too odd." With his lumpy, wounded feet, wild hair, craggy beard and ragged clothes, John Chapman didn't appear to be a very good prospect for a young pioneer woman.

Bitterness followed Johnny, but love never left him. Except for preaching and planting, love was the only thing John knew how to do. That's why his grave in Indiana is always covered with apples of every variety, thank you notes, and an epitaph that reads "John Chapman 1774-1845—He Lived for Others".

Adena Indian Mounds & the State Penitentiary at Moundsville

Anyone who has visited Moundsville, West Virginia knows the town is famous for two things—it has mysterious Indian burial mounds built two thousand years ago and a Civil War era prison with an extremely violent history. The prison closed down in 1994. The Gravecreek Mound is located directly beside the penitentiary. This conical 69-foot mound was well within the view of the prisoners, who had more than enough time to stare out the window and ponder their fates.

When you put these two factors together—the disturbance or removal of human remains and artifacts in one instant, coupled with a

One of the more haunted areas at Moundsville Penitentiary
COURTESY MARK CHAMBERS

place that has seen much violence, evil and sadness, you have the right ingredients for an unpleasant haunting.

The electric chair at Moundsville was once given the name "Sparky." Near the chair, many have reported feeling icy cold spots, having iron doors clanging, the shuffling of footsteps and the disembodied voices of men. Shadow people appear as shadows with no distinct features, and have been photographed in several spots.

Strange apparition in the Sugar Shack area in Moundsville Penitentiary.
COURTESY MARK CHAMBERS

There are now tours and ghost hunts of the old prison; a number of people have even paid to spend the night and investigate its hauntings. On one trip, a group from Parkersburg videotaped one of the guides telling stories from one of the more violent areas of the prison. Slowly, a wailing cry intensified and grew louder as the guide talked. The wailing voices indicated great suffering. Another one of the women in the group felt as if she was being choked by a powerful hand gripping her neck.

Unexplained dark mists have appeared throughout the building. In the Sugar Shack area, where the most violent or dangerous prisoners were placed, strange subhuman looking formations were seen, like creatures from a Bosch painting. Many of these Sugar Shack prisoners were self-professed Satanists, shunned by the rest of the population.

Keith-Albee Performing Arts Center

Built in 1928 as an opulent movie palace, the Keith-Albee Performing Arts Center in Huntington houses not only concerts and off-Broadway productions, but a number of ghosts and presences. The woman's restroom is the most active with spirits. The restroom door has been known to swing open, then close all on its own accord. Muffled footsteps are heard regularly outside the projection booth, and the sound of human voices echo in the building whenever workers enter in late morning or early afternoon. Employees speak of a feeling of "fullness," of unseen personalities or visitors in the theater even when the building is empty. A little girl in a white dress has been seen sitting in the chairs on the third row of the theater and near the balcony. Childish footsteps are often heard skipping through the aisles, along with a feminine humming, as if the girl is looking for someone to play with.

Dark Night of the Soul—Darkish Knob, Parsons

The ghost of a young slave woman is said to return to Darkish Knob near Parsons, West Virginia on the eve of the anniversary of her death that occurred more than 140 years ago.

Hers is one of many spirits of runaway slaves that are believed to haunt Darkish Knob, an area that once was an important stop on the Underground Railroad. This hiding place for the slaves was actually in a house tucked within the dark foliage at the bottom of the mountain, a secluded spot not visible from the road.

The evening was especially foggy, draped in veils that hung over the mountains. For a while the young woman seemed to be reaching her destination with few obstacles to detain her. But on reaching the bottom of Darkish Knob, the slave lost her direction. She came up on the meeting place in the dark and didn't see the house. Instead, she and her horse climbed the steep embankment; she assumed the stop on the Underground Railroad was on the other side of the hill.

Horse and rider went up the path that overlooked the Cheat River. As they started toward the summit of Darkish Knob, the horse lost its footing, causing them to fall into the river below. The horse swam to safety but the girl was killed. They did not find her body for several days, and when they did the look of horror frozen on her face haunted the rescuers for many years.

On the anniversary of the slave girl's death, residents of Parsons claim to hear her moaning cries at twilight. As it grows closer to midnight, the cries turn into earsplitting screams. Some claim the ghost of the horse is a white mare. This may be another variation on the Banshee tale—interesting since the woman was not Irish or Scottish. Such tales get re-told and combined and thus, this ghost story is an intriguing blend of cultures and influences that continue in Appalachia.

Phantom of Tollgate

Early in the evening, during a light, misting rain, a Clarksburg couple drove home after visiting relatives in Parkersburg. They came upon an area called "Tollgate," a place in Ritchie County near the Doddridge County line. There they noticed a man climbing over an embankment, waving his arms wildly as if to flag down a car. Before the couple caught him directly in the beams, his figure vanished. Yet the man's expression told them something was terribly wrong. Perhaps his car had veered off the highway, and he was hurt or in serious trouble. The couple turned their vehicle around and returned to check on the man, but found no living soul in sight.

After arriving in Clarksburg, the couple phoned the state police and asked if there had been an accident or stranded motorist in the Tollgate area. The police seemed puzzled and said no one had reported either. When the couple told a female relative about their strange encounter, she said, "Did you not hear? A man was killed on that lonely stretch of road a few weeks ago. They didn't find his body at first. Emergency workers said he tried to climb up to Route 50, but never made it that far. His dead body lay just a few feet from the road for a couple of days. Good thing it was cold…sounds to me like you two saw a ghost!"

Headless Ghost of Dorcas Hollow

It seems many areas have a bone-chilling tale of a headless ghost such as Washington Irving's classic tale *The Legend of Sleepy Hollow*. One such tale is The Headless Ghost of Dorcas Hollow, near Petersburg in Grant County, West Virginia, where a man was murdered and savagely decapitated.

George Van Meter migrated to Grant County in the mid-1700s from his native Germany. He married a local woman who was also of German descent. They soon started a family and homesteaded in Dorcas Hollow about fifteen miles from what is now Petersburg.

The entire area of Grant County was sparsely populated, but George Van Meter eked out a living for himself and his family by toiling the soil and working as a carpenter.

Perhaps Grant County had appeared like a biblical Garden of Eden to the Van Meters. The Van Meter farm was directly situated in the midst of the blue Allegheny Mountains and green meadows of the Potomac Highlands. No other place felt as peaceful to George Van Meter, or so removed from the troubles of the world.

That is, until one July 4th when the Van Meters prepared to join their neighbors down the hollow for a much-anticipated Independence Day celebration and picnic. George Van Meter and his son David were working in the fields when they noticed a band of Huron Indians coming out of the woods near the edge of their property.

The Indian's faces were painted black, an ominous sign. George told his son David to retreat back to the house and gather up his mother and the children. George Van Meter ordered David to take the rest of the family and run away as fast as they could and to not even take the time to look back!

The Van Meter family fled to the closest settlement, where they learned neighbors had been massacred by the Hurons. After David and the other Van Meters fled, George fought the Hurons valiantly, but not well enough to save his own life. When other settlers returned with David, they found George Van Meter dead, and beheaded. The men searched for the head until dark, but never found it.

But the next day a cooking pot filled with water was discovered just outside the settlement. When the men opened the lid to the pot, George Van Meter's boiled and grinning skull, with lidless eyes, swam to the surface to meet their horrified gazes. Fearing the Van Meter family would be upset by the gruesome sight, the men hastily buried the head on the spot.

The body, with a full burial service, was buried later. Because the scene of George's murder was too painful for the family to return to, they moved to another part of Grant County. For years, no one would even venture near what was once the Van Meter farm.

Perhaps mere superstition about the murder kept people away. The belief that a soul cannot rest if it is missing a part of its body, is a strongly held belief that goes back to the time of the Ancient Egyptians. According to the Egyptians, if the body is not intact, the soul of the deceased will not be able to rest or enjoy the afterlife. Therefore, respectful treatment and care of a corpse is essential for the soul finding peace in the afterlife.

Does the apparition of George Van Meter appear at Dorcas Hollow searching for his missing head? Many locals claim he does.

Throughout the years, some who have traveled along Route 220 have reported seeing the shuffling body of a headless man wandering the fields and woods near Dorcas Hollow. Many say George's ghostly body, with broad, level shoulders, is encased in a glowing blue light. The ghost never utters a word. He never approaches anyone. The apparition seemingly wanders, without direction, as if fumbling for something he might have lost.., lost long ago in Dorcas Hollow.

Headless Ghost at North Bend State Park

The following tale was given to us by Terry Elliott of Cairo:

Another disturbing headless ghost tale comes from what is now the North Bend State Park Road in Ritchie County. About one hundred years ago, between the small communities of Cairo and Harrisville, the headless ghost of a man was said to haunt an area of Park Road near the Jug Handle Campgrounds. But the ghost did not appear on the paved roadway that exists today. It was then a rough and tumble dirt path, frequented mostly by men who worked on the oil wells that flourished in Ritchie County at the time.

North Bend State Park did not exist then. Instead, the rolling hills and slopes were dotted by numerous oil drilling sites, with men more than happy to claim their piece of the proverbial oil boom pie, or at least land a job that paid more than a month of work on a West Virginia farm ever could.

But tragically, one day, a worker was killed in an oil well explosion. This happened not far from Jug Handle Campground, where workers would gather to be driven by horse and buggy to the oil well sites. The victim's body parts were gathered up and later buried, but the unfortunate man's head was never found.

A few years after the explosion, a gentleman by the last name of Furr (first name unknown) drove a buggy from the camp, taking workers up to their oil well sites in what was basically a taxi service. Furr would pick up men at Cairo's train depot and drive them out to their assigned oil wells.

It was nearing dusk one quiet evening when Mr. Furr preceded down the dirt road past the Jug Handle Campground, along his usual route. He came across a low creek that did not have a bridge. It was shallow enough for him to drive his buggy through and allow the horses to drink. Furr let go of the reins so his horses could refresh themselves.

As the horses drank, Furr felt the weight of the back end of the buggy bear down as if someone had just climbed on. He turned to see a man's death-pale hands clasping the back seat. Thinking someone was making a fool of him, Furr raised up to catch sight of whomever it was involved in such foolishness.

But no flesh and blood man was playing with Furr. The figure grasping a hold of the back of the buggy was missing his head. All that lay beneath the shirt collar was what looked to be a bloody stump.

Almost immediately, Furr was convinced it was the ghost of the decapitated oil well worker. Terrified, he drove his horses at a breakneck speed back to Cairo. Amazingly, the bloody torso held on fiercely for most of the ride.

By the time Furr got home, the ghost was gone. Where did the headless man go? Mr. Furr wasn't sure. He knew one thing, though. He'd not be driving his buggy past the Jug Handle Campgrounds near dark again. Furr wasn't about to challenge this grisly apparition, especially one that appeared to him in such a violent and disturbing manner.

Yet Another Headless Ghost!

Pax is located thirty-six miles from the capitol of Charleston and is an isolated village in Fayette County. Sometimes near dusk, the ghost of a man is glimpsed walking along the railroad tracks into town, toward Pax's city hall. The man is reported to be carrying something, at first believed to be a lantern. On closer inspection by witnesses, it is the ghost's own head that he holds!

Many believe the spirit is the residual energy of a man who was decapitated along the railroad tracks many years before. Ghost experts know, however, that headless ghosts do not always mean decapitations. Typically, when an apparition appears solid enough for witnesses to see, he is usually minus some body part. The Pax ghost is missing the most important appendage of all—his head.

The Witch & The Wampus Cat

There is a power witches have called "glamoury" that allows them to transform themselves into any thing that they might choose such as a dog, a cat, a bird or just a more beautiful human being. This is where our term "glamour" comes from. Interestingly, though, the root of the word for "glamour" is "grammar," meaning to recite a spell or incantation. The witch's power of glamoury is shown in the fairy tale *Snow White*, where the beautiful witch transforms herself into an aged crone in order to win Snow White's trust so she will accept the poison apple.

Among mountain folklore in the hills of West Virginia, there is a story passed down about an unmarried woman who had "special powers" who lived in a mountain community. This woman stayed pretty much to herself and she seemed to favor animals over people. It was rumored this isolated woman was in fact a witch endowed with supernatural powers that she could use for both good and ill.

Local livestock started disappearing. The cows dried up and would give no milk. The beginning of growing season suffered a serious drought. This had to be the fault of the witch. The people had noticed her sharp and mysterious looks.

Many claimed it was the witch's power of glamoury that enabled her to turn herself into a large, gold-eyed, tuft-eared cat that many referred to as a "Wampus Cat." Now as a cat, whenever doors would open, the witch would sneak into houses of unsuspecting families and wait until they all fell asleep. She would pilfer objects from the family to be used in future spells. The witch would then cast her spell over the family causing them to be unable to wake up during her nighttime roaming.

As the Wampus Cat she would teleport herself through the walls, then out to the barn where she would take lambs and calves.

For many years, the witch continued her flagrant stealing by using her glamoury spells. She wasn't stopped until some locals caught on to her stealthy, witchy ways.

One night, some village men decided to wait in their barns for the witch, just as she transformed herself into the Wampus Cat. Startled in mid-spell, the witch had only partly changed herself into the cat when the men frightened her. Part of her face and breast was woman but the rest of her was a monstrous cat. The witch yowled, fled the barn and disappeared into the woods.

After that, the witch never returned to her home, but over the years the people in her community have been awakened by a mournful howling in the woods at night.

In Virginia and Tennessee, the Wampus Cat is a Cherokee Indian legend and somewhat different tale. In fact, some believe the entire tale of the Wampus Cat originated with the Native Americans. Among the mountain Cherokee Indians in North Carolina, the Wampus Cat is called Ewah. Its story began with a large wild cat that plagued the hunters of the tribe. It killed off all of the game, causing the people to go hungry.

One Cherokee woman that did not trust her husband during hunts put on a mountain lion skin and tracked the group to see what he was doing. When the Cherokee braves caught her prowling, she was punished by the truth and was doomed to wear the cat skin until eternity. She is doomed to scavenge the mountains as the dreaded Ewah, ready to gobble up bad people's souls.

Another story tells of another Cherokee woman who wore the mask of the cat to spy on her husband while in the woods. She thought perhaps he was lying to her about going hunting and she wanted to catch him in the act of some infidelity.

When she happened upon her husband, he was innocently tracking a deer. But when the husband saw the dreadful mask his wife concocted, he was driven insane by fear. The Cherokee man ran away never to be seen again. As the woman attempted to pull the mask from her face, she found it was stuck to her skin.

Now the young woman, another Ewah or Wampus Cat, must wander the mountain's deep thickets to this day in order to make peace or find resolution with the husband she misjudged and scared away.

Briggs Public Library & Woodlawn Cemetery, Ironton, Ohio

Southwest of Gallipolis along the Ohio River, is Ironton, a modest city with an immodest number of haunts.

For instance, the Briggs Public Library sits on the grounds of the former home of a Doctor Joseph Lowry. His ghost allegedly appears, because Lowry had a business argument with the local undertaker and thus, his body was made a mess of during the embalming (or lack of) process. It seems that after death, the good doctor simply fell apart. Many claim that during the stillness of evening in the library, the doctor's footsteps are heard dragging and echoing throughout. Many are convinced it is Dr. Lowry searching for his lost body parts in the library's rooms and halls.

But the Briggs Library is not Dr. Lowry's only place to haunt. He also appears to startled visitors in Woodlawn Cemetery where he is buried. The doctor's apparition wanders aimlessly, trying to pull himself back together.

There is also a statue in Woodlawn that overlooks the grave of a woman murdered by her husband. A handprint stays on the statue's cheek and many say the statue remains warm to the touch. Some have tried to remove the stain from the statue's cheek, but it always reappears.

Others claim the cemetery also houses the remains of a ballerina who was interred in a mausoleum. It is said the ballerina dances on the lawn of the graveyard under the moonlight, demonstrating unearthly spins to all who are lucky enough to glimpse her form.

THIRTEEN
How Do I Know If I Am Being Haunted?

The appearance of ghosts and other types of haunts often begin in a very subtle manner. You may not even notice them in the initial phase of the haunting unless you are a person who is "tuned in" to these spiritual energies. It is only when the haunts become impossible to ignore that we begin to experience the surreal world of haunted houses and ghosts. And this is where the fun begins.

Fun? But, of course! If you find yourself in the midst of a true haunting, count yourself as one of the lucky ones. Many would love to meet up with a ghost, but never do.

Scared? There is really no reason to be. The vast majority of apparitions are quite harmless. Also, since ghosts are not of this physical world, they are usually not able to harm us in any physical way. Oh, there are a few who may trip you or pull your hair. They may break your camera or twist your ear. But that's about as bad as it gets, except in the case of malevolent spirits where there are some psychological dangers that we covered earlier.

How does one know if one is being haunted? There are certain elements of hauntings that are universal. These happen across the board and occur no matter what country you are in, what language you speak or what culture you live in.

So—do you think you may have met up with an actual ghost or are you living in a haunted house? Read on and see if the following rings a bell. . . some delightfully, frightfully, ghostly bell.

⌘ You feel as if you are being watched. . . You know how it happens. The skin on the back of your neck crawls. Hairs lift. Other souls are watching you—you're sure of it. As soon as you turn around no one is there. Did they leave? Do they no longer watch? Of course, not! Your

ghosts are still watching, enjoying the show. One thing we have learned
from the spirit world, they are just as curious about us as we are about
them—maybe more so. As soon as you realize that spirits are really
no threat, you can learn to live with your ghost. Such spirits probably
haven't been in the world for a while and want to experience it all over
again. Ghosts have feelings, too.

⌘ The sudden appearance of unusual odors or smells. . . The presence
of odd smells or odors that are otherwise unaccounted for is often
the initial phase of a genuine haunting. Smells can be the first (albeit
indirect) way that a spirit makes itself known. Sweet perfumes and the
scent of flowers seem to be a favorite among spirits. Keep a log of smells
turning up in areas of your home or haunted area. This can be a good
clue as to who it might be that is actually haunting your place. Foul
odors, on the other hand, are generally not a good sign. Repulsive smells
may indicate malevolent ghosts and spirits.

⌘ Waking up to a feeling of a presence in your room. . . Many of you
already know the feeling. You startle awake. Your heart pounds. Much
to your horror, you realize you are also paralyzed. You can't move a
muscle—not a baby finger! You sense someone there. A terrible weight
crushes you into the mattress. . . sits on your chest. Now, whatever it
is pulls you by your ankles to the bottom of the bed. In worse case
scenarios, there may even be the sensation of a sexual violation. This
is no doubt the most terrifying spirit experience of all. Not because the
ghostly presence is going to hurt you. It is simply because during such a
state, there is very little you can do to stop it. This state of psychic attack
is called the "Old Hag" or "Night Paralysis."

Researchers think this has little to do with ghosts but I am not so sure.
I've had attacks of this "Night Paralysis" throughout my life and they
always occur in the houses where I've lived that are the most haunted.
They also tended to occur whenever I opened up a bit more psychically,
as well. I believe this dreaded appearance of the "Old Hag" (fear of it
caused me to have insomnia for many years) is both a physical and a
psychic attack. Some researchers believe that paralysis happens when
we wake up during a period when our muscles have been paralyzed to
keep us from thrashing around and hurting ourselves during deeper
sleep cycles. During the Middle Ages the "Old Hag" was associated with
demonic attacks such as the Incubus (a spirit that has sex with sleeping

women) or a Succubus (a spirit that has sex with sleeping men). If you find yourself the victim of too many "Night Hag" violations you may want to bring in a psychic, a healer or some other holy person to try and get rid of it. Prayer often breaks the spell but cursing works almost as well. Recent research shows if you sleep on the left side (and not in a supine position) you will have less of a chance of having an "Old Hag" attack. Why? No one knows for sure. Maybe it is because you are keeping your heart, your vital self, covered and protected. Never sleep flat on your back if you are prone to this strange sensation.

⌘ Drafts and cold spots. The presence of ghosts is associated with cold spots, and that means a significant drop in temperature from one room to the next. However, such drafts or frigid areas are not limited to indoors. The next time you visit a cemetery, for instance, you may notice how much cooler the air seems to be inside the gates. Why? Some theorize spirits use natural heat or thermal energies in order to appear or manifest in such way that they can be noticed. In other words, ghosts may use heat to gain vital energy. Cold spots do occur in most cases of haunts, whether the spirits turn out to be malevolent or benign. But a scarier explanation may be that death is damned cold.

⌘ Hearing glass shattering or ice being dropped into sinks, yet when you check out the area, nothing is there. This is a familiar story once you start investigating or studying ghosts.

⌘ Feeling a weight or seeing an impression at the foot of a bed, seeing the shape of a human body outlined in the sheets, or feeling any kind of weight or impression on a piece of furniture. These are another universal indication of a haunting. Visiting New Orleans a few years ago, we visited the former house of the Voodoo Queen Marie Laveau. Later in the evening, at the Royal Sonesta Hotel, my small daughter gasped and said that there was the shape of a woman's face in her pillowcase. Wanting to reassure her that pillowcases sometimes crease like that, and that it is only our minds playing tricks on us, I was shocked to see that my daughter was right. There was the outline of a very pretty woman's face in the pillowcase. Marie Laveau was quite a beauty. Did the Voodoo Queen visit us? Perhaps.

⌘ Unexplained electrical malfunctions such as problems with television sets, clocks, phones, computers, or lighting. After I attended a blessing ceremony with Tibetan Lamas a few years ago, the energies in my house went wild. The night of the blessing, the television set switched itself on after I walked upstairs to bed. I walked downstairs, turned off the television and went back to my room to sleep. The next morning, I awakened to the telephone ringing. As I sat up, the television in my bedroom suddenly switched on. For this particular week in my life, the TVs turned themselves on two to three times per day. So, what can it mean? Spirits are electrical in nature and in order to become detectable they will often resort to drawing upon various types of electrical equipment to get their batteries charged. Why is this? It is the easiest way. It is so much easier than trying to distract or connect with the mind of a human that is preoccupied by other things. In keeping with this, spirits will also use other electrical items, most especially lights. If you've ever gone into an old haunted theater or library, you may notice how erratically the lights tend to flicker. No need to worry, it's just the spirits saying, "We are here."

⌘ Hearing your name called when no one else is around. Hearing your name being called or whispered into your ear may be explained by one of two things. A person close to you may simply have you on his or her mind. This is one form of telepathy (thought transference) and is fairly common. The other explanation may be that spirits are simply trying to get your attention. This does bring up the question—are the ghostly voices audible to others? In my experience, yes! Other people around usually hear the same spirit voices. This means spirit voices you are hearing as well as other examples of ghosts are not just happening inside your head. Makes one feel a bit less cuckoo, eh?

⌘ Feeling touched, patted or caressed. It must seem odd that a nonphysical being would be capable of human touch, but such is often the case. During our ghost tours each fall, several participants have reported being caressed, fondled and having their hair tugged on around or near the Weeping Woman statue at Riverview Cemetery. It is her job to watch over the graves of Stonewall Jackson's relatives. But the Weeping Woman seems not to like having her picture taken. This was an interesting development since earlier in the tour I dreamed of a woman's icy hand caressing mine. It was not a bad feeling but the hand was eerily cold.

⌘ An awareness of being brushed or touched indicates a pretty intense haunting. It takes a lot of power for a spirit to come across in a physical way. So, if this has happened to you, take your ghost seriously.

⌘ Someone in the home begins drinking heavily. Unfortunately this happens more frequently than most would ever imagine. Many of the most talented mediums throughout the history of Spiritualism ended up alcoholics. Never drink alcohol while communicating with the spirit world. This is extremely treacherous.

⌘ Stuff gets lost and then turns up in unlikely places. Missing objects are often the way poltergeists start out. Researchers have found that where there are poltergeists there are usually other ghosts. Look for objects of significance getting lost and then turning up in obvious places. The items may be family heirlooms, or objects that are associated with a family member who has passed away but now wishes to communicate with the living. The spirit of my maternal grandmother placed one of her hankies on my cousin's pillowcase. My cousin hadn't seen the handkerchief in years, and then suddenly there it was, there on her pillow. Grandmother was simply making her presence known. There are also nonsensical manifestations of objects, such as finding your hairbrush in the refrigerator or your toothbrush in the toilet. In this instance, it's only your ghost trying to get your attention.

⌘ The appearance of poltergeists. "Poltergeist" is a German term with Greek origins, which means "noisy spirits" or "to rap or to knock." The poltergeist attack usually begins out as loud banging noises. Ordinary objects fly about. Things get broken. Beds begin to shake. Typically, the poltergeist will pester one person in the family more than the others. That person is normally a teenager under stress or with an emotional problem.

⌘ But aren't poltergeists actually ghosts? Over the last fifty years, the appearance of poltergeists is believed to be a latent ability that humans have to move objects with the mind. Such individuals are thought to have some inner turmoil, which creates the right setting for the poltergeist to occur. This is a form of "telekinesis," moving objects with the powers of the mind. Such abilities often occur around adolescents in crisis, usually at the beginning of puberty. Often the poltergeist activity goes away or becomes buried around the age of twenty. However, the experiences can continue at various times throughout their lives. Only recently, psychic researchers have begun to notice that poltergeists tend to occur simultaneously with other hauntings and involve spirits of deceased persons. It could be that spirits also use the electromagnetic powers of the human mind to appear, especially in the case of psychics who are very in tune with their powers. In this way, the person acts as a portal or doorway for other spirits to arrive. Poltergeists certainly fascinate, but before you do an exorcism on your home, keep in mind that poltergeists usually lose energy, fade, and almost always go away on their own.

⌘   Certain rooms in a house exhibit dinginess or unexplained shadows no matter how good the lighting is. Houses and rooms absorb all kinds of energies. The minute a person walks into your home, he or she will change the energy in your home. Usually, if the feeling in the room is bright and expansive, no one really worries about ghosts. On the other hand, if your spirits are earthbound and are of a melancholy nature, the room will take on a dinginess or shadowy quality. For some unknown reason ghosts thrive best in the shadows. They may hang out in sunlight, too, but it is possible more ethereal appearances are not as easy to determine in glaring light as they are in subtle shade. But if you find corners in a house that seem impossible to light well, this is probably the area of the house that is the most haunted.

⌘   Dreams that are not typical, involving people you may not know. There are some dreams that are so vivid or real that when we wake up the next morning, we already feel already tired from the dream. Such dreams tend to have a psychic component, maybe involving people we do not know in our waking world. Such dreams can involve the ghosts that have moved into your life, especially if your dream is recurring and the people you see in your dream are detailed and quite specific. You may want to consider the possibility that your dream characters are actual people, either living or deceased. The living people may be ones to whom you have a psychic connection. If you get specifics in your dream such as names, locations or events, go to the library or courthouse and see what you can find out about your ghost. You may begin to understand why your ghost was initially attracted to you.

⌘   Pets or other animals may appear frightened or avoid specific places or rooms in the house. Do you have a room or a corner where pets refuse to go? Arc there certain areas in your home that tend to unnerve your cats or places where dogs begin to growl? Animals rely upon their instincts, and are able to see and hear things that human beings normally do not. Many cases of pets discerning spirits have been documented. If you find your life besieged by apparitions and ghostly energies, take into consideration the places where your pets act the strangest. These often turn out to be "hot spots" of ghostly activity.

⌘ Setting off buzzers and alarms. By this, I mean YOU and not your ghosts. (Well, maybe it's a little bit of both.) If you are in contact with spirits, you may begin to notice that you tend to set off buzzers and other alarms. In my town, this is not a problem because everyone knows me. If I set off the bomb alert at the post office or shoplifting alarms at my local bookstore, no one is too surprised. You may get a few funny glances as you are walking across a parking lot and your car lights come on and the engine suddenly starts up. Just don't chuckle to the stranger beside you and say, "Did you see that? It always does that whenever I come around!" You may also notice streetlights flicker and go out when you walk under them. This is just one interesting aspect of dealing with the paranormal. It's fascinating and usually temporary, so enjoy it.

⌘ Unexplained health problems, specifically headaches or feeling drained. There is little doubt that directly communicating with spirits can wear you out. Disembodied entities will draw upon your resources, draining you. If your spirit gives you the creeps, you can ring bells, or chimes, or clap your hands loudly in spiritually dangerous areas. This may seem ridiculous, but most spirits, like small animals, avoid high-pitched noises or ringing sounds.

One other problem, which is both physical and emotional, is suffering from depressive episodes. This may indicate spiritual oppression where some negative entity has wormed its way into your life. Using bells, burning sage, creating circles of protection and white-lighting exercises can all work to get rid of any negative spiritual influences in your everyday life.

⌘ Seeing shapes that float, dark spots, small lights or shadows. Perceiving ghosts can sometimes be like staring at a faint star. When looking directly at it, the star seems to fade or disappear. But when you look at it slightly askew, it comes into focus. The same is true of ghosts, especially if there are several moving about. Sometimes, apparitions are most visible when looking out of the corner of your eye. Pay attention to quick movements. Ghost orbs can be seen by the human eye, but they most often appear lightning quick. You can train yourself to recognize them; all you need is patience.

⌘ Waking up suddenly at the same time each night. This can clue you in on the hour that ghostly powers are strangest in your home. It can be your haunts are waking you up in order to convey some message. Waking at the same hour can also indicate the hour your ghost may have died and this is his way of reminding you that he is not entirely gone. Continuance seems to be the main theme among ghosts. It is just one way of telling us that we never truly die.

⌘ Hearing music or singing at odd hours when no one else is around. Music seems to remain important to those in the spirit world. Many ghosts communicate through music such as disembodied singing eking through when you're on the phone. It's also not unusual for radios and CD players to start up on their own in haunted houses. Hearing ghostly voices and choruses layered over piped-in elevator music is fairly common. Often, the music has a religious tone, sounding like a Catholic mass or sopranos of angelic choirs. Apparently there is no rock n' roll music in heaven or the afterworld, and for that, I am disappointed.

⌘ When taking photographs, you capture material that looks like mist or fog that was not there when you snapped the shot.

⌘ When entering a room, you feel a presence as if a crowd has just left. It is interesting to walk through a house and realize that empty rooms often feel full. The energy is still present, it seems, from all of the people who've lived or even visited there. Rooms that feel "full" are often the most haunted rooms in the house.

⌘ Last but not least, seeing someone who shouldn't be there! First of all, it's not like in the movies where ghosts appear as filmy, see-through apparitions, with full moon light misting around while the wind blows. Ghosts and apparitions often appear solid and look much as they did in life. Sometimes the spirits are missing a head or their feet. This is because it takes great energy for ghosts to appear, so the extremities (heads and feet) tend to get left behind. However, because the apparition is mostly solid, we are tricked into thinking it is a living person. It is only when the spirit vanishes that we realize we have been in contact with the spirits of the dead. If you think you will die of fright upon seeing an apparition, think again. Apparitions disappear quickly. You won't have time to have heart failure.

What If I Want To Get Rid Of My Ghosts?

You actually want to get rid of your ghost? Even after we have assured you that probably nothing bad is going to happen? Okay, okay, we do have some techniques to banish spirits. Here is a list of a few things that you can do:

⌘ **Smudging**. Try burning some sage. This is an old Native American method for banishing negative spirits. Buy a wand of sage at your local herb shop. Put some in an ashtray or shell, set it afire and let the smoke infiltrate the area. Make sure you blow the smoke in the four directions: north, west, east and south. This is very important in Native American spirituality. Plains Indians believed smoke traveled upward into the spirit world. Ghosts will follow the smoke. It creates a path. It is interesting to note that sage is a natural antiseptic.

⌘ **Using Bells or Cymbals.** Spirits flee from sudden, high-pitched sounds, especially if the spirits are negative. The ringing of bells or cymbals will shatter such ghosts. They hardly ever come back as strong if you keep this up. Brass bells work well. Cymbals from Tibet are the finest ones I've ever used. Clapping your hands loudly, especially around the areas of the haunting, can also be effective in getting rid of your ghosts. Shamans throughout the world often use rattles, bells or clapping in their exorcism and other spiritual rituals.

⌘ **Prayer.** This can't hurt but it may not help that much either. You can use whatever prayer makes you feel the most comfortable. Admittedly, this is not the best defense against ghosts. However, prayer does let your ghost know that you are seriously trying to put him out of your house.

⌘ **Exorcism.** Any number of spiritual leaders or clergy can perform an exorcism such as Catholic priests, fundamentalist preachers, psychics, Native American shamans and even Druids. One fair warning. Exorcism can make matters worse. Why? Many ghosts crave attention. They will gravitate where all of the excitement is. I recommend that you resort to exorcism only if nothing else seems to help. Exorcism can pull in other spirits, and you'll have quite a ghostly mess on your hands.

⌘ **White Lighting Exercises.** White lighting techniques have been popular in New Age circles for years. Each time you feel threatened by your spirits, visualize standing in a lit cocoon of protection symbolized by a brilliant white light. Some see themselves standing inside a white aura. What this exercise does is to help center you so you can feel strong and in control of the situation. Ghosts and other spirits can be amazingly obedient to authority.

⌘ ***Tell your ghosts that they are dead.*** This may sound far-fetched, but earthbound spirits sometimes do not realize that they have already died. They will hang around places where they formerly lived or will gravitate toward people that are psychically receptive. In essence, this means your ghosts are just lost. What do you do? Enter the alpha state by relaxing and put yourself into a trance. As soon as you feel you have made contact, tell your ghost he has died and that he must turn in the direction of the bright light so he can follow it to meet his relatives there.

⌘ ***Ignore your ghost.*** Sometimes the simplest methods work the best. You may have a great deal of ghostly activity for a several weeks or months and then it will stop. The more you worry and panic over your spirits, the stronger they become. This is because the vast majority of spirits thrive on attention, energy and even fear. For instance, if a house becomes well known for haunted activity, other spirits will be drawn there. This becomes the place where all of the fun is, spiritually speaking. It's like throwing a big party for your ghosts. Ignoring your ghosts, or learning to live with them, is the best approach. They generally just go away on their own.

Places Most Likely To Be Haunted

In reading ghost stories, and listening to tales of the paranormal, it becomes pretty clear that spirits tend to choose to visit some places over others. It is important to point out, that in my opinion, there are spirits around us at any given time, but the energies of certain areas create the right atmosphere for the ghost to appear.

1. Cemeteries. This is a given! But when you really think about it, why would anyone want to go back to the place where her or his remains are buried? Cemeteries are places of high emotion, and ghosts are sensitive to this. This can help attract them. Also, some spirits may not completely accept the fact that they are dead and hang around until the body decays. Many ghosts like to be remembered and have their stories told. If people go to graveyards to remember their dead, the dead will often show up. Cemetery ghosts may learn to like it so well, they stick around to see who else is going to show up.

2. Churches. An odd choice especially since most of us are still influenced by the demonology of the Reformation and Inquisition.

With Protestantism, there was no longer a purgatory—all souls either went to heaven or hell. If a haunting started, it had to originate in hell. That's what many people thought.

But the British Isles have a long tradition of churches being haunted. The night of April 24th, St. Mark's Eve, was thought to be a time when the wraiths, phantoms and ghosts of those who will die in the coming year are said to wander through churchyards or pass through the front doors of the church. In Britain many believed those who were not baptized could glimpse dead people hoisting their coffins to the graveyard, perhaps with the idea that those not baptized were not able to distinguish good from evil. Many old churches have graveyards, as well, a good place to start a ghost hunt. As always, get permission first.

3. Battlefields. Gettysburg, Pennsylvania is considered perhaps the most haunted town in the United States. Battlefields are notoriously haunted, as are sites of intense emotion. Battlefields, where many lives are tragically cut short, create an ideal situation for many spirit recordings, and unsettled ghost business. But with most hauntings, battlefield ghosts are usually residual hauntings, where the ghost can't see you.

4. Hospitals and Nursing Homes. Once again, these are places where many people die and families grieve, setting up a perfect environment for a haunting. Of course, going on a ghost hunt or an investigation in a medical facility is about as tacky as anyone can possibly get. However, discreetly interviewing people who work in such places, is okay. In fact, I frequently hear from people who work in these places; they have some pretty amazing stories of people returning from the dead.

5. Museums. Naturally, museums have lots of old stuff of great historical and emotional value that tends to draw ghosts. Objects themselves can be haunted; as there are many famous ghost tales about haunted dolls, haunted boxes and haunted furniture. Some friends and I went on a ghost hunt in a local museum. Interestingly, the only objects that revealed ghost anomalies on our cameras were the Indian artifacts buried away in the basement. Although some of the objects were said to be close to 12,000 years old, they were still the most spiritually active artifacts in the museum.

6. Any area where an act of violence or tragedy has occurred. In these areas, ghost investigators must use their own discretion. For reasons we do not clearly understand, hauntings in such areas can be malevolent. Malevolent spirits seem to be attracted to the negativity of the place. However, if the tragedy or event happened long ago, the haunting might not be quite as intense or as active. It might only be overwhelming to people who are sensitive to such things.

7. Tunnels. Perhaps tunnels create a vortex that pulls in or amplifies ghostly energies, but tunnels are places where spirits love to hide. Some of these hauntings may have to do with fatal train wrecks, accidents in caves, people losing their way and end up dying outside in the elements. If you are looking for a place to investigate and your area has a few tunnels that are safe to visit, you might want to ask around about the stories surrounding the tunnels. They are often quite spooky to visit after dark. You might want to avoid railroad tunnels that are still used, or check the schedule and take plenty of contact gear such as cell phones. You don't want to end up as a ghost on your own investigation.

8. Schools. Children see and draw spirits better than adults do. For this reason, spirits are commonly attracted to schools. I can't begin to tell you how many pictures hit my email box with ghost anomalies that have been taken at school graduations, and children's birthday parties. There is a lot of evidence that shows that spirits thrive on excitement and children often add plenty of energy to the environment. This doesn't mean we should encourage our children to channel, visit graveyards after dark or play with Ouija boards. It does mean that when children start talking about people or personalities that others cannot see, you should listen to them. Abandoned schools, as long as you can get permission to enter, are a good place to investigate the spirit world, especially schools of a religious nature.

9. Crossroads. Universally the crossroads are considered to be a place of spiritual power and danger. Some of the crossroads' powers might have to do with the Christian cross exerting mystical powers over the area. However, the belief in the crossroads pre-dates Christianity by several centuries; the powers believed to be exist at the crossroads are not usually positive. An abandoned house at a crossroads in a rural area might be an interesting place to investigate. Of course, get an okay from the owners.

10. Hotels. Much like hospitals and schools, hotels get a lot of foot traffic. It should come as no surprise that hotels with some age to them are likely to be haunted by one type of spirit or another. The oldest hotels typically have many spirits. It's hard to predict when, where or how a hotel spirit will appear. They rarely appear to novices in a so-called "haunted room." Instead, it seems that the people who don't expect to see a ghost are the ones that invariably do.

11. Historical homes or Estates. Older homes tend to have had a number of owners, some of whom had personalities that attract ghosts. Old houses are interesting to investigate, especially if the owners are open to such things.

12. Theatres. As any actor will tell you "Every theatre has a ghost." Theatres bring out strong emotions in the people who visit them. Couple that with tragic or complex emotional tales and you set up the atmosphere for a haunting. Like bookstores that have their own resident cat, many theatres have their own resident ghost.

FOURTEEN
Are You Ready To Meet Your Ghosts?

Encountering ghosts is endlessly fascinating. Their existence indicates that there are things that we don't completely understand about our world, or even the world beyond. Observe ghosts and experience one of life's great mysteries.

Linking up with the spirit world is really not so difficult and there are many methods that can be used to achieve communications with ghosts. Overall, spirits usually have quite a lot to say. Psychic mediums have the easiest time contacting the spirit world. Many psychics are born with their talents; some never recognize they have them. This form of spirit communication is subtle; you have to be sensitive to recognize the signs that a ghost is present.

Let us look at the more blatant way that ghosts can manifest themselves. These are the kinds of spontaneous appearances that lead to the famous ghost tales. This is when you actually see the ghost right before your very eyes!

This is a type of intrusion from the spirit world. It simply means your ghosts want to get a message across and indicates some urgency. You don't have to be a psychic to see ghosts this way. In fact, ten percent of the population claims to have seen a ghost.

Incidentally, don't buy into all that touchy-feely New-Age stuff that states that only psychics can see spirits. We've found that when ghosts appear in an obvious way, the witness seldom considers him or herself to be psychic.

Truthfully, getting an account of a ghost incident from a salt-of-the-earth type can have more credibility than getting one from people who consider themselves visionaries. That means the spirit has made itself really blatant and very much wanted to make the witness aware of his presence.

With the spontaneous appearance of an apparition, the spirit looks very much as it did in life, wearing the clothes that it once wore (ones you may even recognize) and typically appearing to be around the age of 30 to 35 years old. Some speculate that thirty is an age when the person feels the most vital during physical life.

Of course, small children who have died prematurely will appear as children. If there is something about a particular age the ghost is trying to communicate, they will appear at that age.

Even such full-bodied apparitions appear for only seconds. You typically shudder and think, "Did I just see that?" This is why some eyewitnesses are lead to believe that they may have hallucinated until they meet others who have had a similar experience in the same place.

It is rare to be spoken to by an apparition, but as in the case of Zona Shue, the Greenbrier Ghost, it is possible. Apparitions tend to communicate their feelings or intents through their expressions, such as looking pleased or melancholy. Sometimes the key to their message is in the area where they appear, perhaps near a grave or an old chest, a house, a building, records, or even a piece of furniture.

The sound of a "racket", such as noisy footsteps, voices, thumping noises or even the sounds of water running or ice being dropped into a sink can also be categorized as a type of apparition. Sounds associated with ghosts are really the way most hauntings start out. The other way to perceive spirits is through clairvoyance or a type of inner vision. Psychics have honed their talents and can communicate or visualize such energies, receiving messages, symbols or words that are somehow important to the spirit when he or she was alive. This is more like channeling, as the connection is made through the psychic's cultivated sense of awareness.

Often after visiting a psychic medium, people can experience genuine spiritual contact. Many people miss an attempt from the spirits to communicate because they lack awareness of ghostly happenings that a psychic has learned to look for.

FIFTEEN
Conclusion: Why We Are Convinced the Spirit World is Real, and Why We Believe Spirits Communicate with the Living

We have quickly learned on our journey into the surreal world of the paranormal that there are "presences," and such beings permeate our day-to-day existence. They are not just some rare haunted house incident or report of ghosts. It is also apparent that many such spirits are still interested in interacting with living persons and remain curious about life on earth. They show us this time and time again through their actions and their interest in communicating with the living.

It really doesn't matter what we call our ghosts. If you call them something, they will come. As we have found, spirits are greatly responsive to human beings.

Many years ago the British Society for Psychical Research attempted a unique experiment. Members made up a name for a spirit guide and began to have séances where they attempted to communicate with this self-created spirit. The unexpected happened. Their ghost began to tip over the furniture, ring bells, make noises and was more active than any spirit they had a real name for.

Spirits are eager to communicate, and even if you are the least little bit aware, and if you have an interest in their world, they will let you know.

If you are a Scottish immigrant in the 1800s, and the spirit of a ghostly woman on a pale horse finds you on a lonely trail above some body of water, then she is probably a Banshee whose story was told in ages past. However, if you are near Point Pleasant, West Virginia in 1966 and something large and gray flies over you and then tries to outrace your car, you may want to call what you see after a comic book character "the Mothman."

If you are poor, black and living in the Mississippi Delta in the 1920s, that strange man you met at the Crossroads is mostly likely the Devil. But if you are a Black Dutch West Virginian named Woodrow Derenberger, and you encounter a dark-haired, olive-complexioned man at the crossroads at I-77 and Route 47 south of Parkersburg in November of 1966, it is the alien Indrid Cold.

A few years ago, a paranormal researcher from Virginia named Bo Kitchens drove up to Parkersburg with his wife Debbie. We had a splendid time covering haunts and hunting ghosts that afternoon. Bo and Debbie were genuinely enthused when it came to searching out ghosts. Bo, in particular, solved a number of mysteries that had always intrigued us on our ghost tour, things we never understood until he explained them to us.

When Bo and Debbie left, we thought it might be a great idea to put on a ghost conference in the Ohio Valley, an area so obviously rich with haunted activity. But before we were able to finalize plans, a tragedy unfolded. At only thirty-eight-years old, Bo suddenly died.

Although we only spent a few short hours with Bo and Debbie Kitchens in 2001, we were saddened over the loss of a person as special as Bo, a most kind and decent man.

As the ghost tour became bigger than ever in the fall of 2001, I led a troupe of schoolchildren from Mannington, West Virginia on the ghost walk. Atypically, the tour took place during a bright and colorful afternoon in mid October.

The air was clear and sunny. I thought it might be nice to take the kids directly in front of the Captain's House on Juliana Street. It has an interesting casement window where the Captain's pipe is often seen smoldering with an orange glow. I noticed the house was happily decorated for Halloween, which makes tour guides feel good about neighborhoods along the ghost walk.

As I told the ghostly tale of the sea captain, one little girl turned and commented to her friend, "Why, look there. That sign says 'Bo.'"

Shocked, I glanced over my shoulder to look at the Halloween decorations. I, too, recognized what the sign read. One of the 'o's had fallen off of the word "Boo."

The Halloween sign now read "BO." Beside it was the cartoon of a smiling ghost.

Such mysterious incidents are why we firmly believe in a world of spirits. The real fact is no living energy ever ceases to exist. It is only transformed into something different. And despite the human sadness that is often lost in these tales of haunts, as in Bo's very real story, we feel fortunate in the fact that we know clearly that life goes on.

Life is a blessing, so much so that spirits often have to remind us.

So, have fun while you're here, spirit-seekers. The spirits want you to. Take joy in your meeting up with a few new souls others may refer to as "ghosts." You and I know the secret. *They are our friends.*

Glossary

Anomaly

An event, an occurrence, an image, a materialization or even a sound than cannot be explained by traditional means. Most ghost anomalies appear in photographs. In reference to ghosts, anomalies may be a spirit when the image cannot be ruled out by ordinary means. The West Virginia Mothman might also be considered an anomaly since there was no sighting of any such creature before or after 1966 and 1967. Anomalies are things that deviate from the norm.

Apparition

An apparition is usually a ghost with an identity or a personality that the living can recognize or see—if only for a few seconds. Apparitions usually appear much as the person did in life. Typically, the clothing looks touchable, as does the rest of the ghost—except it may lack legs, feet, hands or a head. Hauntings are not uncommon but solid apparitions are. Supposedly, it takes great energy for ghosts to fully materialize and look as they once did. When seeing an apparition, don't blink your eyes. Many apparitions only show themselves for seconds— just enough time to make an impression.

Anniversary Ghost

Anniversary ghosts are hauntings or spirits that appear on a certain date or a time each year. Usually the date is significant in the spirit's previous life, such as a birth date, death anniversary, a battle or even the date of some important news or happening. The ghost of Irish aristocrat Margaret Blennerhassett tends to appear most often on October 17th and the 18th on Blennerhassett Island. No one knows why. The dates do not coincide with birthdays or dates of death of Mrs. Blennerhassett's family and she did not die tragically on the island.

Aura

A field, thought to be electromagnetic in nature that is said to surround the physical body. It appears as colored lights, bands and energy patterns. Although psychics are usually the ones who see or detect auras, they can also be glimpsed in shadowy areas such as movie theaters or darkened rooms by ordinary people. Health conditions, talents and personality are evident in the human aura.

Automatism

Automatism is a practice, a talent or a discipline that allows communications from the spirit world to flow easily to the living by such means as an Ouija board or automatic writing. Psychic Edgar Cayce accomplished automatism by going to sleep and allowing the spirit messages to be taken down by his secretary. Upon wakening, Cayce had no conscious knowledge of the psychic information that he had been given while in a sleep-like trance.

Banshee

An Irish or Scottish attendant death fairy. Banshees appear as women, young and old, ugly or beautiful, ands mainly with blood red eyes, caused by their endless weeping for the dead. Sometimes the Banshee rides a pale horse followed by a hearse. At other times, she hangs out at waterways, wailing over her dead.

Interestingly, three Irish clans that have been associated with Banshees are the O'Kennedys, the O'Lennons and O'Reagans. These names were later shortened to Kennedy, Lennon and Reagan—names of three famous men who were shot by assassins.

Banishment

Banishment is a type of ritual, spell or form of magic used to cleanse and chase away negative spirits, emotions and outcomes. Banishment is possibly a Wiccan response to the Christian Exorcism. Although the Christian form of banishment has more to do with a belief in devils and driving out diabolical forces, the Wiccan variety emphasizes getting rid of a force that is simply negative, not necessarily evil, or banishing spiritual forces that are not particularly healthy or useful.

Black Cats

Long thought to be witches familiars (helpers), black cats date back to a time in ancient Egypt where cats were worshipped, lovingly cared for and deified—even entombed with Egyptian royalty. There is no evidence that a black cat is more special than any other feline—other than the effects they have on our imaginations as shadowy forms, forever in tune with the mysterious powers of the night.

Black Dogs

Until recently, pretty much a British phenomena, black dogs have been associated with all type of occult powers and the underworld of darkness, seeming to bridge this world with the world of the dead. The legend of the black dog may even trace back to the Greek Goddess Hecate—overseer of witchcraft, the crossroads and night magic—who always traveled with three black hounds at her side. The belief in black dogs as harbingers of death and as watchers of graveyards can be traced in a modern form to Arthur Conan Doyle's Hounds of the Baskervilles. Master occultists say that if you hear more than one hound baying in your neighborhood late at night, you can be sure that Hecate is prowling the streets, working her special brand of witchcraft.

Black Dutch

A mysterious group of dark-skinned, small, colorfully dressed people who settled among the Pennsylvania Dutch. Many later settled in West Virginia. Evidence is growing that the Black Dutch were, in fact, partly German Gypsies (or Rom) who shared their unique form of magic. This includes a belief in the Crossroads, spells, ghosts, powwowing, séances and the practice of witchcraft that dates back to their point of earliest origin, India. Having "Black Dutch," "Black Swiss," or "Dirty Dutch" ancestry in West Virginia is common, especially in the northern part of the state. West Virginia's "Black Irish" are thought to be of Welsh ancestry. But the "Black Irish" have a wedding tradition of "Jumping the Broomstick" that was earlier practiced by Romanian Gypsies in the 1400s. However, the majority of West Virginia's "Black Dutch" are descendants of native Shawnee Indians.

Boggart

Related to the Night Hag, a Boggart is a mischievous ghost that crawls into the beds of sleeping people, sometimes pulling the covers off, or placing cold hands on the otherwise unaware. A horseshoe tacked over the door is said to keep Boggarts away.

Charged Area

An area or a place that has become psychically charged with unseen energies because of it being a sacred place, an area of religious relevance, or a spot that has experienced high emotion is a charged area. Typically a charged area is where a suicide, murder or unsolved death has taken place.

Corpse Candles

Corpse Candles are lights seen over graveyards, churchyards or other haunted areas. In England, they are sometimes called "fetchlights," or "spooklights," and are thought to predict the death of a family member. Corpse Candles come in all sizes and appear in almost any color.

Contactee

A contactee is a person who has one or more direct experiences with alien intelligences connected to UFOs. While some may have a direct, physical encounter with outer-space aliens, such as the claims of Mineral Wells resident Woodrow Derenberger, other contactees report a type of trance-state where they receive messages from other planets, galaxies and civilizations through telepathy or thought transference.

Conjure Book

The Bible was once referred to by some Pennsylvania Dutch as "conjure books" by which hexenmeisters or male witches used to divine knowledge used in their ritual magic and spells. There is no evidence that this unusual form of magic is being practiced today, but there is no evidence that it is not either. The Pennsylvania Dutch have been known to be secretive.

Crossroads

The Crossroads is a place of spiritual danger, where devils, witches, vampires and ghouls lurk. Some evidence suggests that the Crossroads is a haven for evil ghosts brought by the Gypsies to Eastern Europe. Legends surrounding the Crossroads have been incorporated into the Hoodoo practices along the Mississippi Delta. A book about Pennsylvania Dutch magic entitled *The Long Lost Friend* was published in 1820, and later circulated among freed blacks in New Orleans (among them Marie Laveau, "Queen of Voodoo"—1792-1897).

Curse

An ill omen is caused by evil words or thoughts—or—a profane proclamation by individuals with special powers to bring about bad luck upon others by the chanting of words, uttering threats or by using the evil eye, or sharp glance. Curses are fueled by vengeance, avarice or jealousy. The ancients feared curses to such an extent that the tradition of wearing a bridal veil in the beginning was a way to cast off any evil eye or jealous looks by envious women or men attending the wedding. Such an act would surely bring ill luck to the marriage.

Doppelganger

Doppelganger is a German word for a ghostly double that is said to appear to foretell an early death. The poet Shelley spotted his doppelganger outside one of the terraces of his residence in Northern Italy. Shelley spied his soft profile floating by one of the terrace windows and drowned a few days later. President Lincoln also encountered his doppelganger when he was up late and heard a rapping on the door to his study in the White House. When Lincoln opened the door, he met his own image standing there. The image quickly faded. In a few short months, Lincoln was dead.

Earthbound Spirit

An earthbound spirit, for whatever reason, cannot move on, as they did in life. Somehow, they are "spiritually stuck." Such spirits are doomed to return to the places where they lived, or perhaps to the area where their remains have been placed. Many believe such spirits are confused, or they don't know how to "go into the light" or vanish into the arms of God. In reality, this is rarely the case, as oftentimes, spirits stick around to get their message across, or perhaps, to check on their relatives or to just re-experience the happy times.

Saying ghosts are "angels who have not graduated into heaven," as I have heard TV psychics claim, is simply wrong and very unfair to these ghostly manifestations. Many ghosts lived wonderful, productive lives and sometimes, they simply want to return and listen to stories about their lives on earth, how they are still thought of and wish to visit loved ones. Demonizing ghosts is a destructive force in modern ghost theories.

Ectoplasm

Ectoplasm is a misty yet dense substance that turns up during times of communications with ghosts as well as in ghost photography. They tend to look like dense streaks or have appendages. During the 19th and early 20th centuries, any medium worth her salt would always produce ectoplasm at séances. This was a crowd-pleaser but usually fake. The bogus ectoplasm had the consistency of a stringy cheese and was usually made from household chemicals or detergent foam whipped up right before the séance. Real ectoplasm is rarely picked up by the naked eye. In ghost photographs the ectoplasm resembles a whitish or gray misting effect, one that is cloudy and stringy and is denser than what should be present in the atmosphere.

Electromagnetic Field

Electromagnetic field is the electrical force field that surrounds or permeates life. Many believe areas that are haunted will show high electromagnetic readings. Scientists dispute this, saying most areas and all living things radiate electromagnetic fields.

Entity

The presence of a spirit personality that does not have any human-related physical form and in most instances the entity does not actually have a physical body. The word "entity" is often used to describe a spiritual being when we do not know what it is, defying definition. This can be a generic term used in early ghost investigations—before the ghost hunters come to a decision as to who it is really haunting the place. In many instances, they never clearly know and the entity is as good a word as any other while explaining an otherwise, unknown, unseen presence.

Evil Spirits

Humans have had a belief in evil spirits since the beginning of time.

Although evil spirits can mask themselves as something else, they often turn up as foul odors, clammy bone-chilling coldness, drug or alcohol abuse, thoughts of suicide or murder, sadistic fantasies or dreams of violence, rage, jealousy, and any number of negative patterns. The way to have power and authority over evil spirits is to not fall prey to such things.

EVP

EVP refers to a recording of ghostly voices on a cassette or digital recorder. This can be done with a basic tape recorder or digital recorder, but often the sound levels have to be adjusted with more sensitive equipment to pick up the subtleties of spirit voices and their messages. It is always best to address the spirits and communicate with them. Oftentimes the ghostly voices will be recorded on top of the actual human voices and not usually heard otherwise.

Exorcism

A religious rite sanctioned by the Catholic Church used to drive evil spirits out of victims thought to be suffering from spirit possession associated with the Devil. Exorcisms are not common, but a few have been practiced by some non-Catholic faiths. A few victims will improve after the exorcism while others may get worse. Full possession by evil spirits is rare, but being possessed by self-destructive habits and unwholesome impulses may be helped or curtailed by the belief of some higher power or religious authority.

Extraterrestrial

Extraterrestrials are living creatures from other planets or galaxies that visit earth. Also called aliens, most extraterrestrial life appears to have a consciousness that helps them understand the human condition.

Fairies

Especially among the Celts, fairies are intelligent beings associated with the earth, astral and supernatural realms. Some fairies have been thought to be expressions of the forces of nature and other elements. The Celts associated fairies with governing the last earth phase before a soul passes over into the astral. In ancient times, some fairies were linked to the spirits of the dead and many were feared. To slide into entropy, depression or hopelessness meant that you had given up and were being "fairy led."

Fetch

Fetch is an English word for the ghostly double. See *Doppelganger*.

Ghost

The essence of a living being that is believed to have survived death. Most believe ghosts are personalities of people or animals that continue to live on in the spirit world.

Ghostly Hitchhiker

Stories of the ghostly hitchhiker are universal. Usually the spirit is of a young woman that flags down a ride while in a rainstorm. As they near the destination, the driver will turn around only to find the girl gone.

As the driver attempts to locate the young woman, he will often find out that at one time a young woman of the exact same description died—either on the spot where she was picked up—or left at the cemetery where she is buried.

Ghoul

A ghoul is a type of ghost that haunts graveyards and the crossroads and eats human flesh. Ghouls are really more akin to zombies and vampires than to ghosts. One doesn't want to cross paths with a ghoul. They are evil and capable of murder.

Granny Witch

A mountain term for a mature woman who practices various mystical arts passed down through her family or community. The Granny Witch is usually consulted for folk remedies, the use of herbs, midwifery, the right times to plant, or the best times to get pregnant or contact ghosts. Many times young women will consult the Granny Witch for the reading of tea leaves, divining the future with playing cards, mirrors, or tokens, as well as suggestions for special love and marriage spells.

Haint

A southern mountain term used to describe various types of ghosts that haunt the region. Much folklore surrounds stories of "haints" in Appalachia. Most haints are thought to be menacing spirits, much like the 'boogers' that haunt mountain hollows.

Haunting

A haunting is associated with a place of ghostly or other unexplained activity.

Hexen or Hexenmeister

Hexen or hexenmeister are the German words for witch, male and female. Hexens were the bane for the Pennsylvania Dutch. The Pennsylvania Dutch were superstitious over hexing and using hexen "powers"—evidence shows a great deal of spiritual warfare fought between the Hexenmeisters in Pennsylvania, Maryland, Ohio and West Virginia.

Hex

A hex is a magic spell among German peoples that is meant to stop someone from attaining something you'd rather they not attain—such as something that belongs to you. A hex might be used to protect your livestock and your family from evil intentions. Hexes also shield you from starvation and poverty. Hexes can also cause negative events to happen.

Incubus

A spirit entity that many believe to be a demon or ghost that has sex with women while they are sleeping or unable to move, speak or cry out. This phenomenon was reported on widely in medieval times and revealed women as witches for having sex with the Devil. In reality, this phenomena is related to the Night Hag experience, a psychological state, and may be caused by brain patterns firing in the temporal lobe area while women are sleeping that leaves them vulnerable to all types of weird, nightmarish sensations. Women who have had this bizarre, ghostly rape insist the experience is a real attack.

Inter-dimensional Being

An Inter-dimensional being is capable of passing through dimensions, and can slip through space and time, without human detection.

Intuitive

An intuitive is a sensitive person who can "read between the lines." This means, an individual who is able to put two and two together, tally up all of the information and with more than a dash of psychic ability, will come up with the correct answer even while having little information to go on. In most instances, women are more intuitive than men. This probably stems from the fact that the more intuitive one is, the better chance for survival and protecting one's young.

Kinetic Energy

Kinetic energy is thought to be contained within an object that can be released through some psychic means. This is usually associated with poltergeists. It is likely spirits can tap into the kinetic energy of people and other surrounding objects.

Ley Lines

Ley lines are considered to be Earth energy lines that either cross over or are aligned over several strategic spots in compliance with ancient stone or earth monuments. Ley lines are believed to exude great psychic powers along their path, including spirit formations, UFOs and ghosts. Parts of the Mid-Ohio valley are situated along Ley lines formed by ancient Adena and Hopewell Indian burial mounds.

Magick

Magick with a "k" is used to distinguish from stage magic, such as that practiced by Harry Houdini and others. Magick derives from a more ancient form of High Magick related to sorcery and the bringing about of miracles through supernatural means, instead of the usual sleight of hand stage and card tricks. "Magick" involves more endurance and is more difficult.

Mediumship

Popularized in the 1980s as channeling, mediumship is a psychic talent where a gifted individual allows certain spirits to take over his or her consciousness, allowing them to dictate messages for the living. This can occur at a séance, where people are gathered for the purpose of speaking to the dead, or through an individual who does not have to go into a trance to receive the messages. It is very possible that we are all capable of spirit communication with dead relatives and other souls, but we don't take the time to quiet our consciousness minds, nor do we have the faith or insight to understand the information that we are receiving.

Men In Black

Linked with the appearance of flying saucers and aliens, Men in Black are just that—two or three men wearing black, usually dressed in suits—who appear to interrogate and subtly threaten contactees who claim contact with outer space beings or UFOs. Although some have speculated the Men in Black are government agents, their behavior often comes across as downright "alien."

Mothman

A pale, gray creature with the wingspan of about 20 feet and standing more than six feet tall was sighted over 100 times in West Virginia and southern Ohio in 1966 and early 1967. This supernatural being was the subject of several popular books and movies including John Keel's classic *The Mothman Prophecies* and later, the movie in 2002 of the same name, starring actors Richard Gere and Debra Messing.

Old Hag

An extremely disturbing psychological state that occurs during sleep when one wakes up feeling suffocated, crushed, paralyzed and even sexually violated by a demon or a ghost. It happens much more frequently to women than to men. Theorists say that the paralysis is caused by a protective mechanism in the brain that keeps people from thrashing around and hurting themselves during nightmares. Regardless, the Night Hag does seem to be connected to hauntings and many interpret this bizarre experience as an alien abduction.

Since the Night Hag assault often leaves victims exhausted in the morning, there are many who think the phenomenon may have inspired beliefs in energy draining ghosts or vampires in Europe and America.

Necromancy

Necromancy is communication with ghosts or spirits of the dead. Although the Christian and Jewish Bibles warn against necromancy, it is still practiced every day by people who speak to deceased relatives through prayer, use a Ouija board, hold séances or attempt to connect with souls who once lived.

Orb

An orb is a ball of light that is often luminescent but not usually visible to the naked eye. It is associated with all types of spiritual activity, primarily with ghosts. Usually the orb is first seen when pictures are developed. Orbs are usually completely spherical, but the insides may appear different. Some people see faces in them while others see rainbow effects. The orbs may be bright or dull, or changing in color. Orbs are to me, the most fascinating area of the paranormal. They may prove the existence of energy of a spiritual nature.

Orb Trail

An orb trail is a ghost orb traveling at a high rate of speed that is faster than the camera can catch, leaving a comet-like tail sometimes appearing as a rod or rope.

Ouija Board

The Ouija is a board game made fashionable in the early 20th century that was devised specifically to communicate with spirits. Ouija boards emerged out of the popularity of the Spiritualist movement. They can be effective tools in contacting spirits, but can be spiritually treacherous and should never be used while alone. Never allow children to play with them.

Paranormal

The paranormal is a science that goes beyond what we can currently understand through accepted scientific means. Nearly all of the subjects in this book fall under the definition of the "paranormal."

Pentagram

The Pentagram is the mystical five-pointed star that is usually connected with the religion of Wicca, although its origins are considerably older. In fact, the pentagram can be found in most world religions—to Christians, the pentagram represented the five wounds of Christ on the cross. In Freemasonry it is called the "Seal of Solomon."

The five points of the star are associated with the five elements of fire, water, earth, air and ether—the Far East called it "Akasha" or void—the western world saw the fifth element as "Spirit." The pentagram during the Middle Ages was sometimes referred to as the Goblin Cross or a Witch's Foot.

Phantom

A phantom is a mysterious ghost or presence that hides and shows no distinct personality or appearance. Phantoms are often associated with grand old homes and historical theaters.

Phouka

A Phouka is a type of Irish fairy that kidnaps people out of their beds at night to take them on a ride across the countryside. A Phouka often appears as a pale, gray hairy beast. Sometimes the Phouka appears as a big dog or goat or horse. The concept of the nightmare is very much related to the Irish Phouka. Victims are usually tucked safely back inside their beds at dawn. The victim's stories are in many ways similar to reports of alien abductions.

Place Haunting

The same as a spirit recording or residual haunting, but much more tied to a place than to any individual. An example is a house that is haunted by many different ghosts.

Poltergeist

German for "noisy ghost" or "knocking spirit," poltergeists are fairly common in households but are so subtle not all victims recognize them as paranormal. Poltergeists are not actually a spirit or a ghost, but they often appear where other hauntings are being reported. For the past 40 years or so, poltergeists have been linked to the latent telekinetic abilities of some troubled teenagers or very emotional people. Poltergeists appear rather sporadically and usually go away on their own.

Portal

A portal is an opening that somehow bridges the physical world with other dimensions. Some believe portals are really "tears or rips" in our dimension giving us a clear spot to see through to alternate realities. Others believe a portal is a place where the atmosphere is ripe for spiritual forces to come together, bridging the gap between the physical and spiritual realms.

Residual Haunting

Energy left over after a person has died, sometimes in a home or even on a piece of furniture associated with the deceased. These appear to be the kind of ghostly energies that manifest in spirit recordings where ghosts are seen to be doing the same task over and over again.

Sacred Site

A sacred site is an area that becomes spiritually powerful because of religious activity or due to being located along Ley lines or vortexes.

Séance

A séance is a gathering of people who come together with the explicit purpose of contacting spirits. The séance room is normally lit only by candlelight, where members of the séance circle hold hands, or place palms flat to the surface of the table in order to detect the energies. Séances were practiced in the 19th century Spiritualist movement and remain popular even to this day.

Shadow People

Shadow people are fascinating ghost that appear as a shadow with no distinct features, usually appearing as quite tall. Shadow people are typically tied to a place that had other hauntings, but they usually seem to be devoid of personality. When they do have a personality it is usually not a friendly one.

Smudging

Smudging is a Native American ritual where sage or cedar is burned, allowing smoke to rise in order to banish negative energies. There is no evidence that smudging helps much in the throes of an intense haunting, but it smells nice and balances the energies in a room.

Specter

A ghost that is typically transparent or ethereal or appears as veiled wisps. Most apparitions appear much as they did in life while specters have a more shadowy quality, lacking specificity.

Spells

A spell is a ritual that is used to bring about a certain result that the spell-caster has in mind. Sometimes they are cast through incantations, poems, magic herb bundles, potions and other ritual effects. Spells are a very ancient way of practicing magick by bringing about what you wish through imagery, words and intent. Some witches write down their spells in a book that is called a "Grimoire."

Spirit

Spiritual energies are linked to a personality that survives death. Spirit is a more generalized term for ghost. The word ghost is usually associated with a personality. A spirit is too, but not so clearly defined. For instance, if objects in the house start to move of their own accord, we might say our house has spirits. If we see an apparition that looks to be a person, we'll mostly likely say we saw a ghost.

Spirit Guide

A spirit guide is a spiritual being that watches over us in a loving and protective manner, sometimes since birth. Everyone has a spiritual guide. Some have several.

Spirit Recording

Similar to "residual hauntings," ghost sightings, especially those that happen over and over again, can be a spirit recording. They are simply energies that survive death, but no longer have a consciousness. There is rarely any awareness behind this kind of ghost. Spirit recordings usually involve sightings of an apparition whereas residual hauntings have more to do with the playing back of voices and sounds from the past, such as footsteps, doors opening and closing, and even objects moving.

Spiritualism

Spiritualism is a religion based on communications with spirits, founded by the Fox sisters in upstate New York in the 1840s. The teens claimed there was a ghost in their house after hearing a series of rapping and banging sounds in their bedroom. They soon began to communicate with the ghost by rapping on the walls themselves and were surprised that the spirit immediately knocked back. Through a code, they communicated with the ghost and found that it was a man murdered in the home and buried under the house. An investigation did yield the jawbone of a human beneath the foundation of the home.

The Fox sisters then traveled the world conducting séances and performing as famous mediums, giving rise to the Spiritualist movement or religion.

Succubus

As a female counterpoint to the Incubus, the Succubus attacks unsuspecting men while they sleep, often by raping them. Often when the man opens his eyes, he sees a decrepit hag with stringy white hair and boils all over her body. This may well be the male version of the Night Hag, involving a mysterious function of the dreaming brain that causes a person to hallucinate the sexual assault by what, in essence, seems like a female demon.

Talisman

A talisman is a charm used to ward off ghosts, bad luck and evil spirits. Most cultures have talismans, and many people throughout the world would not leave their homes without their talismans. Gems and crystals are the most popular types of charms.

Telekinesis

Telekinesis is an ability to move objects with the unconscious powers of the human mind. Poltergeists, for instance, are thought to be a form of telekinesis. Any real evidence of telekinetic powers is rare because no one— including the one causing it—knows exactly when it is going to occur.

Telepathy

Thought transference through psychic means, telepathy is possibly the most universal psychic talent of all. Many have picked up the phone to call a person only to get a busy signal and find out the friend has been on the phone attempting to call them at the same time. Others have had the experience of thinking about someone from the past all day long, only to encounter him or her on the street or meet the person in a store hours later. These are all forms of telepathy. Telepathy tends to be most strong among relatives and close friends.

Trance

Also referred to as the "alpha state," a trance is a shift in consciousness that allows individuals to enter into and experience spiritual realms and other realities not normally achievable. Such reveries are places where artists and poets receive inspiration and where spiritualists and psychics make connections with the spirit world. Trances are not as dramatic as they are portrayed in movies, books or television shows. In fact, watching television is just another form of a trance—it's just most of the time a television trance is not usually a very productive one.

UFO

A UFO is an unidentified flying object, but not necessarily a spacecraft from another world. Anything that flies through the air, and is witnessed and reported upon, without being explained, is referred to as a UFO.

Ufology

Ufology is the study of UFOs and extraterrestrial life. Contactees, spacecraft, Men in Black, flying saucers, aliens and even crop circles fall under the category of Ufology.

Unfinished Business

Unfinished business, also called unsettled business, is a primary reason some ghosts appear. Something has been left over from, or not realized for them in life and needs to be completed. At times spirits with unfinished business appear sad or melancholy if the living are unable to understand the message that the spirit attempts to convey. Often, when the message is understood or the goal is realized such a ghost will not make any more appearances.

Urban Legend

The urban legend is a mysterious or shocking story that is told over and over again. It is embellished until it creates a reality of its own.

Although urban legends are typically bogus, sometimes the spirit world responds to the telling of the tale and molds reality accordingly. In other words, if one tells that a house is haunted long enough, the attention will most likely attract a spirit looking for a home.

Vortex or Vortices

Like orbs, vortices appear more often in photographs than by the naked eye. Vortices appear as tornado-like funnels in photographs and are usually white. Many believe vortices are orbs in motion, while others think they may imply portals into other dimensions. No matter what the theory is—orbs, vortices and ectoplasm are the most common ways ghosts show up in photographs.

Wampus Cat

A Wampus cat is a type of Appalachian Werecat, believed by locals to be part wildcat and part woman. The Wampus Cat has been associated with the power of witches, stemming from the beliefs of Irish-Scottish settlers in the Appalachian Mountains while other sources trace the legend of the Wampus Cat to native Cherokee Indians.

Wicca

Wicca merges ancient pagan ideas with modern occultism. Currently, Wicca is pretty much a nature religion. It is made up primarily of individuals who believe in and want to develop their psychic powers. They hold the changes of the seasons and the earth in reverence, wear capes, pentacles and other emblems, give psychic readings and advice, heal the sick with spells and herbs, etc. Wiccans give special meaning to places like Stonehenge and other sacred earth sites. One of the most famous witches of the late 20th century was the English witch Sybil Leek, a talented ghost hunter and expert astrologer.

Witch

An individual who has certain mystical powers that reaches beyond the usual psychic ability. Witches have the power to influence events or outcomes or affect changes. This can be achieved through spells or just by concentrating.

In the modern age, a witch can be a man or a woman or a follower of Wicca. But one does not have to be a Wiccan to be a witch.

Witching

Virginia Lyons and the author "dowsing" for ghosts on Fort Boreman Hill, Parkersburg. COURTESY TIM ELLIOT

Also called "water witching," this is a form of dowsing where metal rods are taken (or the forked branch of a certain tree) to divine the areas of not only water, gas, even telephone lines but also graves. In older cemeteries, areas of earlier graves may have been obfuscated, covered up or lost. A "witch" is contacted in order to check areas where houses are being built or new roads are planned to go through, in order not to disturb older graves.

Women-In-White

Women-In-White ghosts are believed to be grieving spirits tied here by a tragic event they have trouble letting go of. It is theorized that such unhappy forces are put into place after a murder, sudden death or a suicide has occurred, but Women-In-White ghosts can also be linked to the death of a child, an unhappy love affair and any number of events that would bring about extremes of sadness. These types of apparitions are reported on all over the world, but seem to be most common in the southern United States.

Bibilography

Books

Barker, Gray, *They Knew Too Much About Flying Saucers* (1956)

Barker, Gray, *Silver Bridge* (1970)

Cartrell, Connie, *The Ghosts Of Marietta* (1996)

Deitz, Dennis, *The Greenbrier Ghost* (1990)

Dougherty, Shirley, *A Ghostly Tour of Harpers Ferry* (publication date unknown)

Eno, Paul, *A Face At the Window* (1998)

Eno, Paul, *Footsteps in the Attic* (2002)

Frost, Gavin & Yvonne, *Witch's Grimoire of Ancient Omens, Portents, Talismans, Amulets and Charms* (2002)

Guiley, Rosemary Ellen, *Encyclopedia of Ghosts & Spirits* (2000)

Sheppard, Susan, editor, *The Derenberger Tapes*, (2002)

Swick, Ray, *An Island Called Eden: An Historical Sketch of Blennerhassett Island* (1996)

Keel, John, *Haunted Planet* (1999)

Keel, John, *The Mothman Prophecies* (1995)

Wamsley, Jeff & Sergent, Donnie, Jr., *Mothman: The Facts Behind the Legend* (2001)

Wamsley, Jeff, *Mothman: Behind The Red Eyes* (2005)

Yeats, W.B., editor, *Fairy and Folktales of Ireland* (1888-1892)

Websites

Haunted Parkersburg Ghost Tours—www.hauntedparkersburg.com

West Virginia Hauntings—http://www.callwva.comlhauntings/calendar.cfm

Mothman Lives—http://www.mothmanlives.com

New England Ghosts.com & Good Spirits Newsletter—http://www.newenglandghosts.com

Parkersburg West Virginia, A Vintage Portrait—http://www.
electricearl.com/parkersburg/
National Trust for Historic Places—www.nationaltrust.org
Blennerhassett Hotel—www.blennerhassetthotel.com
Blennerhassett Island Historical State Park—http:/!www.
blennerhassettislandstatepark.com/
Parkersburg Wood County CVB—http://www.parkersburgcvb.org
Haunted Parkersburg Ghost Hunters—http://www.zzzip.net/hpgh
Mid-Ohio Valley Ghost Hunters
http://www.geocities.com.midohiovalleyghosthunters.movgh.htm/
West Virginia Ghosts.com—http://www.wvaghosts.com/
West Virginia Penitentiary Online—http://www.
shadowsoftmoundsville.com/

Acknowledgements

Grateful acknowledgement is made to the following individuals and organizations that have assisted in writing this book, as well as those who have made contributions to the Haunted Parkersburg Ghost Tours. Without your help, we could not have done this. Thank you for your stories, your leads, and your help!

Doni and Robert Enoch, Ray Swick, Henry Burke, Simone Chiodini, Gary Wolfe, Danette Lemley, Peter Poulos, the Blennerhassett Hotel, Donna Smith, the Blennerhassett State Park, Chris Friend, Gwen Friend, Nellie Ruby and Marilyn, Mark and Kristall Chambers, Lea Wilson, Virginia Lyons, Terry Headley, Chris Stirewalt, The Charleston Daily Mail, Bonita Nichols, Becky Johnson, Bonnie and Craig Wix, Cecil Childress, Ron Nelson, Jim Moore, Joanie and Al Rorick, Richard Southall, Lisa Collins, Ruby Ruppel, Abby Hayhurst, Artsbridge, Jim Chapman, Mr. And Mrs. W.P. Chapman, Jr., Doug Posey and the Grind, Randall Hupp II, Jay Harmon, Brian Kesterson, Brent and Rae Ann Kesterson, Terry McVey, Betty Stewart, Terry Elliott, Greg Leatherman, Jeff Wamsley, Mat Lyons, Glenn Wilson, Regina Metzger, Joey De'Senze, Sandra Moats-Burke, Norma Hartness, Becky Sheehy, Jean Grapes, Shelley Rusen, Walt Auvil, Kirk Auvil, Justin Bernard, Timothy Elliott, Rochelle Lynn Holt, the Dils Center, Dave Ruble, Millie and Forrest McNemar, Connie Richards, Kevin Moorehead, Scarlet Sheppard, Roger Sheppard, Betty Sheppard, Bruce Layman, Michael Sundstrum, TransAllegheny Books, Paul Eno, Tom Moore, Joyce Ancrile, Eleanor Lowe, Teresa O'Cassidy, Marsha Raiguel, West Virginia Public Radio, Don Staats, WTAP-TV, WCHS-TV, Goldenseal Magazine, West Virginia Writers Inc. Pearl Ward, Kevin Moorehead, Beth Lanning, Matthew Devore, Jim Dawson, Josh Danko, Yancy Roush, Jack See, the Frick Brothers, Jeff Stoll, Rosemary Ellen Guiley, Carla, David, Jimmy, Janet, Tyler, Ryan, Amanda, Ethan, and the woman who emailed us the wonderful ghost story from the Parkersburg Elks Club.

About the Author

Susan Sheppard is a native West Virginian and grew up just a few hills away from the first Mothman sighting. She is a writer and artist and the founder of the acclaimed Haunted Parkersburg Tours, as well as the annual Haunted West Virginia Conference. Her poetry and art have won numerous award and she also a popular television host in the area. She is the author of *The Phoenix Cards*, *A Witch's Runes*, *The Astrological Guide to Seduction & Romance* and now, *Cry of the Banshee*. Sheppard is the founder and remains the main tour guide for the popular Haunted Parkersburg Tours that take place each fall. She currently resides in Parkersburg.

Visit her at her website, *www.hauntedparkersburg.com*.